No Fear
in His
Presence

Regal
Books

A Division of G/L Publications
Ventura, California, U.S.A.

The foreign language publishing of all Regal books is under the direction of GLINT.
GLINT provides financial and technical help for the adaptation, translation and
publishing of books in more than 85 languages for millions of people worldwide.

For more information write: GLINT, P.O. Box 6688, Ventura, CA 93006.

Published by Regal Books
A Division of G/L Publications
Ventura, California 93006
Printed in U.S.A.

Library of Congress Catalog Card No. 80-50261
ISBN 0-8307-0753-0

Code Number: 51 089 18

Contents

Foreword

It was a cold December night in Wheaton, Illinois, at the 1978 World Missions Congress, but our hearts were warmed by what we saw and heard. Dr. David Dawson, medical missionary to Zaire, showed slides and told his personal story of being caught in the crossfire of the 1977 rebellion in southern Zaire. His was a dramatic account of tragedy and suffering, played out against the backdrop of God's providence and deliverance.

I was scheduled to address the World Missions Congress following Dr. Dawson's presentation. I was deeply moved by that presentation; it hardly needed anything to complete the evening. I felt that a quiet time for commitment would be an appropriate closing.

As Dr. Dawson spoke I thought of the many servants of God, missionaries and nationals who in this generation have given their life's blood in the work of the Lord. In spite of so-called culture and progress and modernity, people are still dying without Christ and without hope. My prayer is that Christians will become more effective instruments of God to bring the millions of the world to a personal knowledge of Jesus Christ as Lord and Saviour.

I believe God is going to honor and use this gripping account of Dr. Dawson's experiences in Zaire. I praise God that this book is available to speak to the heart of every reader.

Acknowledgments

I am deeply grateful to the Kasaji Family who fleshed out these experiences with me, and particularly to Dr. Peter and Ruth Coates, and Terry Fisher who were valuable sources of information during the writing.

Debbie Archipow painstakingly deciphered the proverbial physician's scrawl, transforming it into a beautifully typed manuscript. I cannot thank my sister enough.

I am very grateful to Isabel Sabapathy for her critical appraisal of the initial draft, and to Keith Price for his enthusiastic support throughout all phases of the book's preparation.

To my parents, Debbie and her husband Heinz go special thanks for their patience, sacrifice and constant encouragement during the months of writing.

These and others have helped me share a story that had to be told.

CASABLANCA

CAIRO

ZAIRE

NAIROBI

KINSHASA

LUANDA   KASAJI

ANGOLA   ZAMBIA

LUSAKA

AFRICA

CAPE TOWN

1
Battle for Kasaji

The footpath to the Davies's house cut through a familiar stretch of bushland. This part of the mission station was usually frequented by many people—African schoolboys strumming homemade tin can guitars, wizened old women returning from the hospital jabbering about Munganga's medicines, and mothers balancing firewood on their heads while their babies bounced along piggyback. Tonight, however, not a person was about. Even the birds and the stray dogs seemed to have taken refuge. All that greeted me as I crossed that 200-yard tract of brush and open field was a strange, foreboding silence.

What made the stillness even more terrifying was the fact that scarcely three hours previously, several hundred Zairian para-commandos had swept into the mission from their base at Kasaji one mile away. In full battle dress, they had stolen stealthily across our compound hunting for the enemy. Expecting an attack by the advancing Katangese rebels, the Zairian troops had taken up positions of defense around our buildings; but now, at 5:30 P.M., they were nowhere to be seen.

I quickened my pace to the Davies's and was welcomed at the door by Brian. A professor at our teacher training institute since 1968, he and his wife Deirdre were the proud owners of their own little nursery school. Three young children kept them occupied, and a fourth was on the way.

"Uncle David," pleaded four-year-old Robbie, "come and look at the crane that Uncle Harold gave me!" Whenever I came for supper, I always inspected the crane and every other plaything that Robbie owned.

Brian, Deirdre and I exchanged glances, hardly knowing what we could say in front of the youngsters. It was Sunday, March 13, 1977, the sixth turbulent day since we became embroiled in the Katangese invasion of Zaire. We were part of an 18-member team that staffed a Christian hospital-college-mission station in Kasaji, Shaba province, southwestern Zaire.

News of the attack had spread like an epidemic, precipitating the panicky flight of thousands. Loyalist troops had flooded into Kasaji and even today several more battalions had arrived from Kolwezi as reinforcements.

Robbie had finished his toy exhibition and was now enthusiastically showing me his *National Geographic* collection. My mind wasn't really following, but two-year-old Ingrid joined us and snuggled in a little closer as we admired historic Edinburgh, toured a South Sea island and visited a snake pit in the Canadian prairies.

Rat-tat-tat! A burst of gunfire broke the uncanny hush. Was this target practice? Were soldiers slaughtering local livestock for food? Or was this the expected assault on Kasaji? *Rat-tat-tat-tat-tat!* There was no time for conjecture.

"Come this very minute, children," Brian called out with typical British sang-froid. "Into the bedroom straight away."

Leaving our supper on the dining table, we each grabbed a child and scrambled to our destination. We thrust the little ones under the bed taking care to crouch down ourselves. It was 6 P.M. and dusk was settling in. A volley of gunfire cracked the air; then a return volley.

The shooting was hard to localize but we crouched even lower when two successive explosions shook the house. Shuddering, we realized that rockets and mortars were supplementing the machine gun fire.

Little Timmy vocalized his discomfort, Ingrid fidgeted, but Robbie clutched his ears and winced with each fusillade saying, "I wish the bangs would go away!" We did too.

Rat-tat-tat! Our watches said 6:15 P.M. It had seemed like three hours.

Outwardly we tried to create a relaxed atmosphere to reassure the children. Inwardly we realized the peril of our situation. If this was indeed the beginning of the battle for Kasaji, we were trapped between President Mobutu's elite para-commandos and the seasoned Katangese guerilla fighters. The town was of paramount importance to each side. It was both a strategic north-south, east-west crossroads and a main stop on the railway line. The presence of the mission pushed the stakes even higher. The large hospital complex was the only one servicing an area of at least 20,000 square miles, and the station's supplies, vehicles, and personnel were of prime interest, especially to the rebels. We were bound to be in the thick of any engagement.

Brian, Deirdre and I looked at each other. In our hearts prayers were silently ascending as indeed they had been for the last six days. The shooting which had begun so abruptly, however, was now settling down, and we quietly talked and played with the children.

"Back in a minute," I whispered, and I crawled from room to room cautiously spying through several windows. I failed to spot anyone lurking outside the house but the occasional discharge of small arms fire was sufficient encouragement to stay low.

"Can't see anything," I reported. *Rat-tat-tat!* We continued to wait. Finally, after another 20 minutes, we considered it safe to leave our refuge. Good thing, too! By this time the three youngsters were ravenous.

With the lights dimmed, we sat half on our chairs and half on the floor, and bowed our heads as Brian prayed, "Dear Lord Jesus, we give you thanks for this day and for this good food. Amen." Our hunger and the threat of escalating danger contributed to the haste with which we consumed the meal.

What had actually taken place in those 45 minutes wasn't very clear to us. Had there been an ambush by the Katangese? Had there been a skirmish amongst Mobutu's own men or were a number of the para-commandos just releasing the tension? The latter hypothesis seemed most likely. The gunfire and mortar explosions were frightening enough but surely the real battle for Kasaji would be louder and longer and more devastating. Of course, we couldn't be sure. Our minds went to our colleagues and our African friends. Were they injured—perhaps wounded and needing help? We prayed again!

Darkness was nestling in around Kasaji. Only a sporadic distant gunshot disturbed the night.

"What are you going to do, Dave?" Deirdre asked, sensing my uneasiness at being far away from the hospital and the Coates's house. The day before the invasion, Dr. Peter Coates had left the mission on a medical trip to our dispensary at Katoka. In his absence I was responsible not only for the hospital but also for his home where I had been staying with our cook Venasi and three students. Would they be waiting for me even now outside the locked house? But how safe was it to venture out? On the other hand, how many wounded were suffering unattended?

I was torn by indecision. The Davies urged me to stay. The inner struggle raged on, then rightly or wrongly, the issue was resolved.

"I have to go!" The words escaped through clenched teeth. I would go—if only my wobbly knees would take me!

"Are you sure?" asked Deirdre.

"Yes."

"Here, take our torch with you," she offered. "You'll need it."

I quickly put on my Windbreaker, grabbed the extended flashlight and strode to the door, giving myself as little time as possible to change my mind. After a hasty farewell, I stepped out into the blackness. It was 7 P.M.

As I eased away from the relative security of the house something within me reasoned that safety lay not in being furtive but in being bold and obvious. So, singing a hymn as loudly as I could and swinging my flashlight in time, I retraced my steps of 90 minutes before. Certainly if any soldier were about he would consider me an innocent even pitiable sight; at least that's what I was counting on.

Rat-tat-tat-tat-tat! I fell to my knees as the fusillade staccatoed to my right. I clutched at my body—everything seemed to be intact. Then realizing that crawling along the ground would make any soldier even more suspicious, I bolted upright and started off again. This time, with heart pounding, brow perspiring, torch flashing and prayer ascending, I broke into a trot and sang even louder. Another volley shook my cadence but I sprinted through the Fisher's garden and burst through their back door.

A startled Terry Fisher appeared in the hallway as I crashed into the kitchen. "What are you doing?" he asked in amazement. Then, without waiting for my response he blurted out, "The rebels have taken Kasaji!"

"What's that?" I replied incredulously.

"The Katangese are everywhere," he continued. "One was just at my door!" Terry was well-known for his stories, but his obvious discomposure was testimony enough to what he then recounted.

When the original shots rang out, Terry and his wife Barbara had sought shelter in the center of the house. The rockets had been launched from near the Coates's property and apparently exploded in that tract of land that I had crossed and recrossed. After the initial clash, the Fishers had heard some rustling near the front window; then a bold voice had called out, "Terry! Terry!" He had shuddered at the mention of his name—who could it be?

"Terry, come on out!" ordered the unknown figure in the pure tones of the local Ndembu language.

Terry had been born in Central Africa, and spoke Ndembu like a native. Warily, yet obediently he approached the front door and stepped out. There, 10 feet away stood one of the rebels in camouflaged dress bearing a machine gun. Emblazoned on the sleeve of his battle shirt were the insignia of the Katangese "Tiger" Battalion.

"Terry, don't you remember me?"

"No," said Terry, hoping that this fellow's remembrance of him had been sweet.

"Terry," he laughed, "why are you shaking? Are you afraid of war?" An unintelligible response fumbled out.

"The Congo is my home," the rebel said, "and the Congolese are my people. We have come to liberate the country from the tyranny of Mobutu and his lackeys. Do not be afraid. We will not harm you unless you prove to be enemies. Go back inside. Put down your lights. We are going to destroy the Zairians tonight!"

With that he turned, joined a comrade who had appeared from nowhere and slipped into the night. Terry charged back into the house and was still recovering from this encounter minutes later when I barged in.

He had just finished relating his story when, suddenly, there was some scuffling on the back porch. Who was it? Were some soldiers about to force an entry? Before we could get there, the door flew open, and in stumbled a dazed-looking native with a bleeding right forearm. He had been shot in Kasaji town and somehow had made it to the mission. Without further discussion we dashed next door to Hazel and Anne's where some emergency medical provisions were stored.

Hazel Macfarlane was an Australian, a veteran missionary with many years of nursing experience. She was a take-charge type of person whose strong will and faith had ridden her through many crises. We silently moved to the dining area where the medical supplies were stashed—sutures, needles, anesthetics, scalpels, dressings and more. Under the light of two 60-watt bulbs and the gaze of 10 African friends we set to work.

The patient was seated at the table looking on stoically as Hazel washed down the wounded area. The bullet had ripped through the distal forearm smashing the ulna.

"He really should have an x-ray, but not tonight," I said. "We'll cast him anyway and get one later."

"There's only one problem, Dave," said Hazel. "All our plaster of paris is at the hospital."

I groaned inside and then debated the obvious. Should I try to get the materials? After all, this man might be the first of many needing plaster tonight. Besides if I went I could see how the hospital and on-duty staff were faring. The gunfire was distant and there was no sign of soldiers. I had talked myself into it.

Hazel, and especially Anne, let me go only with great reluctance. I dashed down the back path, passed the widows' homes and cut towards the operating theater, once more with hooded jacket, scanning flashlight and lusty song.

"Lord," I prayed as I hurried onward, "may I find the hospital untouched by the battle. Oh God! May the staff be filled with your peace though encircled by war!"

I flashed by the maternity ward. Ahead was the road, now the embankment. Only my footsteps broke the deathly silence. I thrust the key into the main door of the operating theater and the lock that never worked opened on the first try. I slipped in, closed the door behind me and hastily gathered several four-inch and six-inch plasters.

I stopped still. What was that outside on the passageway? It sounded like the shuffle of feet on the cement. I took a deep breath and waited. The door inched open. Then, relief swept over me as three of our orderlies crept in, their faces showing both surprise and joy. I hugged each one in turn—Tshihinga, Nunes and Lotani. They had watched my mad scramble to the theater and decided to investigate. I told them about the wounded man at the girls' house; then I continued with Tshihinga, our head orderly, in the work-a-day language we had in common—French.

"How are the patients?" I asked.

"Safe—all under beds!"

"And what about the hospital?"

"No damage."

"Any soldiers around?"

"All over the place," Tshihinga replied. I swallowed hard. "The Katangese are everywhere. One of them called me out and asked where he could find the wounded Zairian soldiers. I told him that they had all fled. Then he said that the camarades had come home to liberate the Congo. After that he disappeared."

I thanked the Lord for His hand of protection over the hospital and for these three faithful orderlies. After praying with them, I headed back into the night. As I stumbled across the uneven terrain, more than once I wondered if this were a dream. Then I heard the guns still sounding—some from Kasaji and some from the direction of the leper camp.

Past the widows' cottages, I thought. *Now just up the back path to the house.* Anne was waiting for me at the door. I darted past her and unloaded my precious cargo on the table. Three 200-yard dashes on a warm African night were more than enough to raise a sweat, especially under the circumstances. As I stripped off my drenched shirt, I shared the good news about the hospital.

The patient's forearm had been scrubbed and was ready for repair. "Hazel, the xylocaine, please."

"Don't waste the anesthetic," she replied. "These men are tough." I shrugged my shoulders—Hazel had been in Africa for over 20 years; I, six weeks. She should know.

After debriding the wound, I closed it with nylon sutures. The patient sat unflinching and as I positioned the forearm and rolled on the plaster, his story was unfolded to me.

He was a Christian from a small village located nearby. Two days previously his young son had died and a simple funeral was held just north of the college at our cemetery. After the service he was lingering at the grave when some Zairian para-commandos happened by and accused him of being a spy. He was brought into Kasaji and thrown into a makeshift prison with 70 other civilians who had been rounded up on similar charges. There they all stayed without food and in complete isolation.

That evening when the attack had begun, the prisoners were hastily lined up to be shot but the encircling Katangese had surprised the guards and averted a massacre. Our patient was hit by a stray bullet during the melee. Ten years back he had been with the rebel forces but had long since abandoned that way of life for farming and a wife and family. However, this ex-Katangese gunman recognized amongst the guerillas one of his old buddies who escorted him through the combat to the mission for medical help. What an incredible tale!

I finished molding, then smoothing out the cast, while Hazel prepared a sling to support the arm. Anne spirited an amazingly rapid clean-up.

"Do you think Venasi and the students are waiting at the Coates's for me?" I pondered aloud.

"Of course not! As soon as they heard the shooting they would have started running and may still be," replied Hazel in her own incontestable fashion.

I remembered that all my possessions including my photography equipment and my diary were lying out in the open at the Coates's house. If any soldiers were to break in, some of these goods would certainly disappear and perhaps with disastrous consequences. Therefore I ventured out again, this time to rescue my valuables. I covered the 50 yards like a veteran sprinter. Once inside I felt my way through the blackness to my room, bundled together my personal effects and scrambled back to the door. Heaving a deep sigh, I plunged out again. I didn't like what I heard—the shooting seemed to be closer and more frequent. Back at Hazel and Anne's, I vowed not to go out again.

I joined Hazel and Anne and our African friends on the living room floor. Together we recalled a similar desperate situation recorded in 2 Chronicles 20. At the time, the Jews were faced with invasion and pleaded to God saying, "For we have no might against this great company that cometh against us; neither know we what to do: but our eyes are upon thee" (v. 12). Our gaze was certainly fixed in the same direction.

It was 8:30 P.M. We sat in silent reflection. The struggle seemed to be escalating. The guns of war drifted nearer. *Boom! Boom!* The dwelling shuddered as a couple of rockets plowed into the ground behind it.

"In there!" Hazel exclaimed. All 14 of us, including a tiny baby and four other children, squeezed into a 4x6-foot stairwell in the center of the house. On all four sides of our refuge stood at least one brick wall and overhead were wooden stairs and a tin roof.

The firing became more furious. *Rat-tat-tat! Rat-tat-tat-tat-tat!* Soon we could recognize the sound of launching rockets and braced ourselves for the inevitable explosions. *Boom! Boom!* Boots scuffled along the back walk. The soldiers were now behind the house yelling almost constantly while their machine guns rattled on. We huddled there on the floor making our bodies smaller and smaller. The ex-Katangese gunman swore in hushed tones that the combatants we heard outside were the rebels. That was just the way they fought—shouting, shooting, making noise—doing anything in fact that would terrify their enemies.

For two hours we lay there while the struggle alternately intensified then tapered off. We endured with suspense the launching and explosion of rockets. Many frenzied voices called out from the bushes around the house while land and sky were peppered with gunfire. The ministers of death and destruction carried on relentlessly, each fresh wave of volleys appearing more merciless than the last.

I looked at Hazel and Anne. Hazel was no stranger to the face of death. In 1973 she had gone to England to have chemotherapy for what was diagnosed as terminal cancer. After a truly miraculous recovery she had returned to her lifework in Zaire. Anne too had confronted death. As Hazel's closest friend she had suffered by her side during that terrible illness, watching her sink lower and lower, and then dramatically restored to health again by God's grace. Being a doctor had repeatedly exposed me to death but the violence which engulfed us and our African friends was a completely new experience.

The night wore on. The shooting waned. We finally crawled out of our little refuge and bedded down on the floor in various corners of the house.

Deep inside my sleeping bag I scrawled into my diary a brief account of the events of the day. Then I stretched back on the floor. Innumerable questions flashed through my mind. What was so important about Kasaji that drew me here anyway? Was it worth all this trouble? And what happens if I don't make it? Am I really where God wants me to be? Groping in my pre-somnolent state, I reached back thousands of miles and several years for the answers I knew to be there.

2
A Prophecy Fulfilled

"David, you're a bonnie laddie. One day you're going to be a missionary doctor in Africa—just like David Livingstone!" Grannie Durnan had an earnest yet not too subtle way of informing her grandchildren exactly what she expected of them. As a youngster I protested initially but better judgment ultimately prevailed and with time I learned to smile weakly. After all, it wasn't worth losing favor with the one who supplied maple walnut ice cream, delicious licorice treats, and fish and chip dinners at the neighborhood restaurant.

Nevertheless our trips to see relatives in Toronto always left me with something to think about. Doctor? Not me. Much as I liked our family practitioner, I hated the idea of having to hurt people with needles. Moreover, ever since I had witnessed a friend of mine struck by a car, I couldn't imagine facing, even less treating a torn and battered human body. In Africa? Never. Books and films and stories about the continent were fine but in my boyish mind I dreaded living in a tropical jungle with wild animals as working companions.

My academic interests in high school were quite varied. Latin and literature, mathematics and music, history and physics—each had its own attractions. However, the one subject which all aspiring physicians select I completely disregarded. Biology did not require the sort of mental gymnastics that intrigued me so I opted for the maths and the physical sciences. On completion of high school training I couldn't have had less of an interest in medicine as a vocation despite Grannie's relentless recruitment.

Those early years were happy ones, being brought up with my sister by loving Christian parents. My father worked with the city newspaper and used to preach extensively in the Montreal area, in addition to his involvement at our own church in Rosemount. As I grew older, I saw that his life-style matched his messages. How compelling this became when through school, the media, and my own experience I was exposed to a society where servile speech, duplicity and cover-up were commonplace. I had recognized that the privilege of having Christian parents did not register me in God's family so I had personally made a decision to become a Christian. Now, in my sixteenth year, I realized that my principles and beliefs based on the Scriptures were countercurrent to popular thinking.

Never silent about my convictions, I was soon pitted against my intellectual peers in the Rosemount High School cafeteria during lunch hours. It must have been an absurd spectacle for all onlookers. There sat a dozen young men huddled around sandwiches, school books, and, amazingly enough, several open Bibles. It was a truly combustible atmosphere complete with fierce cross-examination, passionate rebuttal and wild gesticulations. When the school bell terminated the veritable verbal donnybrooks, we would leave for class all the better friends for the debate and already planning strategies for the morrow's collision. Defending the Christian faith was a lonely task but I enjoyed being the underdog. It drove me to honest inquiry and extensive reading on the subject, and I became increasingly convinced by the evidence for orthodox Christian belief.

It was halfway through an undergraduate maths program at McGill University that my very intellectually-based Christian faith underwent a profound metamorphosis. After a period of doubt leading me to a fresh examination of the resurrection of Christ, I emerged fully overwhelmed by God's incredible design for man and His world and fully desirous of laying my life before Him. I stopped playing a defense lawyer with God as my client. Instead Jesus Christ became my Friend, my joy and my life. What a thrilling encounter with the living God!

This spiritual revolution came at a time when I was reevaluating my university program. Math was still challenging but I seemed to be losing the fervor with which I used to attack theorems and equations. Now I preferred talking with people, working with people, helping people. I recognized that I was a "people man," and so my mind turned to three areas—law, theology, and yes, medicine.

Law and theology would be at least two years off but there was a slight possibility of entering medical school one year earlier. I began to consider it. As I examined the lives of Christian physicians in the Quebec community, I found that they had accomplished great things—the establishment of youth camps, orphanages, and senior citizens' homes at the same time as playing leading roles in church growth and conducting thriving, respected medical practices. They were "people men." Medicine stood in a new light—me helping people in the name of God.

I applied to McGill Medical School in my third undergraduate year and continued to reflect and pray over my choice of vocation. During those semesters I was deeply involved with McGill Christian Fellowship as well as other university affairs and my home church Ebenezer Gospel Chapel— and all the while, my interest in medicine was escalating. At last I made my decision. I had only to wait for McGill.

Final exams came and went; my results were the best of my university career. It was now the fourth week of June 1971 and I had just turned 20 years old. Mail arrived from McGill's Faculty of Medicine and with pounding heart I ripped open the envelope. The letter began, "We are pleased to inform you . . . " Thank you, Lord! Thank you! The jubilation of that moment, however, was subdued in the light of some three-day-old news. My mother had cancer.

The hallway was crowded with first-year medical students impatiently waiting before a locked door. Sporting bright white laboratory coats they jested nervously and fidgeted with their newly-purchased set of surgical instruments. It was the first anatomy lab.

The double doors swung open and the more confident ones strolled ahead while the rest eased their way inside. The room reeked of preserving fluid and contained 50 slabs on which lay 50 corpses draped with morbid green sheets. Overcome by the sight and smell, a few students were helped back against the flow into the hallway. At our table, my lab partner and I reached out bravely and pulled back the covering to reveal the corpse of a 60-year-old man. This was my "formalinized" introduction to what was later to be torn and battered living bodies.

I was highly motivated that first year. Having virtually no biological science background, I had to put in extra hours of study. Despite the heavy load I was resolved to stand by a God-given promise in 1 Samuel 2:30 which says, "Them that honour me I will honour." I kept up my commitments at the assembly and hard, disciplined work paid rich dividends that first set of exams.

Christmas was approaching. Mother's surgery was well behind us but she was suffering from the ill effects of a prolonged course of Cobalt therapy. One Saturday night I was directing an open-air carol service in downtown Montreal when the news came. Father had collapsed with chest pain and was in the intensive care unit of the university hospital with a presumed diagnosis of acute myocardial infarction.

It was a difficult time. I trudged the streets around my home wondering why the Christmas lights twinkled merrily. Didn't they know my parents were both sick? Didn't the Lord know? Would my folks be alive to see me graduate? Would they even see me finish first year? Then it occurred to me. How could I be so sure that I would ever complete my training? What guarantee did I have even to live through next week? I saw before me life in all its fragility and uncertainty—as brittle as the Christmas tree ornament that shatters at the slightest impact. There on the snow-filled sidewalk I stopped and turned to the only certainty I knew: *Lord, my tomorrows are far too distant to see but I give them all to you whether they be many or few. I will serve you with or without parents, with or without medical training.* The Lord drew very near that night.

It was several days before my father's condition was sorted out. Idiopathic pericarditis was the very welcome revised diagnosis. The disease lingered unusually long, but by the summer Father was showing flashes of his former vigorous self and Mother's disease seemed under control.

In December 1972, I drove to Wheaton College, Illinois for a congress on world missions. The challenge was clear. The third world had vast educational, medical and spiritual needs. Who would teach the children, heal the sick and share the gospel of Christ if not believers like us? The message was not a new one. I had heard it frequently before but the urgency of it all was something I couldn't ignore. I knew that my own province of Quebec had tremendous spiritual need as well, but if the door opened up, I decided to go overseas during my training to get at least a feel for Christian medical mission work.

Exactly two years later during my final semester at medical school an amazing set of circumstances cleared the way for just such a trip. Under the auspices of Medical Assistance Programs and with a scholarship from *Reader's Digest,* I found myself in south India at Tiruvalla Medical Mission. For three months I worked beside Drs. Kunjappan and Vimala John both of whom had extensive training in America—he, in general surgery and urology; she, in pathology and anesthesia. A dedicated British nurse named Mary Bardsley labored with them as did a large associate staff of Indian physicians and nurses.

Tuberculosis, typhoid fever, cobra and viper bites, elephantiasis, rabies, scorpion stings and leprosy were all a part of this Indian experience—as were three personal encounters with dysentery.

Patients often arrived when their disease was too advanced for treatment. This was partially due to neglect and fear but also related to the local peoples' practice of first consulting the village Ayervedic doctor with his herbal brew and incantations. His influence pervaded every aspect of native life. Witchcraft, voodooism and magic formed the fabric of society. Yet out of this spiritual darkness many had been delivered by the power of Christ and there was a strong indigenous Indian church in the area. I returned home with deep admiration for the Johns and Mary Bardsley, a real love for India and a heightened understanding of a world in need.

The remainder of my final year was humdrum by comparison. The weeks dragged but graduation finally came and with it one of the prizes. Most important of all, the whole family was present—Father, Mother and Debbie.

My internship at Royal Victoria Hospital exposed me to many situations I would later face: trauma, postpartum hemorrhage, minor surgery, cardiac arrests and diagnostic dilemmas. There were satisfying moments such as working night and day on a moribund Eskimo baby—what a joy to see him recover! There were also times of frustration such as attending the young mother with terminal choriocarcinoma. I found medicine to be not just a science but an art as well—the art of helping people recover, cope or die with their disease. Many were the times I drew close to my patients and prayed with them. I realized that many needed me as much to hold their hand as to hook them up to an intravenous solution. I began to see my role as a Christian physician more clearly than ever before.

On July 1, I left the Royal Victoria after the last sleepless night of my internship. Having decided to take off one year before pursuing specialty training, I embarked on a busy summer program of camp work, and in the fall I looked for a posting in general practice. My intent was to pay off my debts and finance a medical trip overseas by February 1, 1977.

All summer I had prayed for a September job that would meet three criteria: first it would be in the East End near my home; second it would let me work for just three or four months; and third, it would provide a largely French clientele so that I could improve upon my fluency.

The obvious specific answer to my prayers came in the form of a small unilingually French clinic in a dingy area of Rosemount. With fear and trembling, I took my place in a swivel chair behind the big oak desk. A French-English dictionary in my left hand and a pen in the right, I braced myself for each new patient. The tension soon dissipated however, and I became deeply involved with the medical and social problems of the poor working class. In fact I grew so attached to the French community that I even expressed regret at leaving it to go overseas—but I had to go overseas.

India, of course, was my planned destination and February 1, 1977 was the target date. There was nothing magic about the first of February: any later than that would mean less than adequate tropical medicine experience before returning to McGill in July; any earlier would break my obligation to work at the clinic for four months. Throughout the fall I had committed my proposed medical trip to the Lord. "Father," I prayed, "please open the door for me to be overseas by February 1, 1977."

In early November, Dr. Jim Rennie spoke at our chapel. Since he had just returned from Zambia, I quizzed him on medical mission life in that country. Almost as an afterthought I asked about mission hospitals in French Africa.

"Well, there's Dr. Peter Coates in Kasaji, Zaire," he said. "I don't really know much about the work but it's quite large and he's the only physician. Why don't you contact him through the Missionary Service Committee in Toronto?"

He handed me the name on a slip of paper and I put it into my back pocket. I had no conviction to follow up his suggestion—India was foremost on my mind.

The next weekend I was visiting friends in Ontario, and on Sunday morning, I met Dr. Donald Curry at Central Hall in downtown Toronto. He had worked for a short time in India and was able to supply the address of the New Delhi-based Emmanuel Hospital Association. I determined to write immediately for information about hospitals needing help in north India.

That very morning, however, Doris Pitman, a veteran Angolan missionary talked with me about my intended expedition. I told her that I was most likely going to India but was sorry there were not any French-speaking regions in that sub-continent.

"Have you ever thought of French Africa?" she asked. "There is a British doctor in Zaire named Peter Coates who may be happy to have some help. Why don't I give you his address?" This time the name plus the address ended up in my back pocket. The story was becoming familiar!

Two days later on November 23, I wrote an impassioned letter to the E.H.A. in New Delhi stating my deep and immediate interest in working in some needy part of north India. I listed a few hospitals that I preferred but indicated an openness to serve at others. The deed was done. All I could do was pray and wait.

The next week, I received a message to telephone Dr. Leslie Bier in Toronto. I knew him by reputation. He had run a hospital in Angola for many years and recently he had been associated with the Missionary Service Committee. I had never met the man and, unless he wanted to offer financial assistance to a fledgling short-term missionary, I couldn't imagine why he would call.

"Dr. Bier? Hello. This is Dave Dawson in Montreal. I believe you wanted me to call you?"

"Yes, I did," a soft and friendly voice began. "Dave, I heard you were interested in going to Zaire."

What? It sounded like a conspiracy! "Well, not really. I am planning on going overseas shortly but expect to work in India."

"When are you supposed to start?" he asked.

"Nothing's definite," I had to reply.

"Where exactly are you going?"

"I don't know that yet either."

"Who are you going to work with?"

"I'm not sure," I answered with growing uneasiness.

"How's your French?"

"Quite good."

"Let me tell you something, Dave. I've just received a letter from Dr.

Peter Coates in Kasaji, Zaire.''

A shiver swept up my spine.

"Dr. Coates is going on furlough in the New Year and wants me to replace him. I've done it before and I really love the people but I am in my seventies. The Lord has been good to us, but I don't know if my wife and I could take the strain of the trip. Would you consider going, Dave?"

I was staggered at the rush of events. I had been asking about French Africa and three times Dr. Coates had been suggested to me. Now there was a specific need at Kasaji. I could speak French and I was available. Was this the Lord's will?

"Well, I'd consider going," I replied cautiously.

"Good. I'll write him tomorrow and let him know."

Not to be railroaded into it, I said, "Dr. Bier, for a long time my heart has been set on India and that is where I still believe I should go. Perhaps the Lord has other plans. I'll pray about it and ask Him to make it clear. But as it stands now, India is my destination." I wondered if I had been too firm.

"The Lord will have His way, Dave," he replied gently. "I'll be in touch if there's any news. Good-bye!"

I calculated from my previous experience with letters to India and Africa that my answer from New Delhi would arrive before Dr. Bier's correspondence ever reached Kasaji. Sometime in mid-December I expected a reply. None came. Christmas arrived. No answer. My prayer was still that I be overseas by February 1, but time was running out. I wrote about the dilemma in my diary: "Do I go to the first place that responds? How long should I wait for the second letter after the first arrives—one week, two weeks, more? What if both arrive at the same time and are decidedly yes? Or worse still, both decidedly no? I do lean towards India because of my previous trip there, but I am beginning to realize that my 'time and places are in His hand.' " I didn't know how prophetic these words would eventually become.

Wednesday, December 29, 1976. An evening telegram arrived from Africa. I trembled as I read the following words, "Accept Montreal doctor. Meet me in Kitwe, Zambia, February 2, 1977. Dr. P. Coates."

I was stunned! How could Africa reply before India? How long do I wait for India's response? What should I tell Dr. Bier? It was amazing the way the Lord had answered my prayers—only one day off! And Dr. Coates sounded so positive. If this was the Lord's will, He had worked it out well—but how could I be sure? Could India's answer be even more specific? There was a fierce inner struggle that night! I had no peace about the direction I should take. Finally, I fell off to sleep.

At noon the next day I phoned home from the clinic.

"Hi Mother, I just—"

"There's a letter here for you," she interrupted. "From India!" I was speechless. "Shall I open it?" she continued.

"No, I'll see it when I get home. Thanks."

What a wonderful God! From eight and ten thousand miles away, answers to my future had arrived within 12 hours of each other. The rest of the day dragged mercilessly on but when I finally arrived home at 9 P.M. a strange spectacle took place! I couldn't open the letter right away! I changed, washed, then ate my late supper while the envelope sat beckoning on the mantle. I read the newspaper in great detail while my parents watched incredulously.

Finally they retired for the night. I knew that they were both aching to know the outcome yet I wanted to face it by myself. Even then, I looked at the rest of my mail first, leaving the critical document to the last. With a sigh, I opened it and read it through once, twice, three times. The message was warm and clear. Distilled it said: Yes, we have a place for you . . . not at any of the hospitals you mentioned . . . perhaps at this other one . . . first there is the need for correspondence with these places to get further information . . . will be in contact. It was evident from the letter that a position would be found but not until March or later.

I curled up in the chair and watched my return to India slowly dissolve before my eyes. The Lord had prepared me to accept this moment and now I praised Him for His leading. I prayed earnestly for that poor country of India and I prayed for that unknown land of Zaire. And even though it was only for a few months, Grannie Durnan was right—I was on my way as a missionary doctor to Africa!

3
Not a Day Late

The early morning sun struggled up over the horizon, its dazzling rays splashing across the cloud tops and inundating the giant bird that winged effortlessly over the primeval jungle. Far to the east a rugged chunk of land pierced the ceiling of cumulus displaying its face to the sun and its shadowed, sinister nape to the plane. Mount Kenya stood solemn guard over the heart of the country but let our aircraft pass unhindered. The thrill of finally standing on African soil would soon be realized.

My final days in Canada had been hectic but I made time to read about Zaire. Previously known as the Belgian Congo, the country had been plunged into turmoil at independence in 1960. Led by Moise Tshombe, the mineral-rich province of Katanga had seceded but the revolt was eventually crushed by the United Nations which was committed to maintain Congo's national boundaries. The Katangese troops had fled into Angola where they were employed as mercenaries by Portugal to quell local uprisings throughout the colony. Since an abortive attempt to retake their homeland in 1967, the Katangese had remained in Angola fighting first for the Portuguese, then for the newly established Marxist regime.

Lumumba, Kasavubu, the Simbas, Dr. Carl Becker, the martyred Dr. Paul Carlson—all were prominent figures in Congo's story. Since 1965 however, Joseph Désiré Mobutu had dominated the political, social and religious life of Africa's third largest nation. He was president of the government and of the country's only legal political party. He was chief of the armed forces and the police, and he presided over the Cabinet, the Legislature and the Supreme Court. Mobutu was in complete control.

Under his rule the country was renamed the Republic of Zaire and the Congo River became the Zaire River. His Africanization policy forced all citizens to drop their Christian names and adopt African ones, he himself becoming known as Mobutu Sese Seko. The Catholic Church was severely

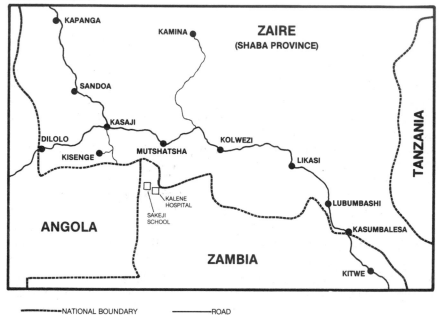

KAPANGA

KAMINA

ZAIRE
(SHABA PROVINCE)

SANDOA

KASAJI

DILOLO

KISENGE

MUTSHATSHA

KOLWEZI

LIKASI

TANZANIA

KALENE
HOSPITAL

SAKEJI
SCHOOL

ANGOLA

LUBUMBASHI

KASUMBALESA

ZAMBIA

KITWE

------------NATIONAL BOUNDARY ————————ROAD

Diagram 2

criticized and all Protestant groups were required to merge into one national church. Easter, Pentecost and eventually Christmas became working days. All religious youth organizations were banned and Mobutu's portrait re- placed crucifixes throughout the land.

His government forged friendships with both East and West in a politics of expediency. Economically Zaire was propped up by the wealth of the mines in Shaba province, the old Katanga. Industries had been nationalized and foreign traders' businesses handed over to Zairians; but these and other policies had led the country to the brink of financial ruin. My reading on Zaire had not painted a very glowing picture.

Tickets, visas, and other plans finalized, I was left with the good-byes—the hardest task of all. On Friday, January 28, a small party of family and friends struggled to the airport through a blinding snowstorm. The farewells were quick. I was off. A day in Amsterdam and touch-downs in Munich and Cairo had brought me to Sunday morning and a slow descent into Kenya.

I was exhausted. My body was not designed to slumber in a seated position and I had managed less than three hours of sleep in two days. It felt as if I had worked all weekend in the intensive care unit. Moreover there was little prospect of rest before my 3 P.M. flight to Lusaka—a Canadian missionary named Judith Perlick was to meet me at the airport and bring me to one of the Nairobi assemblies for Sunday worship. Tonight in Lusaka, I would catch up on my sleep—or so I thought.

Thrilled as I was to arrive in Nairobi and meet some of the Christians, and impressed as I was by the city's skyscrapers, parks and boulevards, I was happy to head back to the airport. Judith had been delightfully hospitable and I promised to take her out for a leisurely meal on my return through Nairobi in June.

It was 2 P.M. when I strolled through a surprisingly empty terminal building to the Zambian Airways booth.

"I have a ticket for the 3 P.M. Lusaka flight," I said to the agent.

"Sorry, sir. It left 15 minutes ago," he replied.

"What? It's not supposed to be off for another hour!"

"Well, we had enough passengers so it left early." I couldn't believe it! This method for determining departure times was certainly novel and would make a good story back home but it thoroughly upset my travel arrangements. Not only would some poor fellow be left waiting for me in Lusaka that evening, but I would miss tomorrow's connecting flight to Kitwe where the Coates were to meet me. I couldn't fathom why the Lord was allowing all these complications to intervene.

"Will there be any flights to Lusaka tomorrow?" I asked.

"Maybe."

"When will you know?"

"Call us in the morning. If there is a plane, we'll guarantee you a seat. Here, let me adjust your ticket." By now physical exhaustion had overtaken me and a pounding headache dulled my senses.

"Well, Judith," I mumbled absently, "what next?"

"Come on. We'll go back home. You can sleep at a neighbor's house. I guess the Lord wants you to get some rest before you move on. And don't worry about the Coates in Kitwe. We'll telephone them later tonight." Her resourcefulness in this setback was a real blessing.

Half an hour later I tumbled into bed. At the limits of fatigue while on hospital duty, I often found a little extra strength to open the Scriptures before falling asleep. That afternoon I read the following words from Proverbs 30: "Who hath gathered the wind in his fists? who hath bound the waters in a garment? who hath established all the ends of the earth? . . . he is a shield unto them that put their trust in him" (vv. 4,5).

What an encouragement! The One who established and controlled the elements could doubtless care for His own children—even those who missed their connecting flights. With a truly thankful heart I put out the lights and fell fast asleep.

It was dark. I strained through aching eyes at my watch. Nine o'clock, the luminescent hands revealed. What day was this? Where, who and how produced equally vague responses but finally I became reoriented. I hastily dressed and plodded next door.

"Welcome," said a cheery voice. "There's a little food here ready for you to eat."

Together we enjoyed the meal then shared some Scriptures. We tried unsuccessfully to telephone Mrs. Turner's home in Kitwe where the Coates were staying. Instead, we contacted Jim and Ruth Hess at nearby Chingola and they promised to relay the message. Then, before retiring for the night, I wrote a letter home detailing the auspicious beginning of my adventures.

How glorious it was to wake up the next morning refreshed and ready for the next leg of my journey. Breakfast was a hearty preparation of eggs, cereal, toast and that delicious British spread, Marmite. We drove downtown to the Zambian Airways head office where to my joy I learned that a Lusaka flight was newly scheduled for 11:30 A.M. My reservation was confirmed and we hastened to the airport arriving at 9:30 A.M. I approached the same ill-fated wicket as the day before.

"Good morning! I have a seat on this morning's Lusaka flight."

"Sorry. We are full—the flight is booked up. We have turned many away," he replied. How could that be? I excitedly repeated the whole story while Judith underscored the important points. After a hasty consultation with some colleagues, he apologized for the mix-up and processed my ticket. I wondered if the real obstacle was that I had not offered a bribe.

Judith had been such a help. I reminded her of that June supper engagement.

We soon boarded and when the jet took off there were still several seats available despite the ticket agent's story. In conversing with fellow travelers I learned the amazing details about the previous day's Lusaka flight. The plane had not in fact gone to Lusaka but had been commandeered by a delegation of politicians for a trip to Tanzania! The unfortunate passengers waited in a crowded lounge all evening and most were actually aboard this flight. How wonderful the Lord had been to give me all that rest instead of hours of frustration and discomfort in a waiting room!

We arrived in Lusaka to hear some exciting news. The plane to Kitwe had been delayed so that we could catch the flight! The only problem was that the destination had been switched from Kitwe to Ndola. From there, we would be bussed 30 miles to our original terminus. There was no alternative—I would call Mrs. Turner as soon as I arrived.

I clambered aboard as with growing excitement I anticipated my encounter with the Coates. What would they be like? Dr. Peter Coates had been just a name on a piece of paper in my back pocket yet I knew that he had been awarded the M.B.E. from Queen Elizabeth in 1973 for his record of distinguished medical service in Zaire. About Ruth Coates I knew nothing, but soon I would meet them both.

"Attention. This is your captain speaking. Our plans have changed. We will land at Kitwe first then proceed to Ndola. Our estimated time of arrival is 3:30 P.M."

By now I could believe anything. Even when I learned that the airport was 10 miles from Kitwe and had no taxis, telephones, washrooms nor waiting rooms, it hardly surprised me. Somehow I would make it.

Up ahead in the middle of the bush with no town in sight sat a tiny airstrip with a small hangar and a little office—the famous Kitwe airport. On landing we were told to retrieve our own baggage from behind the cockpit. I organized a task force and within minutes the luggage was unloaded and distributed. Finally I disembarked.

I had no idea what the Coates looked like but no one seemed to fit the imagined description and no one approached me. I would simply have to wait in this desolate place until they came. In the meantime I pulled out my camera for a photo of the plane. As I adjusted the settings, a raspy voice with a thick German accent breathed, "Put it away—quickly! Come here!" Obedient, I thrust it into my sack and walked over to a fellow passenger who stood with his family and a younger brother.

"You're lucky that you're not already arrested and your camera confiscated," whispered Mr. Egger, the younger. "This is a restricted area where absolutely no pictures are to be shot. Don't so much as take out the camera again!"

I was aghast at the admonition but very relieved as the moments ticked by and no military arrived to whisk me away. This unusual introduction to the Eggers was most providential for when they discovered my predicament, they offered me a lift into town. I thankfully accepted it.

On the way to their construction firm in Kitwe, the Eggers bemoaned the flagging economy, the difficulty attracting foreign engineers, the worthless "wallpaper" currency and the scarcity of whisky and cigars. According to them, life in the Copper Belt was not what it used to be.

After a half hour ride, we arrived at their large industrial complex. As we stepped out of the car and opened the truck, several African employees were quick to reach for our baggage. Feeling equally capable to the task, I carried my own suitcases inside amidst incredulous looks. I was ushered into an empty suite and given some coffee while the receptionist was commissioned to ring Mrs. Turner.

Mr. Egger the younger soon joined me. Relaxing in his swivel chair, he recounted in greater detail the problems of the Copper Belt. When I told him that Zaire was my destination, he shook his head saying that the situation was even worse there. He was completely baffled when I further mentioned that there were no wages waiting for me and that it was God's love that constrained me to come. It saddened me that he had no real understanding of a personal God and man's responsibility to Him.

Twice, Mr. Egger telephoned the front desk to see if my contacts were reached. Twice the reply was that the calls couldn't get through and twice he gruffly ordered the African to make the connection or else. On turning to me, however, he was as mild-mannered as could be. In one breath he swore at the African and with the next he offered to put me up in his home. I was shattered by this double-standard treatment of two persons equally made in the image of God.

A third effort proved just as fruitless. He slammed down the phone with cursings and said, "Well, Doctor, it's five o'clock. What would you like to do?"

"Frankly, Mr. Egger, I appreciate your offer but I must find my friends tonight. Perhaps I could get a taxi and track them down. They live at Itempi near Kitwe."

"No taxis here, my friend—but follow me."

The firm's large garage contained several vehicles. Mr. Egger bellowed for a driver and soon a pudgy African in a tattered suit and beat-up fedora appeared.

"Take the Doctor to Itempi and if he cannot find his friends, bring him back to my place. Understand?"

"Yes, Mr. Egger."

"Good!" Then turning to me, he extended his hand and said, "Good luck, young man."

"Thanks for your help! I'd like to meet you again." There was much more that I wanted to say but the time was inappropriate. I would write him later on. In the meantime I was grateful for his kindnesses to me.

The pickup roared down the national highway towards Itempi while billows of black cloud poured from the exhaust system like a stream of smoke signals. After a few moments of silence, the African chauffeur announced in his thoroughly amusing thick German accent, "All Americans are very rich, eh?" He seemed to be moderately satisfied when I explained that I was neither American nor rich but was in Africa to serve the people without prospect of any monetary gain. He listened as I told about God's free gift but he seemed to doubt the existence of such an offer.

The sign for Itempi appeared on our right. We swung off the main road and at the first intersection decided to turn left. In the drizzling rain and early dusk I peered out the truck window at the first house. A little sign sat on the front lawn and I barely made out the words "Christian Missions in Many Lands."

"This is it!" I exulted. "Turn in here." My joy was boundless. I had made it from a desolate airstrip to an unknown industrial office to my expected destination—all without public transport or telephone. My heart bowed in quiet worship and thanksgiving to the Lord.

The truck stopped behind the house to the noisy barking of the dog and the wild fluttering of the chickens. An astonished woman stepped outside.

"Mrs. Turner? My name is David Dawson." Poor lady! Her chin dropped with amazement and she fumbled for a few words before regaining her composure.

"We must bring this luggage inside," she said, reaching for one of my two bags. I thanked the chauffeur and asked him to convey my appreciation once more to the Eggers. The old pickup rattled off leaving a smokescreen to cover its trail. I followed Mrs. Turner into the house.

"You've beat the Coates. Well, I never! Imagine that—all on your own steam. They left early this morning to fetch you and it's now, let me see, 5:30 P.M. Never mind. Put your cases in that room. That's where you'll sleep tonight. You'll be off in the morning. If you want a bath here's a towel and there's the bathroom. Now make yourself at home. Poor Peter and Ruth!" Mrs. Turner had all the answers even before I submitted the questions. I was especially grateful for her invitation to get freshened up. I certainly needed it.

It was 6:30 P.M. A vehicle rumbled up the driveway and stopped behind the house. Trying to control my intense joy I strolled out to meet the Coates. A lean, determined-looking man walked briskly away from the Land Rover.

"Dr. Coates? I believe you were looking for me."

"Dr. Dawson! It's good to see you. I'd like you to meet my wife Ruth." It was all so very formal. I shook hands with Ruth. She was of slight stature but looked every bit as energetic as he and she had such a radiantly warm and winsome smile. We went inside where the story unfolded. The flight changes had sent the Coates racing back and forth between airports. When I actually arrived, however, their Land Rover had broken down on the highway and there it stayed for three hours. Finally, with the vehicle repaired but without a trace of me they had returned home quite exhausted and discouraged. I was glad that my presence provided them with a little cheer to an otherwise exasperating day.

After supper, the conversation switched to Kasaji. "Three months ago I had never heard of Kasaji and was fully expecting to go to India. Then I was bombarded from every direction with the suggestion to write Dr. Coates. All this time I was praying to be overseas by February 1, 1977. When I received your telegram to be in Kitwe on February 2, you can imagine my reaction. Then came the letter from India, and surprisingly it was very vague by comparison. Anyway, now I'm here. When do we go?''

Peter chuckled. "Not so fast. There's plenty of traveling to be done. We'll have a good night's sleep and be off early in the morning." He paused for a moment then continued, "You mentioned something interesting about the telegram. Ruth and I had to be here now to send our eldest child Annie to school in Rhodesia. We in fact wanted you here by February 1 but you see the Belgian and French numeral one looks deceivingly like a seven to North Americans. Since we didn't want to chance you arriving a week late we changed our original telegram from February 1 to February 2.''

My heart leapt to my throat. I was overwhelmed by this revelation. My prayers had been answered so specifically. I knew I was in the center of God's will and went to bed that night praising Him for His goodness to me.

Early the next morning we headed for the Zambian-Zaire frontier. The two-lane national highway took us to Kasumbalesa on the border and at 11A.M. we entered Zaire. I lowered the window and took a deep breath of fresh air. Wide-eyed I scanned the rolling terrain and the lush green vegetation. I was finally here. It was February 1, 1977.

4
"*Jambo!* Welcome to Zaire!"

Scarcely 200 yards ahead was a roadblock. "Let me do the talking," Peter cautioned as a soldier stepped out of the bushes and lumbered into our path. A rifle nestled in the crook of his arm, he stood motionless, almost defiantly, while the Land Rover eased to a halt.

"*Jambo,*" Peter began most congenially. Although I didn't understand Congo Swahili it took little imagination to catch the gist of the conversation. The soldier stared in at us and demanded a search of our luggage but Peter resisted saying that we had already been certified entry by customs. Of course that meant little to him. Each military man was virtually a law unto himself.

While the dispute continued, a second member of the roadblock squad emerged from a nearby wrecked car. Straightening his clothes and stretching his arms, he shook off a late morning snooze. Fortunately he was more amicable than his colleague and seemed to be satisfied by Peter's explanations for our travel. He motioned us on much to the disappointment of his confrere who fully expected to exact some payment from us whether in money, food or seized goods. The angry soldier dismantled the barricade and glowered at us while we edged past him and carried on our way.

"I don't believe it! That guy actually wanted us to pay him something—and he brandished a gun to make him even more persuasive!" I exclaimed.

"Don't get too upset. Roadblocks and barrier fees are part of life here," Peter replied. "Just be thankful that the soldiers are lenient on physicians. Any other traveler would have had to pay a tidy sum, especially an African!"

The conditions of the highway had markedly deteriorated since we crossed the border. The road was now single lane and in many places the tarmac had been completely washed out. Even though this was the main thoroughfare from Zambia to Lubumbashi, traffic was almost non-existent; every one or two hours we would meet another vehicle. Signs of life were few

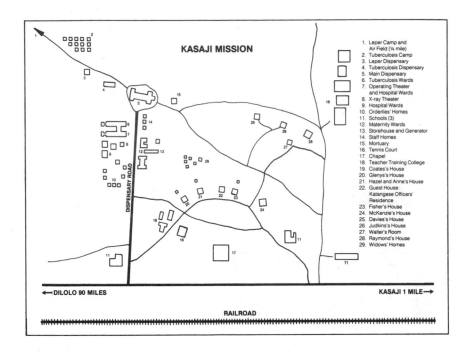

KASAJI MISSION

1. Leper Camp and
   Air Field (¼ mile)
2. Tuberculosis Camp
3. Leper Dispensary
4. Tuberculosis Dispensary
5. Main Dispensary
6. Tuberculosis Wards
7. Operating Theater
   and Hospital Wards
8. X-ray Theater
9. Hospital Wards
10. Orderlies' Homes
11. Schools (3)
12. Maternity Wards
13. Storehouse and Generator
14. Staff Homes
15. Mortuary
16. Tennis Court
17. Chapel
18. Teacher Training College
19. Coates's House
20. Glenys's House
21. Hazel and Anne's House
22. Guest House:
    Katangese Officers'
    Residence
23. Fisher's House
24. McKenzie's House
25. Davies's House
26. Judkins's House
27. Walter's Room
28. Raymond's House
29. Widows' Homes

DISPENSARY ROAD

←—DILOLO 90 MILES   KASAJI 1 MILE—→

RAILROAD

Diagram 3

in this region but the Kasaji area supposedly had a much more substantial population. How had the Coates come to Zaire?

"Well, David," Ruth began, "I grew up in Bern, Switzerland. After teaching for several years near my home I was led by the Lord to work in Nyankunde in northeast Congo. That's where I later met Peter. When he had finished his medical training he came out here to replace mission doctors who were on furlough. We were married in 1961 and went for what was to be a short time to Kasaji. We're still there." Finishing medical training, replacing doctors on furlough, short time—it sounded all too familiar.

"Peter, I've been meaning to ask you when you're returning to England," I asked.

"The first week in April," he answered.

"That's when the children finish their classes," Ruth explained. "We're picking up Lizzie and Jimmy across the way at Sakeji School in Zambia, and Annie's flying home on her own from Salisbury."

The first week in April, I mused. That would give me two months before being on my own. "Peter, tell me about the hospital."

Peter turned on the windshield wipers as a gentle rain began to fall. He guided the Land Rover around a pothole and finally spoke. "Well, the hospital is a busy place. We treat 350 lepers, over 300 active tuberculosis patients and perform more than 800 deliveries a year. Beyond that, there is the regular medical and surgical work."

"What?" I protested. "How many nurses do you have?"

"Five one for the TB's, one for maternity, one for surgery, and two for general ward and clinic work."

"And the lepers?" I asked incredulously.

"I run clinics for the lepers regularly but Ruth and one of our orderlies attend to their day-to-day needs," Peter replied. "Besides all this, each year we take a thousand x-rays as well as perform 260 major operations and 300 minor ones. Four hundred outpatients are treated each day and a thousand new files are opened monthly. The general medical and surgical cases fill up another 75 hospital beds. In addition, we conduct monthly medical trips to our dispensaries at Mutshatsha and Katoka. Are you getting tired already?"

Tired? I was terrified! How had I managed to inherit this? Kasaji needed a team of experienced physicians and surgeons not a rookie medic. I began to fantasize impending emergency situations—shock, poisoning, acute intestinal obstruction, ruptured ectopic pregnancies. How could I cope alone?

I was snapped out of my wild imaginings as Peter muttered, "Road-block ahead!" Another hastily constructed barrier was thrown up across our path and another couple of soldiers began to question us. When they found out that we were physicians, one of them began to complain about his health.

"I have a terrible headache and stomach cramps," he moaned. "For several days I've suffered with diarrhea, vomiting, fever and fatigue. I can't go on this way any longer." Peter handed over three white pills with instructions to take two that day and one the next. The now smiling and recovered Zairian soldier let us through the barrier.

"What could you possibly have given him?" I asked Peter.

"Aspirin," he replied through a smile ever so slight. "He's not sick. He'll probably sell the drug on the black market where it will fetch him a good price. Anyway it was better than him rummaging through all our medical supplies."

Soon we spotted Lubumbashi, the old Elizabethville, now Zaire's third largest city. Slag heaps, smoking chimneys and shaft houses surrounded the provincial capital and reminded us that Zaire's wealth lay in these Shaba mines.

We proceeded to our local mission along city streets that were filled with speeding, weaving, honking vehicles. There were no traffic lights to speak of and the whole situation reminded me of a demolition derby. We also saw cars lined up for blocks on the main roads and side avenues. They weren't locked in traffic jams; they were waiting for gas at their local Petro Zaire filling stations.

What struck me most, however, were numerous signs exalting the president in almost divine fashion: "Mobutu Sese Seko, Our Only Hope"; "Mobutu Sese Seko, Our Salvation." Such tribute was sadly misplaced. Christ was man's hope and man's salvation. These government proclamations flatly contradicted a life-style that I was following and which I intended to preach.

At supper I was still troubled by those billboards I had seen. "Peter, do you remember those signs in town?"

"Which ones?"

"You know, the ones about Mobutu being the only hope and salvation. Don't they bother you?" I asked.

Peter paused then slowly replied. "Most people don't take them as seriously as you have, David. To the Africans they're more a figure of speech. However, as missionaries in Zaire we are guests of the country, and as guests we obey the laws of the land. Our task is to supply medical and educational assistance and to share the gospel. Not everyone may agree but politically we remain silent, praying that the changed lives of Africans may become instruments of righteous change for the nation. As long as we can continue with this work we are thankful to the government in power."

The mission headquarters at which we were staying was called "Restawhile" and had been established by the Rews. Mr. Rew was 91 years of age and through his pioneer efforts about 40 assemblies had been planted in Lubumbashi. The old warrior was still a going concern. Recently he had traveled to Katoka where he had conducted a 10-day Bible conference for African church leaders. We visited him that evening and a couple of hours later had to pull ourselves away from his fascinating stories in order to allow him sufficient sleep for the night.

The next morning we picked up some measles and smallpox vaccine at the provincial health bureau. The medical officer warmly greeted us and showed us a map which pinpointed the location of each of the 153 physicians serving Shaba's population of 5 million.

The Kasaji area was noteworthy by its lack of doctors. At Kapanga, 160 miles north of Kasaji was Dr. Glen Eschtruth, an American Methodist missionary. At Kisenge, 50 miles to the southwest and at Mutshatsha, 65 miles to the east were hospitals for the mines but medical care was mostly limited to employees and their families. There were no doctors to the south of us. Kasaji was thus responsible for much of southwest Shaba province with a population of at least 250,000 people.

Our final stop before continuing our journey was the post office. "We won't be long," Ruth promised.

"Don't leave the Land Rover for anything," Peter added. "It takes only minutes for thieves to do their work."

I reclined in the back seat and watched Lubumbashi's mid-morning activity. There was an almost leisurely atmosphere that prevailed. Men in flashy Western attire stood idly on the sidewalks. Young African beauties peacocked across the square while a few late model cars cruised around and around this downtown hub.

After a while the time began to drag and I decided to take some pictures of urban African life. A young macho pranced down the sidewalk. *Click.* I was fascinated by the African hairstyles—puffballs, medusa-like braids, and massive Afros. *Click. Click.* Suddenly my whole viewing field became blurred. I looked up. An angry face stared back. Around the vehicle were eight similar countenances.

"What are you doing?" growled the spokesman in French.

I lowered the camera to the floor and, determining to stall as long as possible I replied, "Waiting."

"Waiting for what?" he retorted.

"Who are you anyway?" I asked, ignoring his question.

"Security agents," asserted the Boss, thumping his chest. "We have been watching you all morning. What are you waiting for?"

"The arrival of the doctor."

"Which doctor?"

"Dr. Coates from Kasaji. He is in charge of a large hospital two days' journey from here."

I rambled on and on about how many lepers, and tuberculosis patients he had, about his outpost dispensaries, about his awards from the Queen and capped it off by declaring that I too was a physician, newly arrived to help him out. They were duly impressed and began to repeat the details quite excitedly amongst themselves.

"Where are you from?" the Boss continued. My story had not satisfied them. It had only made them hungrier for more information.

"Quebec," I replied, but seeing their blank faces I hastily added, "in Canada." They looked at each other and grunted knowingly but somehow I wasn't convinced.

"Where's Canada?" I asked the Boss.

"In the north."

"Where in the north?"

"In Africa of course," he snarled.

"What about you?" I asked turning to his associate.

"It's in Europe." The gravity of my situation became more clear with each passing moment.

"Show me your passport," the Boss ordered. I held it up for him to see. "Give it to me!" he barked.

"No! You must wait until the doctor arrives." I knew enough not to surrender my passport.

"We have caught you spying!" the Boss charged.

"What?" I was startled at the obvious fabrication.

"You were taking pictures of the military installation," he announced exultantly.

"What military installation?"

"The post office," he declared.

"The post office?" I stammered disbelievingly.

"Yes. There are military antennae on the roof." From my vantage point I couldn't even see the front door of the post office, let alone the roof.

"I took no pictures of the post office whatsoever. You'll have to believe me."

A young man jumped out from the group of security police and exclaimed, "I saw him lean out the window and take a picture of the antennae—like this," and he pretended to snap a photo through an imaginary camera.

I was incensed at this damning falsehood. Glaring at him I breathed softly, "You're a liar," and he melted back into the gathering crowd.

The situation was becoming hopeless. Turning to the Boss I politely said, "Dr. Coates will be here soon. I am going to wait for him." With that I moved away from the window and opened a book. I wasn't reading, however, I was praying. How would we ever disentangle ourselves from this mess? Poor Peter and Ruth!

After some time the Boss gathered his men together and left three of them to handle the affair. Minutes later the Coates arrived. I quickly explained the situation to them, hoping that with Peter's prestige and experience he would have more success. Not so. He tried the soft approach then the hard approach, then the appeal-to-reason approach and the rev-your-engine-and-pretend-to-leave approach, but all to no avail. The more we squirmed the worse it got. Finally they insisted that we accompany them to military headquarters for interrogation. Peter adamantly refused.

"Well," repeated one of them, "there are only two things to do—go to the military headquarters or . . . " and his voice trailed off. He said it again and then it struck home. They wanted a bribe! The audacity of these rogues! No wonder Peter was so opposed to going to their offices; there would be more mouths to feed. We prayed for deliverance from these unreasonable men.

Just when all seemed lost, along came Mr. Shakespeare, the British consul. After hearing our story he lashed into the security men with a vengeance. "Why are you harassing tourists? Don't you know the government is trying to encourage them? This young doctor is in the country for 24 hours and you're already pestering him. Don't you have anything better to do?'' Even I cringed at the consul's barrage.

"But he took photos of the post office with its antennae!" they countered.

"Did you?" he asked me.

"No."

"There we go," Shakespeare continued. "He didn't. And even if he did, what would it matter? You or I or he could go into any one of the shops around this square and buy a post card with a full-sized photo of the post office including the antennae. What's the difference?" he argued.

There was a stony silence. "Good, I'm glad that we agree. Now they can leave for Kasaji."

"No!" one of them fought back. "There are only two things to do—go to the military headquarters, or . . ."

The consul turned to Peter and said, "These men are not interested in their own people—they only want a fast bribe. Why don't you send Dr. Dawson back to Canada? The Zairians do not deserve to have him. Let the people of Kasaji suffer and die!" Shakespeare's ploy was brutal but it brought a swift response.

"Wait a minute!" one called out and the three of them pulled away for a quick conference.

Within moments they returned. Angrily one of them scowled, "We have two things to tell you. Mr. Consul—you go! And Mr. Doctor—you go too!" Then, softening, he grabbed my hand and shook it warmly saying, "Work hard for our people. Thank you for coming to our land. We need you."

After a round of hand shaking and well-wishing with all the secret police we left Lubumbashi, still dumbfounded at the amazing turn of events but deeply thankful to the Lord for bringing the consul to us at our bleakest moment.

The next leg of our journey was anticlimactic by comparison. Roadblocks became a welcome distraction to our travel. As long as we encountered no mechanical trouble we expected to arrive at our next stop, Kolwezi, by supper.

"Peter, what happens when the Land Rover breaks down on the highway?" It was an innocent question.

"I fix it." It was a truthful answer. Being handy was essential in the bush. There were no telephones, tow trucks, or garages. The missionary was on his own. In the pioneering days there were no cars either. The early missionaries had to be rugged sorts—like Grannie Fisher.

"Tell me a little about Grannie Fisher," I remarked.

"Grannie has been in Africa for over 60 years," Ruth began, "so there's more than a little to say about her. She and her husband Singleton Fisher are almost legendary figures amongst the Lunda people. They traveled in canoe and on foot from village to village winning the hearts of the Africans to themselves and to the Lord. Together they translated the Bible into Ndembu, and Grannie herself translated *Pilgrim's Progress* and created the first Ndembu dictionary. Singleton died back in 1961 but Grannie stayed on and still does translation work as well as conduct reading classes for women. Except for her deafness and her weak legs she's remarkably well for 83. Grannie's anxious to meet you, David, and I'm sure she'll fill in the details.'' I certainly looked forward to that time.

Kolwezi was a mining center. Gigantic craters had been gouged from the surrounding countryside. Dynamite blasts shook the earth and caravans of lorries streamed from the bustling quarries. Modern homes, street lamps and tennis courts could be seen in the affluent sections of town. Several thousand whites still lived here staffing Belgian, French and American mining interests in the area.

It was dusk when we arrived at the mission house. Our co-worker Terry Smith was overjoyed to see us and invited us for supper to the home of Ken and Lorraine Enright. Pilot, evangelist and senior missionary with the American Methodists, Ken was an inveterate storyteller whose infectious laugh crowned each rollicking tale. It was sheer delight to spend the evening with them, and to sense their love for the Lord and for the African people.

The next morning we stopped at the Enright's as we left Kolwezi. They had been in radio contact with Kasaji and informed us of a robbery at the mission overnight. A thief had broken into the Raymond's home and had stolen a clock, a radio and Mr. Raymond's mobylette (moped).

''Poor Robert,'' Ruth said as we continued our journey. ''Just three months ago his car was stolen. It was found but we couldn't replace the missing parts. When Robert ordered pieces from overseas they were lifted in the mail. All of us have been victimized and there is little to be done. The local police never find anyone.''

''What about the hospital supplies? Do they get stolen too?'' I asked.

''Regularly,'' Peter answered. ''If our boxes arrive at all, they arrive half empty, the most valuable drugs having disappeared in transit. Complaints never reach the right source and if they do, nothing happens. It's a way of life and we've had to cope with it.''

What a way of life! No amount of legislation or terror or reason could reverse such deep-seated malignancy. Legislation encountered loopholes. Terror was met by counterterror. Reason faltered in the face of monetary gain. Only the life-changing Christ could give man a solid foundation upon which to reconstruct from the chaos of that old way of life; only His blood could cleanse men's sin and guilt; only His power could sustain and drive the new creation. That was our message for the people. That was our hope for the community.

We were now deep in southwest Shaba province traveling in a steady downpour on the most terrible highway I had ever seen. Only big trucks and four-wheel drive powerhouses like our Land Rover could get through. Even then a great deal of skill was needed as evidenced by several lorries lying entrapped in ditches along the route. The rain fell more heavily and streams of water cascaded down hilly sections of the road carrying gravel, rocks and sand; no wonder whole sides of the highway had simply disappeared! Other stretches of road had a treacherous clay base over which the vehicle skidded and lurched as it battled onward. A blitzing thunderstorm now cut visibility to 10 yards. What a ride!

Soon the rain stopped and the sun shone, but the highway was worse than ever—and this the main east-west thoroughfare of southern Zaire. We passed through many small African villages creating quite a stir in the communities. Little children would scramble towards us from their homes screaming, *"Jambo,"* and many adults excitedly called out *"Munganga, munganga,"* as they saw Peter go by.

After driving for almost four hours we arrived at our Mutshatsha mission. The town had been a major railway center under the Belgians but in recent years it had undergone a general decline. However, Peter maintained a dispensary here and that afternoon we saw several interesting patients: a man with a "watering-can" perineum; a woman with newly-diagnosed tuberculosis; and children with herniating irises secondary to vitamin A deficiency. Some would come to Kasaji for treatment while others would be followed at Mutshatsha by our trained African orderlies.

About 2:30 P.M. we finished a late lunch and pushed off to Kasaji down washed-out roads, through isolated villages, over swollen rivers, across grassy plains and under interlocking jungle. Mile after weary mile we pressed on. Conversation lagged. We all wanted to arrive.

At 6:10 P.M. we rolled through the main intersection of Kasaji town and five minutes later swung into the mission proper. Peter tooted his horn the length of the station before finally pulling up behind his house. We had barely unloaded when Harold McKenzie roared up on his motorcycle and invited us over for the evening meal.

Supper at the McKenzie's was the first of many similar refreshing times. Harold and Norma were New Zealanders—she a nurse, and he the mission maintenance man. The meal was hardly underway, however, when the hospital sent word that a woman had just arrived with a fractured femur. Peter and I gobbled down our food and started off. I was bone weary from the six-day journey but my heart was doing cartwheels and thanksgiving filled my being.

Kasaji was not only a place—it had become a call to obedience and service. Obedience had brought me here. Service was just beginning.

5
The Sweet and the Bitter

Cock-a-doodle-doo! Cock-a-doodle-doo! I jerked the blankets over my head at the swelling chorus: *Cock-a-doodle-doo!* "How can anybody sleep with that racket?" I moaned. Throwing off the bedclothes, I staggered to the window and shut it. "That should do it," I mumbled as I hopped back into bed. *Cock-a-doodle-doo!* More awake than ever, I nevertheless determined to fight on. My head now buried under the pillows, I pulled the blankets tightly over everything. *Cock-a-doodle-doo!* I had to surrender. The Alarm Cock, or so I called him, had won again. It was 5:45 A.M. and clearly time to get up. I rolled out of bed.

In my first day at Kasaji, I had met most of the staff as well as toured the more than 100 buildings. A host of new faces and places still blurred my mind. Today was my baptism of fire—I would see my first African patients.

After a time of reading and prayer I joined Peter and Ruth at exactly 7 A.M. for breakfast. The Coates were a model of punctuality.

"Good morning, David," Ruth chimed.

"Good morning."

"How did you sleep?" she asked.

"Great—until the rooster crowed."

"Was it a foul sound?" Peter was an incurable punster.

Breakfast was typically English. A bowl of porridge, two cups of tea with a dash of milk, one piece of toast with marmalade—this was Peter's daily immutable fare. It was all very nourishing but my advent would soon introduce such abominable breakfast alternatives as rice cakes, papayas and homemade peanut butter on toast. Peter would be scandalized.

"We round at seven-thirty," Peter announced, "then it's off to the dispensary. There should be quite a crowd today. The word's passed around that another doctor is here and everybody wants to see you."

I gulped.

Rounds were conducted in a curious mixture of Swahili, Ndembu, Chokwe, French and English. The average native spoke either Ndembu or Chokwe and probably Swahili while the more educated also knew French. None of the Africans spoke English, however, and we could use it to discuss delicate issues in front of the patients.

In one hour we saw more than 70 patients with a variety of conditions: hydrocephalus and hip fractures, malaria and malnutrition, pelvic inflammatory disease and paraphimosis, measles and melanoma. With scarcely a moment to collect my thoughts, and without visiting the maternity, tuberculosis and leprosy wings of the hospital, I followed Peter to the dispensary. Several hundred outpatients had been gathering there since early morning. Although many had already been seen, others were referred to the doctor and now jostled for position as they saw us coming. We slipped in through a side door and stumbled onto Sue Judkins and Norma with a dozen or so Africans in their examining room.

"Good morning," shouted Sue over the din.

"Good morning," I replied. "It's a little noisy, isn't it?"

"Don't worry, you'll get used to it," she called out. "By the way, Colin and I want you over for supper tonight. Glenys and Walter are coming too."

"That sounds great," I said. "Thanks a lot." I stepped over another couple of patients and entered Peter's office. "Am I confused! I'm totally lost with all the names and when it comes to who's married to who, forget it."

"It takes time but it'll come. Sit here while I call the first patient." Peter strode to the door and opened it wide to reveal a sea of black faces, brown eyes and white teeth all directed at me.

"Ndala Kapenda!" Peter bellowed. An elderly man broke through the crowd and hobbled into the room. Peter shut the door behind him and took a seat at his desk.

"*Kuya, baba. Ikala hapa,*" Peter said in Swahili. The man came closer, sat down and excitedly began his story.

Many patients were whisked through that morning: a woman with a massive splenomegaly, a man with cirrhosis, and several new surgical candidates. Then at 10 o'clock Peter jumped up. "Time for break." Back at the house, Ruth had prepared biscuits and, to my surprise, not tea but coffee.

"Ruth, don't you have tea in the morning?" I asked.

"Oh no-o-o," she intoned. "Coffee at ten, tea at three. Don't you drink coffee?"

"Well frankly, I rarely have it at home. It's not that I don't like coffee. I just don't drink it often."

"That's too bad," Peter replied matter-of-factly. "When we heard that a North American was coming we bought 40 jars of coffee.'' I almost choked on my cookie and then all of us broke into laughter.

"Would you prefer tea?'' Ruth continued.

"Oh no,'' I said. "I'll take coffee, but if you're ever in doubt, I always respond well to a glass of cold water.''

I was still working on my biscuit when Peter stood up and strode to the door. "Time to go,'' he announced.

"It's hard to keep up with him,'' I muttered as I washed my cookie down and charged out after him. Ruth smiled knowingly.

By noon we had seen 40 outpatients. Peter had a sympathetic ear, a friendly quip, a treatment and an appropriately stern or kindly word for each. It was a pleasure to watch him work but my head was spinning with the sounds of a new language and I had been overwhelmed by more than a hundred fresh medical and surgical cases in one morning. I couldn't imagine being left alone to handle all this.

The Coates and I were invited to the Raymond's for Saturday lunch. Mr. Robert Raymond was headmaster of Institut Kamanyi, our teacher training college, and for his 38 years of educational service in Africa he had recently been awarded an O.B.E. by Queen Elizabeth.

His son Walter taught at the school as did Mr. Raymond's wife Phyllis. She was also a very good cook judging by the meal I had just finished.

"David, would you like some more fruit? Walter?'' She received a yes on both counts. Walter and I could always finish the leftovers.

"Now, who wants tea?'' Phyllis asked. "David?''

"Oh no-o-o,'' Peter said dramatically. "Just fill his cup with water, thank you.'' Peter, Ruth and I grinned then began to laugh heartily. From then on the Kasaji folk would set the table with a tall glass of water at my place.

That afternoon Peter introduced me to our x-ray facilities. Our American-made GEMCOM-30 was a 25-year-old piece of equipment, yet it did the job. In less than half an hour we performed numerous fluoroscopies and rattled off a score of films which we then processed manually. Back in Canada, an x-ray was a phone call away; here it was up to us from start to finish. If it came out poorly I had no one to blame but myself. I was determined to master the technique.

It had been an exciting day. Before my supper engagement at the Judkin's I took time to reflect on the overwhelming challenges that faced me. First I needed to prepare myself for Peter's departure. That meant several things: learning routine surgical procedures; becoming familiar with management problems in leprosy and tuberculosis; acquiring proficiency in radiography; developing clinical acumen for local problems; establishing rapport with the African staff—the list was endless.

Then too I wanted to be involved in teaching Scripture. This would mean helping out at the students' and the African teachers' Bible studies. There would also be countless opportunities on the personal level amongst the patients and the hospital staff.

Learning about African culture and life-style as well as watching local Christians interact in their society was another area of interest. The more I mused, the more I realized how much lay ahead. I was glad that it was time to go to the Judkin's.

Colin and Sue had been in Zaire for two years. She was a nurse and he a Cambridge graduate with a Masters in chemistry. Rachel and David, three years old and sixteen months respectively, were both very bright, squeezable children. I was reading a story to Rachel when our surgical nurse Glenys arrived.

"Auntie Glenys, come sit beside me," Rachel implored. Rachel skillfully deployed her charm keeping us both busy while brother David raced up and down the hallway, his chubby face grinning broadly and his arms raised victoriously to the ceiling. When Walter showed up we had our meal then spent the evening chatting, sharing and getting acquainted. Such companionship at Kasaji was a real joy.

I was still rounding on Sunday morning when the tom-toms began to thunder. Their rumbling signaled the start of chapel services and hastened the tardy on their way. About 200 African believers were gathered around the Lord's Table: the singing was harmonious and strong; the prayers were impassioned yet reverent; and the exposition of the Word was inspirational and Christ-exalting. One after another, as prompted by the Spirit of God, different worshipers rose to praise the Saviour. The anthems of adoration and thanksgiving crescendoed to a climax—the partaking of the bread and wine. As I shared the loaf and the cup that morning with my African brothers and sisters, I sensed afresh that tremendous oneness in Christ with all true believers of every tongue, nation and race.

My eyes were still moist when I noticed an old, bent African woman leave her seat and shuffle past me ever so slowly to the nearby door. When she reentered the hall my eyes flooded with tears. Her labored gait finally brought her to the central table where she humbly placed a bucket overflowing with peanuts as an offering to the Lord. It was all she had. It was all she could give. It was the scriptural widow's mite. That hour of worship and that act of devotion were indelibly printed in my memory.

The next day was the start of a very trying experience that threatened to ruin my joy at Kasaji. We had scheduled a medical trip to our dispensary at Katoka where Mary Ratter ran an incredibly busy clinic and where William and Kathy Rew were active in the school and church work. I had looked forward to this visit ever since meeting old Mr. Rew at Lubumbashi. During the three-hour journey, however, I began to experience malaise and cramps, both very uncommon for me. As the day wore on my condition worsened and by the evening I was miserable. Even William's exciting account of a recent two-day hippo hunt couldn't keep my interest. I didn't eat supper; I was forced to leave the room on several occasions, and finally I excused myself early.

All that night I tossed and turned with severe abdominal cramping and spent much of the time agonizing in the bathroom. Then came the shaking chills and the fever, and by dawn I was really sick. Strangely enough, Peter had come down with malaria during the night and was confined to bed as well. The only bit of interaction we had that morning was over my diagnosis. Peter called it malaria and diarrhea; I preferred to call it malaria and Zairrhea. My memories of those two groggy days at Katoka included the barking dogs and slamming doors that disturbed my slumber, the sumptuous meals I couldn't eat, and two comforting signs on the wall of my sick bay—"Smile, God loves you" and "Hang in there," both good pieces of advice.

Back at Kasaji my fever disappeared but the cramps and the Zairrhea persisted. I continued to fast. Over three or four days the abdominal pain gradually changed in character and soon I recognized what it represented— hunger. In my diary I could write, "I am thankful that the Lord has spared me from the gnawing ache which so much of the world knows as its constant companion."

By Saturday my condition was improving and I started to eat. I had become increasingly disheartened at having abandoned Peter to all the work at the hospital, but now that I was feeling better, I hoped to make up for lost time. And then disaster struck. All night long I raced to the bathroom. By morning I was both exhausted and thoroughly dejected. Having come to help at Kasaji, I found myself a liability for seven of my first 10 days. At the rate I was going I'd never get enough experience before Peter left. Moreover, the Fishers were to come that noon for a special meal, and I rued the fact that I wouldn't be able to eat. Why was this happening to me?

It was Sunday morning. I read the story of Jesus washing His disciples' feet and it became alive as never before. Jesus wanted to rid His disciples of the grime from their journey. Had I been gathering dirt in the form of self-pity and lack of trust, and did the Lord want to rid me of these? Peter balked at the Lord's efforts to cleanse him—was I? Jesus told him that without this cleansing he was not fit to participate in the Master's work. Was my little trial to prepare me likewise for His work?

Many other searchlights probed my inner man and I soon repented of my selfishness and unbelief. My attitude was revolutionized. I went to worship with a humbled, thankful heart and then enjoyed the company of the Fishers at the noon meal even though I had to abstain from the food—and Grannie was the charmer I had expected.

"My new hearing aid is absolutely marvelous! For the first time in years

I heard what was said at the meeting. And Terry, I was so proud! You spoke so well in Lunda—just like a native!''

''Mother, I was born here, you know,'' Terry answered, a little embarrassed.

''Of course, I know,'' Grannie chuckled. ''But it is quite a pity about the hearing aid. Poor Terry and Barbara will have to put up with so much more now that I can hear what's going on!'' She laughed even harder.

''David, did you know that Singleton's father, Dr. Walter Fisher, built Kalene Hospital, the first hospital in Central Africa? In fact . . .'' She then went on to give a highly informative and very eloquent account of the pioneer days in Lunda country. Her love for the people was unmistakable and her zeal had not waned but had surged. It was only her weary body that frustrated the devotion of her godly heart.

Then, sympathizing with my recent illness, Barbara remarked, ''The first days are not always easy, David. I had hepatitis and accomplished nothing for several months.''

''Yes,'' added Grannie, ''Barbara's right. When I first sailed from England to Africa, my fiancé was supposed to meet me. We had planned to get married here and work on the mission field together. By the time my ship arrived, however, he had died of Blackwater Fever. The first days were difficult, but the Lord was faithful and here I am 63 years later!''

I felt like crawling under the table at these revelations. That Sunday marked the end of my sickness and a new beginning to my service.

6
Rumblings of War

Kasaji mornings during rainy season have a sparkle all their own. Then as the burning sun rises higher in the sky thunderclouds form and quickly shroud the heavens. By midday a violent storm bludgeons the earth, scattering man and beast for cover and creating a network of rivulets where before there was none. Then, as swiftly as it comes, the tumult disappears and in its wake the early afternoon sun arrives to sponge up the fury of an hour. The cooling rains, however, breathe into the land an invigorating freshness which lingers until the morrow when the drama is reenacted. With this backdrop our work at Kasaji carried on.

It didn't take long for me to discover how much the nurses and the African personnel actually performed at the hospital. Hazel and her midwives handled all the obstetrical cases and called us only for emergencies. Although Peter and I regularly attended tuberculosis and leprosy clinics, Barbara, Ruth and their teams followed these patients on a day-to-day basis. Norma, Glenys, Sue and a dozen orderlies were saddled with the general medical and surgical work, and this was where most of our time was spent.

My days were filled with many firsts—my first solo hernia repairs, my first urethral dilatations for strictures, and my first African cardiac arrest. I saw tuberculous pericarditis, disseminated fungal infections and an ovarian tumor weighing 15 pounds.

Then there was my initiation to witch doctor medicine. A local Zairian soldier complained of a swollen right leg. He had twisted his knee two days before and had wrapped it so tightly with an elastic bandage that the circulation was compromised. The diagnosis was clear, but as I examined his leg I was horrified. From knee cap to forefoot was a series of 20 razor-thin lacerations still oozing blood. Ostensibly these were designed to let out the poison. The soldier grinned when I told him whom he had just visited. Releasing the bandage, I explained the cause of the swelling but he would attribute the resulting cure as much to the medicine man's treatment as to mine.

There was our first vaccination expedition. We traveled in Terry's old pickup to a distant village where a clinic was set up in a school building. In short order, several hundred measles and smallpox vaccinations were administered to the young children, but in the process we encountered an alarming collection of significant pathology: cerebral malaria, nephrotic syndrome, nutritional disorders, and many more.

Then the local headmaster asked me to see some of his schoolboys who had sores on their feet. I happily agreed and followed him to a classroom.

"Musenga," he called out. A young boy rose from his seat, and as he approached us I noticed a dirty cloth wrapped around his lower left leg. He instinctively unraveled a filthy homemade bandage tearing off a scab with the last pull. I withheld a gasp as a large, putrid tropical ulcer came into view. What was even more repulsive was the mass of intertwined herbs, mud, and grasses matted down over the bleeding ulcer. This was the handiwork of the witch doctor.

There was nothing I could do for Musenga on this trip. Although I was uncertain that the headmaster would comply I insisted that he send this boy and others to Kasaji for hospitalization and treatment.

Two days later I was working in the clinic when I heard an African excitedly exclaim, "Look at that!" There in solemn procession down the dispensary road marched a string of schoolboys led by an older man. I rushed outside where the teacher triumphantly pointed to his charges and handed me a letter from the headmaster. In it were listed the names of 18 students who had walked those 20 miles for treatment of their leg sores. I now had my share of tropical ulcers!

My first days at Kasaji had exposed me to a new language. I discovered that a flashlight was a torch, a truck was a lorry, soccer was football, and to steal was to lift. With time I assimilated some of these expressions but there was one cultural change I resisted. All the Britishers were bath-takers but I considered showers more hygienic. The peace was kept when we found an old shower house built years ago by Swiss folk who obviously had convictions similar to mine.

I first met our college students through Walter. He had a real love for them and devoted a great deal of time outside of class hours to being their friend. On one occasion I was with him when they asked me, "Doctor, why won't you play football with us? Why won't you come?"

"I never said I wouldn't," I objected.

"Good! We'll see you this afternoon." Roped in again. The game of course was not football but soccer, and to my surprise it was a league match against a team from Kasaji town! From the top of a 40-foot anthill the local collegiate commentator bellowed out the play-by-play action. Down on the field, my performance was far from stellar, but the crowds were most gracious. They whistled and cheered at my most mediocre moves and kept silence at my obvious and frequent miscues. I was happy when it was over and we had won, but my legs ached for days.

My first letters from Canada arrived at the end of February. What a thrill to get news from home after a month of waiting! A few days later I was sitting on the porch replying to this mail and conversing with our parrot when I was called to the hospital. On my return I found Percy the Parrot chomping away at my precious letters and at a prized medical text. I was not pleased. The damage was not that extensive however, and later on the episode brought many a laugh. After all, Percy did have good taste.

During those first few weeks I read the journal of Frederick Stanley Arnot, mostly at the insistence of Grannie Fisher. What a challenge it was to follow this missionary pioneer on his eight journeys across Central Africa. On his first expedition from 1881 to 1887 he had explored this vast area discovering the formidable slave trader Mushidi and his mighty empire. Arnot's diary was replete with stories of near-starvation, raging epidemics, wild animals, unfriendly natives and treacherous white men. Not least among his incredible hardships were the lengthy separations from family and friends that he had endured. Yet, in his steps hundreds of assembly missionaries had followed, establishing centers just like our own Kasaji. I was inspired by the lifework of this man of God. Having read his journal, I went back to Grannie for his complete biography. She was delighted!

It came time for Peter to take his first trip to Mutshatsha leaving me alone in Kasaji for two days. The night before he left I stayed up until 2 A.M. taping some messages to send back home. At 4 A.M. Peter and I were called down to the hospital to treat a newly arrived patient with an accidental gunshot wound to the head. Drawing upon our vast, combined neurosurgical experience, we worked on the literal hole in his head through which we could see a pulsating frontal lobe. His neurological status remained amazingly stable and around 6:30 A.M. we finally finished the debridement and dressing—just in time to freshen up at home and return for rounds and a busy morning in the operating room.

The Coates left for Mutshatsha in early afternoon. Exhausted, I had just gone to bed when I heard the *whirr* of an approaching plane. That meant only one thing—an emergency for me to deal with. The patient was a 70-year-old male in acute urinary retention. He was in agony. A Foley catheter didn't work. Urethral sounds didn't work. A special type of abdominal operation would be successful but I had never done one. Perhaps I could put in a supra-pubic catheter. Back in Canada the complete sterilized set for such a procedure would be available in minutes. Here I would have to rummage around and create my own. With Hazel's help I found what I needed and moments later the patient was resting comfortably. So were we.

By early March, Kasaji had become home. I had come to know and love my co-workers both white and black. There was increasing confidence in the operating theater and in the outpatients department. I was pleased with the potential of the Bible teaching work amongst the college students and Walter was emerging as a trusted friend.

One Sunday afternoon I took a long stroll during which I was overwhelmed with the quiet beauty of the land and the sense of purpose and personal peace that I had found at Kasaji. On returning to my room, I wrote a letter to Peter Fenty, a friend of mine in Montreal.

Sunday, March 6, 1977
Kasaji, Zaire.

Dear Peter,

I just finished taking a quiet walk around the outside of the mission station and have a few minutes before supper so I thought I'd drop you a note. The walk was beautiful. We crossed the main hospital block and went toward the leper camp (see map I sent Wooley Ikuda), then up the air field and back via the graveyard beyond the college.

We saw a giant eagle hovering a thousand feet above the ground eyeing its prey; a little African boy sitting on top of an anthill trapping flying ants for a future meal—delicious; a rainbow hidden amongst the clouds reminding us of the early afternoon downpour; wild flowers and insects; neck-high elephant grass so sharp that it nicked our legs and arms; girls carrying manioc along narrow paths to their villages; avocadoes, guavas, papayas, bananas and pineapples growing in abundance; army ants marching in orderly column to a destination known only by the queen.

We then passed the graveyard. Here lay the earthly remains of many missionaries and their children—Mr. Singleton Fisher who founded Kasaji station over thirty years ago, Mr. Robert Raymond's first wife and one of his sons—reminders of the sacrifice that others gone before had made for the spread of the gospel.

A little later we finished our walk filled with praise for God's creation, esteem for His servants' dedication and challenge for our personal meditation.

Give my love to all. God bless!

In Christ,
Dave

On Monday the Coates and Glenys left on their regular medical trip to Katoka. There was an uncanny foreboding about this departure but I was soon steeped in my work and forgot about it. That night I began to read Dr. Carl Becker's book *His Hand on Mine*, which described his experiences in northeast Congo through the troubles in the 1960s.

On Tuesday I ate lunch with the McKenzies.

"What happened to your tennis court?" Harold inquired.

"Yes, David," Norma added, "you were so 'hep' on that."

"As a matter of fact, the court is finished and I'm planning to put up the net today at rest hour. We'll have our first match when Peter comes back."

"Bravo!" Norma exclaimed. "Here are some white socks to help you win."

"Thanks. See you at tea," I promised as I hastened off to set up the net. I was proud of my tennis court. About three weeks previously I had been chatting with the Coates and had raised the subject of physical fitness.

"Peter, what do you folks do around here for exercise?" I had asked.

"Keep busy."

"I don't mean that. I mean physical exercise, sports, that sort of thing." I saw I wasn't going to get a reply, so tongue-in-cheek I added, "You know, there's nothing worse than a flabby missionary!" Did that ever get a response! Within days the old tennis court lying under three feet of grass and topsoil was being resurrected. The land was surveyed, the ground dug up, the sand brought in, the surface rolled and now I was putting up the net. The lines would be painted later today and we'd be rallying on the morrow—or so I thought.

After finishing some work at the hospital, I returned to the McKenzie's for afternoon tea. Harold wasn't there, and when I looked at Norma I knew something was wrong.

"David, there's been an invasion," she said with controlled emotion.

"What?" I gasped.

"Terry just received a distress call from Glen Eschtruth at Kapanga. Perhaps you'd like to go over and . . ."

Before she could finish I dashed out the front door and bolted to the Fisher's. Barging into their dining room, I found Terry and Harold huddled around our radio transmitter straining to catch a fading signal. For several minutes they switched from one band to another but were unable to pick up any more messages.

Finally, Terry turned and looked solemnly at me.

"The Katangese have spilled across the border from Angola and have captured Kapanga," he disclosed. "For years they've threatened to return and overthrow Mobutu. Now they're back—we're in for quite the fireworks!"

7
No Escape

The fall of Kapanga on Tuesday, March 8, was a stunning blow. We were still reeling from the shock, however, when African friends hurried by with even more startling news. Dilolo, the regional capital, had been overrun! Kisenge, a manganese mining center just 50 miles away, had surrendered! Three border towns had been captured by Katangese rebels in one afternoon—this was some military undertaking!

The local adjutant immediately radioed Kolwezi to send reinforcements for his 20-man garrison. Back came the promise that President Mobutu's crack para-commando battalions would arrive that night. Kasaji was to become the headquarters for Zairian troops. Here they would stave off the guerilla offensive.

Panic gripped the community. Within hours, literally thousands of terrified Africans had disappeared into the bush carrying their hastily made bundles. The rain mercilessly pelted down on the fleeing and their goods but they continued to stream along flooded roads and muddy paths to distant fields. Several hospital patients were spirited away on bikes by their families. Women in labor fled to a wet jungle. The students nervously finished out their day of classes and some of the hospital staff didn't show up for their duties.

That night the missionaries met to review the situation. Our family was separated—the Raymonds were in Kolwezi on business and the Coates and Glenys were in Katoka—but we had to make decisions. We knew that Kasaji was a strategic military target for at least three reasons: it was a railway center; it had a large hospital; and it was the crossroads for two national highways which plunged north and east into the heart of the country. Undoubtedly it would be the rebels' next goal on their three-pronged drive eastward.

Despite these chilling considerations we realized that we couldn't leave

Kasaji. Not only did our responsibilities at the college and the hospital keep us there, the Zaire army had closed down all the roads. We were obviously trapped between the advancing Katangese rebels and the oncoming Zairian reinforcements.

Our position was desperate, and yet as we turned our eyes away from ourselves and our circumstances and fastened them on the Lord and the written Word, a settledness descended on our gathering. Together we read Psalm 91. It gave us no details about the future; instead it pointed us to a shadow, the shadow of the Almighty. Here alone was our refuge and fortress. Here alone would be freedom from fear.

Despite these assurances, I wasn't able to sleep that night. My mind wrestled with weighty questions. Why had God allowed me to get into this mess? Was I really in the center of His will? Would I actually face war, and if so would I live to walk away from it? Innumerable speculations, reasonings and fears jammed my thinking process. Restlessly, fitfully, I endured the night, watching the clock strike at one, then at three and again at 4 A.M. I finally crawled out of bed in the five o'clock blackness. Quivering and laden with anxiety, I washed, changed and made my bed.

If ever I needed a word from the Lord, it was now. Should I look to the psalms for encouragement or should I meditate on the beautiful promises of Christ in John 13—17? No, I decided to pursue my regular studies in the book of Acts. It was there in chapter 17 that I read Paul's discourse with prominent Greek philosophers.

The apostle had seen countless idols in Athens and on one altar an inscription "To the Unknown God." This, he told his illustrious audience, was a myth. The unknown God was in fact known and had intervened in space-time history. He was a personal God and therefore had dealt with the world and mankind in a personal way. Moreover the Creator God was Sovereign God, Lord of yesterday, today and tomorrow; it was He who had given men life and breath and everything else. My heart was stirred as I recalled the many goodnesses I had already experienced in my life.

My eyes fell upon the next few words that Paul used in describing the personal, knowable Lord God, and then I could see no longer. Tears streamed down my face while I read, "He determined the times set for them and the exact places where they should live" (v. 26, *NIV*). My weeping turned to cries of joy as I recognized that my time was March 1977 and my exact place was Kasaji, Zaire. The message could not have been clearer had a finger from heaven etched the words on the wall before me. My times and places were in His hands! I was in the center of His will—of this I was absolutely certain.

What a dramatic impact this had on me! I was free. No more fear, no dread, no panic—just deep superabundant peace at being where He wanted me to be. It was amazing. My longevity, my safety and my career were no longer issues. Far better it would be to live briefly with adversity and without acclaim, yet be in the vortex of His will, than to survive long, comfortably and with recognition if paddling in the backwaters of His best purposes for my life. What a liberating realization!

I burst out of my room into the awakening morn. All was quiet. The dispensary road was virtually desolate at a time when it would normally be crowded by the feeble and infirm. Although the wards were almost full, the OPD was quiet, and from my vantage point in the dispensary I could see the continuing flow of Africans down the back paths behind the hospital. In my diary I wrote: "The sight is quite pathetic. Their destination is a wet bush with little drinking water and less food. They face it in large numbers, poorly clothed, weak and disheartened, knowing that they will have nothing left if and when they return."

That morning we reestablished radio contact with Katoka. The night before we had warned Peter against his proposed trip to the rebel-held Dilolo but wonderfully the Lord had already cut short the journey because of car problems.

"Forty-one, forty-one, do you hear me?" Terry called.

"Roger, Roger. Loud and clear," Peter replied.

"What should we do with the mad dog broomstick? Over."

"Could you repeat that please? Over."

"The mad dog broomstick. Repeat. The mad dog broomstick. We'd like to dispose of it. Over."

Peter owned a rifle which he used for shooting rabid dogs. In spite of having a valid gun license, we would be in real trouble should either side discover it in a house search.

"Roger, Roger," Peter answered. "The old well should do. Perhaps some emergency medical supplies could find a safe place as well. Over."

"Roger. Roger. A few red caps were to come last night but didn't show up. Now expected at noon today. Others to follow. Any news from the West? Over."

"Just a few firecrackers far away. Over."

"Roger, Roger. I believe you should stay until the situation is clear. We're all praying. Over."

"Thank you, thank you. We feel the same. Will contact at noon. Over and out." Peter's signal went off the air.

"We'll have to look after the gun and the drugs," Terry said. "You should put your documents in a safe place too, Dave, while you have the time."

While I was hiding my valuables at the hospital, our head orderly Tshihinga came by with the latest information. Two soldiers had escaped from Kisenge and had made their way to Kasaji through the bush. They reported that the Kisenge troops had been disarmed without a fight and that thousands of Katangese were now amassing for the conflict. Such news dealt another blow to the sagging morale of the Kasaji militia and the population.

Tshihinga continued, "Doctor David, the orderlies are very afraid. They want to leave the hospital for the bush. What should we do?"

The orderlies were understandably fearful. During the 1967 invasion, mercenaries and Katangese gendarmes had overrun the countryside and, brandishing their weapons, achieved popular support. Then, when the rebels were routed the Zaire soldiers returned with a fiery vengeance, wreaking havoc on the local population. These happenings were seared indelibly on the memories of the orderlies.

Despite these dangers I made it clear to Tshihinga that the hospital work would carry on. We would not hold back any who felt they must flee but we firmly believed that the Lord would look after the mission, its patients and its staff. Because of this confidence we invited the orderlies to move onto the grounds of the station. Tshihinga and several others did.

Very little happened that afternoon. Our only piece of hard news was that an advance guard of Mobutu's red-bereted para-commandos had arrived. One lonely jeep made half a dozen frantic rushes along the highway bearing a paltry few of these soldiers to checkpoints west of the mission.

What was lacking in substantiated reports, however, was generously furnished in rumors. Some said that Dilolo and Kisenge had been seized by Katangese riding bicycles—a much more reliable mode of transportation in the rainy season. Stories had it that trains and planes were pouring across the Angolan border with tons of military supplies including heavy artillery. Another account described the recent shipment of an inordinately large supply of gas (40,000 liters) to Dilolo for the use of the Zaire army. All of this would now be in rebel hands and some charged that this was the work of a highly placed fifth column. A student claimed that the railway man had heard cannon fire over a telephone line to Dilolo. All this talk prompted me to write in my diary: "In war there is no true story, only a mixture of fact and fear and fancy."

By Wednesday supper there was still no sight of Mobutu's troops even though they had left Kolwezi the previous day. That the Zaire army was stuck in the muddy roads somewhere was a distinct possibility; but whatever the delay the local adjutant was rapidly becoming panic-stricken.

Before more para-commandos roamed about the mission than already did, Terry and I decided to dispose of the "broomstick." We waited until dusk. I strolled towards the hiding place leaving Terry in the shadows of the house. When all was clear I signaled and he emerged carrying the rifle case. He ducked into the garage and there stood watch while I wandered past the well. In a flash I clambered over the side and down a rickety steel ladder. Terry noiselessly passed the case through a window to my upstretched hand

and I slowly lowered myself into the damp dark hole. At the bottom 15 feet down was a little tunnel whose entrance was blocked by a rusty oil drum. I placed the rifle on the drum, scampered up the ladder and swiftly returned to the house. The deed was done.

By the time Terry and I arrived at evening prayer meeting, almost everyone was there and an animated discussion was taking place. Apparently the two soldiers from Kisenge had vanished and were now presumed to have been Katangese in Zairian uniforms. They had managed to reconnoiter the Kasaji defenses on their visit and their disappearance now generated even more terror than their arrival.

Our ensuing discussion revolved around the many things for which we could be thankful. We talked about the Lord's intervention in Peter's trip to Dilolo. There was also Terry's return from Kolwezi just one day before the invasion. His knowledge of the people, the language and the country was invaluable especially in the light of the absence of Peter Coates and Robert Raymond.

Anne then reminded us of what had been happening recently at the college. "Remember that last week alone, six students prayed to become sincere Christians. And how many bought daily Bible study notes, Walter?"

"About 90," he replied. "That's more than we've sold in a long time."

"I really believe," Anne continued, "that this was the Lord's way of equipping our boys to find comfort from His Word."

"Did you hear about the flour?" Barbara asked. "Our supply of manioc meal for the patients was running low so last week we ordered the usual half a dozen sacks. When I received the stock last Saturday, was I ever surprised! Thirty-one sacks of flour! That's three times as much as we've ever ordered! I thought it was a mistake but now I know it isn't. The Lord was simply filling up our storehouse before the troubles began."

After a refreshing time in prayer we headed home. On the way, Hazel said to me, "David, Anne and I don't think you should wear your khaki shorts anymore—not with all these soldiers who are to come."

"Yes, and do get rid of that dreadful army sack with your camera," Anne was quick to add. I dared not argue with them. There was in fact some grounds to their fears.

Before falling asleep that night, I pulled out Dr. Becker's book to read the next chapter. It was entitled, *A Time to Live and a Time to Die*.

A stock car race? What a preposterous dream I was having! I opened my eyes but the sound wouldn't go away. Obviously it wasn't a dream. I pulled the curtain only to see blackness; but the noise I heard was unmistakably a lone jeep tearing back and forth along the highway. It was 5:30 A.M. and since I was fully awake, I decided to get up.

Before breakfast I walked over to the Fisher's. The jeep was parked in front of the house and the haggard adjutant was pacing the floor inside. He blurted out the bad news.

The Zairian troops had not yet arrived. Their trucks had become stuck on the muddy roads forcing them to wait for a relief train. Even that should have been here by now. Meanwhile the guerillas were doubtless advancing without resistance toward Kasaji. Terror had crippled the will of his soldiers. Many had deserted and he himself hadn't slept for 48 hours. His sad predicament and righteous protestations reminded me of the prophet Elijah who once said, "I, even I only, am left."

The conflict was already two days old but the radio still had nothing to say about beleaguered Shaba province. At least that meant that our families back home would be spared the anxiety.

The morning dragged into the afternoon. Although we kept busy at the college and at the hospital our minds often turned to our situation. We realized that at any moment something could happen. The Katangese were pushing unmolested towards Kasaji and it was only a question of time before they reached us. Would Zairian troops be here to stop them?

We had our answer that afternoon when the sudden screech of a locomotive whistle pierced the air. The troop train had arrived and hundreds of soldiers poured off the coaches into an empty town. A handful of military greeted them—no one else. Most of the poor fellows hadn't eaten for two days and Kasaji's abandoned shops made easy pickings for the first ones there. Late arrivals were less fortunate.

Another visitor took us by surprise. At 3 P.M. Ken Enright flew in unannounced bearing three Zairian army officers. We raced down to the airfield and approached the plane. Ken was sporting his customary open neck shirt, golf hat and happy smile. The corners of his mouth fell for an instant as he whispered, "We know what it's like and we're praying for you. Robert and Phyllis send their love. They wish they were here. Can't say any more." With that he took his leave.

The officers stepped into the waiting army jeep and sped off but the adjutant came over to me virtually in tears.

"Doctor," he implored, "please give me some pills to calm my nerves and make me sleep!" He followed me to the dispensary where I gave him some Valium. He would sleep well.

On my way home I was stopped by a speeding military vehicle whose occupants demanded medical supplies for the army. The most officious of the soldiers told me repeatedly that he was the big chief; he wanted to get into our stocks and he would take what he wanted because he was the big chief. Sensing trouble, I sent off for Terry's help then contacted Hazel and Sue who administered the store room. They all joined me at the hospital.

It didn't take long to discover that the medical officer in charge, Big

Chief, was stoned on local weed. That meant trouble. With a flourish he produced a list of drugs that looked more like the index of a pharmacopoeia than a requisition to a small jungle hospital.

Beside him stood an assistant in full battle dress grinning vacantly and wearing an over-sized green helmet. In his hands was a metal receptacle the size of a school child's lunch box. It was meant to carry all the supplies they were demanding from us.

I scanned with disbelief the list of medications:

1. Ampicillin	*500 mg*	*5,000 tablets*
2. Coagulin		*20,000 ampoules*
3. Penicillin G	*1 x 10⁶ units*	*10,000 ampoules*
4. Penicillin G	*5 x 10⁵ units*	*10,000 tablets*
5. Quinine	*600 mg*	*10,000 ampoules*
6. . . .		

There were 88 drugs in all, some in quantities that we did not even stock at the hospital. Both anger and amusement welled up inside as we continued to study this preposterous requisition: laxatives and constipating agents, sedatives and stimulants, antacids, antihypertensives, vitamins, deworming agents and 200 kilograms of cotton. All inside a little lunch box? The cotton alone represented about 40 cubic feet. Yet the list went on and on.

"We can't give him all this lot," said an indignant Sue. "We'll have nothing left for our own patients!"

Agitated, Big Chief interrupted in French, "Hurry up! I have to go off to battle!"

"But we cannot give you all that you want," I replied.

"What? Of course you can. I need everything that you have for my army—and right now! Where's your storeroom?" he growled pulling himself up to his full five feet four inches.

"It's over there and it's locked," Hazel responded just as authoritatively. "I have the key and no one but me or my associates can go in." The matter was settled right there.

"We'll give you what we can but we don't have everything," I continued softly. Meanwhile Hazel and Sue were checking off a few drugs with which we were willing to part.

"Why don't you have these drugs? What is this place, a dispensary or a hospital?" His face was screwed up in fiery anger. I noticed his right hand dangerously close to the pistol at his hip.

"Many of our drugs are stolen before they get here," Terry reasoned. "Those that do arrive are used for the thousands of patients we treat each month."

"Besides," I countered, "why didn't you bring supplies with you from your big government hospitals in Kolwezi?"

"They didn't have enough," Big Chief blurted out unthinkingly.

"Then how do you expect a mission hospital to supply what the government hospitals cannot? You had better send word back to Kolwezi for medical reinforcements."

"And do you really want these," Hazel inquired, "15,000 anti-hemorrhoidal suppositories?" Everyone grinned except for Big Chief.

"Of course!" he thundered, then launched into a tirade while the women slipped away to the stockroom. Big Chief was deathly afraid of the battle that lay ahead. With blazing eyes and flinging arms the drunken officer raved against the rebels, against reactionaries, against Mobutu's enemies and against all who withheld aid from the Zaire army.

At the most heated moment, Hazel and Sue arrived bearing two card-board boxes full of supplies. Even Big Chief was unable to conceal his obvious delight at the generous contribution. However, there were a few important things that he had failed to request. Before I could return with them, Big Chief sped off in his jeep cradling his boxes of supplies oblivious to the fact that he had sutures but no needle drivers, scalpels but no blades, and syringes but no needles. I wondered if I'd ever see him again, but was thankful to the Lord that we had emerged unscathed from such a tense confrontation. It would require increasing wisdom knowing when to stand our ground to protect the livelihood of the hospital and when to yield to the unreasonable demands of crazed men.

After supper, the first truckloads of Zairian troops rumbled westward out of Kasaji. Forty, fifty, sixty soldiers were jammed like cattle into the open backs of Gécamines lorries that whisked them towards a hidden enemy on an unknown battlefield. One after another, seven trucks hurtled off into the night followed closely by ten speeding tanks. The battle was imminent but hopefully very distant.

At our evening fellowship time we learned that contact with the Katoka folk had been broken. They had decided to dismantle their transmitter for fear that the advancing rebels should catch them using it. We could hear from them no more and so we committed each one lovingly to the Lord. There had been no word from Kapanga since Tuesday and we continued to pray for reassuring news about our Methodist brothers and sisters. We also remembered the Raymonds who were longing to be back with us. We didn't see any prospect of their return but we brought it to the Lord.

Psalm 46 was read to us. "God is our refuge and strength, a very present help in trouble. Therefore will not we fear, though the earth be removed, and though the mountains be carried into the midst of the sea" (vv. 1,2).

The whole psalm was beautiful, containing as it did so many parallels to our situation. Tanks had rattled across our property; drunken, angry sol-diers had fondled their pistols in our presence; gunshots had broken the silence; yet we had no need to fear because God was our refuge and strength, a very present help in trouble. We prayed for help to keep on trusting.

That night before I fell asleep I listened to the BBC. What we had dreaded for the sake of our faraway relatives was now a reality. We were on the international news: "Thousands of troops from Angola invade Shaba province in Zaire. . . . Three border towns are shelled . . . Sophisti ated military equipment used by attackers . . . Mobutu appeals to UN and OAU."

The last words scrawled as a prayer in my diary that night were, "God, please calm the folks!"

8
The Paw of the Lion

Despite Friday morning's radio broadcasts, the Katangese had not yet appeared at Kasaji. According to the BBC, both Kasaji and Divuma had been taken by the rebels but after a night of bombardment, had been recaptured by loyalist troops. As far as we knew we hadn't been captured nor bombarded nor recaptured, so from the start we learned to be skeptical of news reports.

The clinic was keeping me surprisingly busy that morning when the hum of an engine and the rapid-fire *tic-tic-tic* of chains grating against turf caused me to look outside. There, large-as-life, was a Zairian tank crawling down the road. Its long front gun pointing at the dispensary, the great green machine maneuvered into a parking position in front of my window. It jerked backwards and forwards, turning this way and that while the gunner in the turret shouted out directions with increasing frustration to the driver. Finally, after two or three minutes he seemed to give up and the engine was shut off. Half a dozen soldiers piled out of the tank and into my office— medical complaints, grenades, machine guns and all. We treated their malaria and other ailments then sent them off quickly before an accident with the grenades converted my room into a charnel house.

Soldiers looking for food began looting homes in the local villages. The men were obviously hungry and had fully expected the civilians to provide mushes for them. Remembering their shoddy treatment in the past, however, the people had long vanished and the troops would have to fend for themselves until adequate rations could be brought up. The only army foodstuff in plenteous supply was grog, and although it was meant to keep up the soldiers' spirits for combat it would transform many of them into swaggering bullies.

Around 10 A.M. two Zairians walked into the dispensary, one with a broken wrist and the other with a sprained thumb. They related almost cheerfully how they had injured themselves by falling out of a Gécamines truck while on the way to the front lines. As I set and examined the fracture, my patient sat there beaming. For him it meant a trip to Lubumbashi away from the conflict. Meanwhile, his buddy insisted that his thumb was broken despite the normal x-ray. When he saw that I was not impressed he pleaded with me to put a cast on his thumb anyway.

"Of course not!" I replied sternly. "You must go back and fight for your country." I was not about to set a precedent.

Soldiers and military vehicles roamed the mission at will but the army did not seem interested in searching our houses or confiscating questionable personal property. What surprised me even more was that the military did not seize our transmitter! Whether because of trust or oversight, we kept it and for this we were thankful because at 1 P.M. that Friday afternoon the transmitter communicated a real answer to prayer.

Terry had left the set on continuously and was in the house when a familiar voice attracted him to the receiver. It was Dr. Eschtruth! "We are all safe and well. Repeat. We are all safe and well. Officials of the FNLC have a message for the Zaire government."

There was some muttering and clattering and then another voice took over.

"We are the Front National de Libération Congolaise. We are exiles from all parts of the Congo but we have returned to free our people from the bondage of Mobutu. The missionaries will be safe in the new socialist state as long as they cooperate. Black and white will work together without class and without distinction. At Kapanga, Dilolo and Kisenge we have begun. At Kinshasa we will finish!"

The communiqué ended as abruptly as it had begun. There were many mysteries left unanswered; yet for the moment we praised God. Kapanga was safe! Our brothers and sisters were alive!

More troops pushed on to the front lines that evening while others settled into the ghost town that Kasaji had become. Our cook Venasi as well as three college seniors now joined me at Peter's house where our collective presence would provide some measure of safeguard for the Coates's belongings. The students, moreover, would be able to translate for me should unknown soldiers arrive during the night.

Before going to bed, I composed a letter to my family just in case there would be opportunity to send it out before the situation worsened. It had to be brief and very discreet lest, intercepted, it bring trouble upon us. The letter read:

Kasaji, Zaire,
March 11, 1977,
9:30 p.m.

Dear folks,

All is well in Kasaji this night—eating and sleeping and keeping well. This letter doesn't go by the normal channels.

Peter Coates, his wife and our surgical nurse are not here. They went out on a medical trip this week and couldn't get back. They are well. No other doctor (besides Peter) for 50 miles radius.

It's strange how plans are all in God's hands—not strange, really, because we can't improve on His designs for our lives. An exciting, reassuring passage came to me just when needed a few days ago!

"The God who made the world and everything in it is *the Lord of heaven and earth* . . . he himself gives all men *life* and *breath* and *everything else* . . . he determined the *times* set for them and the *exact places* where they should live" (Acts 17:24-26, *NIV*).

I have no doubt that this is where God has set me so I would rather be nowhere else. By the time you receive this, things may be resolved and plans for return may be worked out, but nothing can be counted on for now.

Can't really say much more.

Give my love to all back home.

David

On Saturday morning, rounds were much like those of previous days. Our wards were three-quarters full but the overall morale was, if anything, somewhat better. A few soldiers had already been by to report a crushing victory over a disorganized band of guerillas. How they acquired this information was not disclosed, but it did lend hope to the local people that the struggle might never reach Kasaji.

Such aspirations were short-lived. At 9:30 A.M. a Zairian armored personnel carrier tore down the dispensary road and skidded to a stop in front of the operating theater. As I reached the vehicle, several wounded soldiers stumbled out and an officer blurted something about others who were coming. I quickly looked at the men. Two of them had sustained skull injuries while three others were suffering from burns and shrapnel wounds. By now, Hazel and Norma had arrived.

"Could you take these three to the men's ward?" I asked Hazel. "The orderlies will give you a hand. Mostly soft tissue trauma I think. The others need x-rays." The girls were great. Off they went with three wounded para-commandos in tow. Later on I'd examine the soldiers more thoroughly.

At the x-ray theater I pressed the military officer for more information. He stated that some of his men had been shot up around midnight while the others had been blown up in their tank that very morning.

"Where did all this happen?" I casually inquired.

The officer eyed me and replied, "On the Kisenge plain." Another soldier pinpointed Malonga as the site of the ambush. That was 45 minutes away. A third said some other place. They obviously didn't know where it had happened, but each one insisted that the battle was going well and that the advance was steady.

I positioned a burly six-foot-tall para-commando on the x-ray table. While he lay there, I couldn't help but remember stories of the arrogant soldiers who in times past had bled the local people. Yet, when he began to moan and cry out, my heart melted.

"I'm going to die!" he wailed. "Mama, mama! I'm going to die!"

How many more like him were lying unattended on some not-too-distant battlefield? How many others still in the arena would have their groanings silenced by a single well-placed bullet? Inside I agonized, *Oh God! They're only weak, frightened men; not swarthy braggarts, not malevolent bullies, just human beings like me. And they need help. And they need you. Help me, Father, to help them!*

It was a haunting spectacle. I saw in that man a picture of all men everywhere stripped of their power, their position and their defenses. I saw a human being clinging as it were to life itself. What a picture of despair! I thanked the Lord for the hope that was stronger than life or death.

The first soldier's films showed a depressed fracture of the base of the skull with no identifiable intracranial foreign body. His injury had been mediated through a dull object without soft tissue penetration. I had no choice but to treat him conservatively. Happily, the second patient's x-rays were normal.

Hazel arrived. "The others are all fine. I pulled out a few pieces of metal but none of the wounds are deep. The burns patient is the worst off. What about here?"

I told her quickly then expressed my concern about where we should place the soldiers. "I don't want them with the regular patients. Our people are already terrified enough."

"They're not the only ones who are terrified," Hazel replied. "All the paras are wearing civilian clothes underneath their uniforms."

While we talked we became aware of some commotion in front of the operating room. Turning around the corner and stepping up his pace as he spotted us was none other than our friend Big Chief. I was not anxious to see him.

"Doctor," he called out excitedly, "I have some very important specimens to analyze. Where is your microscope?"

"Down at the dispensary. The orderly will take you."

"Thank you. I have some urine samples," he continued earnestly. "Some of the officers are sick and I suspect schistosomiasis. Yes, schistosomiasis!" He spun around and strode off. Incredulous, Hazel and I watched him go. Here he was, the chief medical officer wanting to look at urine samples when some of his colleagues were seriously injured. It was all so improbable, yet so true.

Later the orderly told me what had happened at the laboratory. Spying some white blood cells, Big Chief had made the grand pronouncement, "Schistosomiasis!" Trying to be helpful, the technician told him that he didn't think so.

"What could it be?" quizzed the mystified officer.

"Only one thing—gonorrhea," was the innocent response.

"Impossible! Not our officers!" Big Chief stomped off not to be seen again.

Our five commandos were resting comfortably on a special ward. Two of them could have returned right away to their companies but we agreed to let them stay with us until the next day. A fellow soldier was posted by their front door and their own rifles were at the ready by their beds.

I was still on the wards at 10:30 A.M. when gunfire suddenly broke out. Many patients hopped under their beds and others ran for the bush. Three of the wounded soldiers grabbed their guns and crouched at the end of the building poised for action. Was this to be the battle?

And then the shooting stopped. Some said that the army was just killing goats. Others swore that a rebel-driven tank sneaked into town and blasted headquarters before being knocked out. There was no final explanation offered but similar volleys of small arms fire repeatedly broke the stillness that day and added to the mounting tension.

The morning would not allow us a moment of rest. A heavily armored tank soon appeared and in it the wounded commandant.

"*Docteur, j'ai e'te' touche'*," he whispered holding his wounded left side. Three military nurses carried him gently into the theater. I noticed that his men were visibly shaken but it seemed that something more was bothering them, something more than the condition of their superior officer. Were they being pursued? Was the struggle sweeping towards us?

The commandant lay grimacing on the table, his left hip maximally flexed. I exposed his abdomen discovering that he too wore civilian clothes under his uniform. A bullet had pierced his left flank and then exited through two large holes in the lower abdomen. All three wounds were bleeding freely.

"These wounds are fresh. When were you shot?" I asked.

"Thirty minutes ago," the spokesman nurse replied.

I shuddered at the disclosure. I shuddered even more when I realized my therapeutic predicament. The commandant had probably suffered significant injury to the bowel, bladder and other internal organs. What dare I do?

The nurse interrupted, "Doctor, we want you to give him first aid. We plan to take him back to Mutshatsha far from the front lines. Just do what you can to help us get there."

Quite relieved, I quickly found some sterile dressings while Hazel used Kotex pads to make a perfect pressure bandage. While we were working, several soldiers stated that the battle was going well, that we had nothing to fear. However, when we had finished and the commandant was being transported back to the tank, one military nurse lingered to wash his hands.

"We passed through village after village. All of them were empty. Then suddenly we heard shooting behind us, then in front of us, then on both sides." His eyes became fierce and his tone bitter.

"They mounted a terrific attack—we left many dead. It was a terrible ambush." The commandant was already back in the tank as were our five wounded para-commandos. I tried to give them their x-rays but they wouldn't wait. The moving fortress rumbled off into a driving rain.

The morning had been filled with discouraging reports but the afternoon began with good news. In a trip fully authorized by Kolwezi, Ken had flown in the Raymonds and whisked off our mail! What a thrill it was to have the Raymonds back with us! In our minds they had left safety and walked into danger; in their minds they were only doing what was right. Their presence cheered the students and uplifted all our spirits. We praised God for bringing them home.

The panic of the morning appeared to be ill-founded. The guns of battle were definitely not within earshot. However, several observations were troublesome. Some rebels were clearly 30 minutes down the road. None of the Ge'camines trucks and less than half the tanks had come back from their Thursday night expedition. Moreover, there had been no massive return of the several hundred soldiers who had left on that first attack. Either the loyalist troops were faring very well or very poorly. Only later would we receive confirmation of their massacre in a bloody ambush.

The waiting seemed endless. Evening came and I retired early to catch up on my rest. That day had been physically and emotionally draining, leaving me exhausted in every way. The Lord had upheld us through all the strain yet I prayed for renewed strength to carry on.

Early Sunday morning another troop train arrived swelling the already considerable numbers garrisoned at Kasaji. Eyewitnesses described in distressing tones the many hundreds of soldiers digging in for the fight. The Zaire army was not marching out to engage the Katangese. It was preparing for their assault!

The Lord's Supper was attended by the few villagers still left in the community. As we sat there during that morning hour, sporadic rifle fire and a tank on maneuvers reminded us of our peril. The rainy season thunderclaps shattered the stillness simulating the boomings of heavy artillery; yet our hearts were drawn in worship to the Saviour above these distractions. When the service concluded I wondered if this had been Kasaji's "Last Supper."

That afternoon I strolled home from the hospital. The walk up the dispensary road was always beautiful and today even more so. The sky was cloudless and the sun tingly warm. A fresh breeze from the southwest rustled through the bushes that lined the route. All was quiet. All was still. It was the idyllic Kasaji that I had first known.

Unknown to us, the Katangese had already encircled Kasaji and were watching our every step. That afternoon they also saw several hundred Zairian para-commandos fan out across the mission taking up positions behind our homes and around the hospital. Then, at dusk, the rebels launched their bloody assault sending us scurrying for cover.

The tumult raged outside our houses for several hours and as I sprawled there on the floor at midnight, numerous questions invaded my mind. What was so important about Kasaji that drew me here anyway? Was it worth all this trouble? And what happens if I don't make it? Am I really where God wants me to be? Yet, when I reached back in time and space, I found I had many answers for each intruder. Even in the heat of guerilla warfare in an African jungle, with the paw of the lion poised to strike, I knew I was in the palm of the Lord.

9
Hearts of Darkness

The first light of dawn poked through a break in the curtains and danced along the ceiling to the far wall. I rolled over to escape its glimmer, then suddenly woke up to my surroundings. I peered at my watch—6 A.M. I must have fallen asleep! The last I could remember was the noisy arrival of the rebel troops down the road. Their trucks had rolled into Tshisangama's village one mile to the west and their jubilant singing had provided an eerie accompaniment to the guns of war. Volleys of rifle fire had kept me awake for some time longer, but I must have given way to exhaustion. I strained to hear some noise of battle. There was none. Instead, the musical chatter of birds was heralding the new day.

I crawled to the window and peeked outside, half dreading to look down the barrel of an unfriendly rifle. All was quiet! There was not a trace of a soldier, living or dead. I leaned back against the wall for several minutes of quiet prayer. Soon there was stirring in the other room and the baby began to cry. I saw our ex-Katangese gunman pacing the hallway holding his cast—he was obviously disturbed by the stillness. Then Anne appeared, her cheerful face bringing morning greetings.

"How did you sleep?" she asked.

"Not bad. Have you heard anything?"

"No. It's been quiet for the last few hours. Hazel thinks we should wash up as soon as possible and then have breakfast. You can use the bathroom now, if you like."

"Thanks, Anne. I'll go right away." As I walked down the corridor I saw the cook come in the rear door carrying provisions from our outside storeroom. I was glad to see him return; I wouldn't have ventured outside this morning.

"Look at the soldiers!" Hazel exclaimed from her room.

A patrol of about 40 Zairian commandos had appeared in the clearing in the front of our homes. Sporting their red berets and carrying their rifles over their shoulders, they strolled leisurely across the open ground. Their casual air defied explanation. Didn't they know about the battle?

Suddenly, the fury of a thousand firearms seemed to be unleashed. One Katangese guerilla jumped from cover on a nearby anthill and machine-gunned the surprised Zairians while several other comrades surfaced to pound them as well.

We dropped to the floor and within seconds were at the cubbyhole. Then, realizing I had seen the rear door open, I scrambled to the back of the house, closed the door and barred it just as I heard army boots scuffling roughly along the walk scarcely five paces away. In a moment I was back at our refuge.

With heaving respirations, I surveyed our motley bunch. Our quarters could not fit four comfortably, yet 14 bodies huddled closely and uncomplainingly. Our expertise from the previous night was of no help. We agonized through each fusillade, each exchange of rocket fire. The pungent smell of spent gunpowder drifted cloudborne into the house enveloping us in a stinging haze. Once more we heard combatants charging around the house. Once more we heard angry voices shouting at the enemy.

But another voice spoke. Anne handed me a verse which she had torn from a calendar just that morning. It was the Lord's promise to Joshua, as true for us then as it had been for him millenia before. It said: "Be not afraid, neither be thou dismayed; for the Lord thy God is with thee whithersoever thou goest" (Josh. 1:9).

For nearly two hours the fighting raged. There was no way of knowing which army was winning or what buildings had been destroyed or how our family was faring. Once more we committed everything to the Lord while around us the guns still thundered.

And then there was silence! We could hear each other breathe. How deafening! We had become used to the noise—its terror we could handle. But stillness was a new experience. How should we react to this uncanny hush?

"*Kuya!*" The voice behind the house was firm and the message unambiguous. Even in my limited Swahili I couldn't mistake it.

"It's a Katangese," our wounded ex-rebel whispered.

"*Kuya!*" This time the pitch was higher and the tone was more gruff. We decided to go out before he decided to come in.

There he stood near the back door. On the side of his head sat a wide-brimmed army hat while a faded camouflage uniform draped his slight frame. He clutched a machine gun at the ready and several belts of ammunition dangled from his neck to his boots. A blinded right eye and a menacing scowl completed the picture. Was this to be it?

Hazel, Anne and I stepped onto the cement walk. We must have looked a helpless lot, especially me wearing only white tennis shorts. He glowered at us.

"Where are you hiding the Zairian soldiers?" he challenged.

"There are none here," Hazel replied quickly in Ndembu. "Only missionaries and African friends." As if on cue, out came our wounded Katangese gendarme waving his cast and telling his story. The rebel soon lowered his rifle to the ground and leaned his elbow on the muzzle. That was a welcome sight.

"I need your car," the Katangese said to the girls.

"Gladly," answered Anne running off for the keys.

The Katangese were now emerging from innumerable sites and we were ordered to the mission roadway in front of the house. What a joy it was to greet Terry and the McKenzies, a joy only to be magnified when Brian appeared with news of the safety of all the other households. Not one occupied home had been stormed by the soldiers, and aside from one fair-sized hole in Hazel and Anne's roof, none of the houses had been damaged by the fighting! Our hearts praised the Lord.

But what would the rebels do with us now? First of all they commandeered all our cars and trucks including the Fisher's Chevy pickup. They also seized all our motorbikes except for Harold's and Glenys's which escaped detection. Then they decided to search our homes but couldn't agree where to confine us in the meantime. Some were obviously distrustful, and when we supplied them with water for their canteens, we were made to drink of it first in case it had been poisoned. Others were openly friendly and told us not to worry about their more suspicious comrades. It was abundantly clear that authority amongst these men belonged to whoever seized it. In the end, after a token inspection of our homes they left quite satisfied.

Hazel's phone rang. It was from the midwives at the maternity. They reported that the fighting around the wards had been fierce but no harm had come to any patients or staff and all the buildings were intact. They had only one piece of bad news—a wounded man was waiting for us at the theater.

Two rebels escorted Hazel and me along the main road. We dared not travel alone nor along the back paths because the Katangese were combing the property for wounded or hidden Zairians. Any rustling of bushes would first be greeted with a burst of gunfire, then an investigation. This they called their *nettoyage* or mop-up operation.

As we passed by the Coates's home, several comrades emerged laden with household goods which they carried to a waiting truck. I was sickened at the thought of our home being plundered but this didn't seem the right time to protest. Further along, just beside my shower house lay one of the Zairian dead. He was sprawled face down, his body riddled with bullets. I was getting my first sobering look at the ugliness of war.

At the operating theater stood the wounded man clothed in a white hospital gown. He was young, only a teenager, and his badly shattered right arm lay limp in a sling. As I looked at his face I recognized that his features were not those of the local Lunda people.

"What are you?" one of the rebels growled. "A soldier or a civilian?"

The youth glanced down at his torn limb then replied, "A soldier." The next question was inevitable.

"Are you Katangese or Zairian?" The tension was almost unbearable. The answer was written on his face. Would he lie or would he beg for mercy?

"Zairian," was his meek response.

I didn't wait for the rebels to react but, grabbing the soldier by his good elbow, I led him into the safe confines of the theater. Hazel seated him on the operating table then looked at me.

"Well, what next?" she asked.

"He needs an x-ray but I doubt he'd make it there and back. Let's just—" The doors of the theater crashed open as three rebels angrily stomped in and leveled their guns at us.

"Give him to us!" they clamored. We stared down their rifles, horrified and speechless. I turned to the boy.

"Doctor, save me!" he pleaded with eyes fixed on mine. He was only a youth and he was hurt—certainly they'd understand. I began to speak again but the guns jerked back at us and the guerillas' tone became more threatening. To interfere would jeopardize everybody's lives not just our own, but how could we let him die?

He began to weep. "Doctor, do something! They're going to kill me!" His words pierced me through like a thousand daggers and his imploring gaze tortured my breaking spirit. Hazel whispered to him that God was love. Could he believe it?

The rebels grabbed him by the shoulders and hauled him out the door, his heels dragging behind. All the while his eyes were riveted on mine and his shrieks became more frenzied.

"Hazel, stay inside," I said. Moments later we heard it. *Rat-tat-tat-tat-tat!* Oh God, why? The answer came in a flash from the prophet Jeremiah: "The heart is deceitful above all things, and desperately wicked." Its terrifying capabilities were just surfacing.

We knew we had to be an inspiration to the Africans especially in the light of this story that would now be spread. We prayed for multiplied strength, then walked out of the theater and toured the hospital. To see all the buildings intact and to converse with our unharmed staff and patients was wonderful beyond imagination. It was not just a welcome distraction from the horror we had just witnessed. It was a marvelous vindication of our earlier exhortations to the people to trust God for His protection of the mission. More than that, it was a personal fulfillment of an Old Testament promise: "The angel of the Lord encampeth round about them that fear him, and delivereth them" (Ps. 34:7).

On the way back to the girls' home I met Terry and recounted to him the sad happening at the hospital. He too was stricken at the news and offered to bury the young man and the other Zairian dead on the grounds. Then he told me that both his transmitter and Peter's two old ones had been confiscated by the rebels. The officer in charge of this operation, however, had been a most pleasant fellow named Henri who claimed to have been raised on one of our mission stations years ago. He promised to help us with any problems and when Terry mentioned the break-in at the Coates's, he asked for someone to list what had been taken so that he could retrieve the missing goods. I decided to do it.

The house was a shambles. Both doors displayed big boot marks halfway up where they had been kicked in. On the front wall were scrawled misspelled slogans praising the liberators and denouncing Mobutu. The inside was ransacked. Cupboards were smashed, cabinets turned over and clothes strewn across the floor. Besides the wanton destruction there were many articles missing including clocks, cameras, a record player, kitchen utensils and much more. The drawer where my camera and diary had been hidden was pulled out and its contents scattered. The fact that I had rescued these was a small mercy in the midst of greater tragedy. I had barely started to clean up when one of the orderlies found me.

"*Munganga*, there are many wounded at the hospital!"

For the next four hours, Hazel, Norma and I worked steadily on the war victims.

Safi was one of our patients. She and her family had been fleeing down the Sandoa Road when they became trapped in a crossfire. Besides a mutilated right hand and a blinded left eye, she had sustained an extensive soft tissue loss to her thigh. Her baby's leg injuries were even more serious.

A husky truck driver was brought in with a partially severed arm. He had another much graver problem, however, in that he was suspected of being a Zairian soldier.

Other cases defied both the few available textbooks and our combined experience but we did the best we could—even with the anesthesia. I had refused to use ethyl chloride as a general anesthetic when Peter was there. I had once read a text that only mentioned the drug to condemn it as unsafe. Yet for several patients I had no option that day. We strapped them down, then lay across them as they thrashed through the excitement phase of anesthetic induction. We performed the procedure then watched them wake up as quickly as they had gone under. Hazel and Norma smiled as they saw my growing enthusiasm for the drug I had once openly scorned.

Beginning around noon there was almost continual gunfire on the station. Soldiers were casually walking in and out of the theater so we knew that the noise was not that of battle. We continued to operate but the shooting only intensified the incredible strain under which we were already working. Anne sat on a stool praying for us throughout much of the ordeal. What a pillar of strength!

When we learned the significance of the gunfire we were almost crushed. Some of it was just an expression of jubilance on the part of the Katangese. Some of it was the slaughter of three of our cows by rebels who had requested and received written permission to do it. Some of the shooting, however, was the execution of captured Zairian soldiers. I realized that such practices were not new to the history of man but the brutishness, the pitiless savagery of it all was never more apparent to me. While I was wielding a healing scalpel, scarcely yards away man and beast were being destroyed with equal relish. Whereas a beast's death required written permission, a man's did not. Passionate reaction to such atrocities would be a sure path to insanity or martyrdom. A measure of detachment would be necessary until we confronted the authorities. But would they listen?

We finished surgery around 2:30 P.M. and stepped out of the theater into the afternoon sunlight. The Katangese were everywhere. Lounging on the grass, conversing with the women, distributing meat to the hospital patients—they were decidedly more relaxed than in the morning. Several stopped me on my way home and with inexplicable affability wished me well. I was dumbfounded at the unending string of incongruities I had encountered that day.

Two more rebels greeted me near the Coates's house. One looked like a high schooler and the other had a greying beard. While I was exchanging a few pleasantries with them, gunfire erupted nearby and I threw myself flat on the ground. Their hearty laughter embarrassed me as I lay at their boots. It was obviously a false alarm. Crimson, I regained my vertical posture and hastened off. I wasn't afraid to die but neither did I plan to stand merrily chatting while bullets were flying around. Only time would condition a more controlled reaction to the shooting.

What was left of the afternoon passed quickly but the evening brought more tragedy. Safi's husband was a veterinary student and thus a member of Zaire's armed forces. In his possession was found an army cap and he was summarily executed on the hospital steps in front of his family and a horror-stricken crowd. Hazel and I were dragged down to the wards and accused of sheltering an enemy soldier on our premises. Only vehement protestations of innocence extricated us from the affair.

Our sorrows had been many that day, and Safi's dreadful loss only hit us where we were already numb. There was no court of appeal for us on earth but our heavenly Father listened to the anguish of our hearts. Yet, as we thought about that day, there was much cause for thanksgiving. The mission station and its occupants had been miraculously preserved despite the extensive damage in Kasaji town and the untold scores of dead. We recalled numerous other mercies: help during the surgery, news of Katoka's safety, the friendliness of Henri, and many more; but most of all a loving God whose compassions were stronger than the terror of ... ...

Since hundreds of heavily armed para-commandos still lurked in the surrounding bush, the Katangese established a network of sentries around the mission. The Zairians didn't counterattack, however, and we all enjoyed a quiet night—all of us, that is, except the Fishers.

Until this time, Grannie had thrived on the excitement. So much intrigue had filled her days that a little war was not about to upset her. But that night she was terrorized by a drunken toothless soldier who banged his gun on her window and fired wantonly in the air. Terry finally rescued her by dragging her upstairs out of danger. Poor Grannie! She would soon bounce back.

On Tuesday our homes and the hospital were plastered with posters glorifying the new president, Nathanael Mbumba. A few of us were drafted for service—such as Harold who was forced to repair military vehicles—sometimes at gunpoint. All of us were soon instructed on two important practices of the FNLC. Firstly, we had to address each other as "camarade." To call someone "citoyen" as decreed by Mobutu, was imperialistic. Secondly, we were taught to use an old tribal handshake which was composed of three maneuvers. A palm-to-palm shake slipped smoothly into a palm-to-thumb grip and then back. These two practices symbolized the expedient combination of socialism and tribalism that were at the basis of the Katangese movement.

Shortly after lunch the action started once more. A van from the Catholic mission five miles away arrived carrying a young woman just shot in the abdomen. Her pulse was up, her pressure was down and blood was flowing freely from high in her left side. Her spleen was probably hit.

"Will you take her?" the nun asked. The woman needed opening but I had never done a solo laparotomy before, and certainly not a splenectomy.

"If you don't take her, we'll drive on to Kisenge or to Angola. I don't mind. Just make a decision," the Catholic sister pressed. What a predicament! If the patient's spleen was hit she could die on the way to those distant hospitals. It seemed her only chance was our inexperienced hands.

"Okay. We'll do it!" I gritted my teeth.

At that very moment an army jeep sped up and a young man with multiple burns was roughly pushed out. "Here's a Kinshasa boy for you," a rebel scowled. "He says he's not but I can tell by his smell."

The prisoner was so weak that I had to secure a stretcher. He had been languishing in the bush for days, and though his burns were minor, I became nauseated when I examined his badly shattered left forearm. A score of maggots freely moved inside a grossly contaminated wound. The hand and wrist were swollen to double size and were covered with infected craters. The condition of his arm was serious but his overall prognosis was worse. Would the Katangese let the Kinshasa Boy live long enough to receive treatment?

While x-raying the new patients, I read the splenectomy chapter of Hamilton Bailey's *Short Practice of Surgery*. Back in the theater I gave our lady a spinal anesthetic hoping it would be sufficient. Hazel draped the patient. I prepped the field. Norma counted the scalpels and clamps. Anne sat in a corner poised to read aloud the open textbook when needed. Tshihinga stood ready to fetch extra instruments if called for. Then, with the backdrop of sporadic gunfire, soldiers' guffaws, and racing jeeps, I prayed, "Lord, if ever we needed your help, it's now. Preserve this woman's life. For your glory. Amen."

Only minutes after we had started, two rebels entered the building insisting to see me. Tshihinga tried to reason with them but they barged past him into the theater with their guns.

"Camarade Doctor, we must talk with you right now," they demanded.

"I can't. I'm busy."

"This is important, Camarade," they replied threateningly. I was forced to break scrub and join them in a side room.

"This hospital now belongs to the new socialist state and according to Article Three in our protocol, several changes will be made." While they pointed to their crumpled official document, I grew more angry and resentful at their unreasonable intrusion.

"Four army nurses will join your hospital staff. Every test and every treatment will soon be free to the people. Just make out a bill and the state will pay." And on they went with their string of new improved regulations.

Finally, I could take it no longer. I indignantly told them that the patient was going to die unless I returned immediately and that it would be their fault. They backed off and agreed to meet later.

I had to extend the incision upwards, and since the spinal was no longer holding her we had to give a general anesthetic. Only ether was available but I had never seen it used. With Barbara's help in its administration, I witnessed another first in that operation. That wasn't all—a self-avowed military nurse visited us. Before I knew it, he had poked his head over Barbara's shoulder into the operating field while puffing a cigarette. Hazel and I exploded before the gas did and he was banished from the room. Perspiration streamed down my body while prayers mounted to God. The tension was incredible.

Two or three times we heard shouting on the front steps where different groups of guerillas would stop and threaten to kill the Kinshasa Boy. Tshihinga would go out to plead for him on our behalf before they would move on. Meanwhile we had discovered the bowel and spleen to be intact. A large hematoma of undetermined origin was present but active bleeding had stopped. We decided to be conservative under the circumstances so closed up quickly.

I dashed outside to confront the next group of accusers. One of them waved a piece of paper at the wretched Kinshasa Boy and shouted that he would die. "I checked out this man's name," the tormentor argued, "and found that he is not with us. He is listed in our files as a Zairian soldier. This paper from the commandant verifies it." I didn't believe the rogue.

"Let me see the paper, Camarade," I growled.

"No," he retorted.

"Give me it!" I grabbed it from his hand and quickly read it. Then, raising my voice for all to hear, I said, "You have lied, Camarade. The commandant has ordered this man to be treated not killed, and I am going to treat him." Silence ripped the air as the guerilla jerked his rifle.

"When you have finished, camarade Doctor," the rebel grinned, "we will look after him."

As we helped the poor fellow onto the operating table, Hazel remarked, "He doesn't have a chance. They'll get him yet."

It was 7 P.M. and quite dark when we finally emerged from the theater. Wonderfully, the rebels had disappeared! Our work of an hour was only a start for this young man but we knew that the work of a moment might still finish him off.

We picked our way home along a back path stepping over an unexploded mortar that lay behind the girls' house. "Thanks, Hazel," I said. "All of you were great this afternoon."

"We all need each other," she replied.

We certainly did. Only two days of rebel rule had passed yet we had already struggled through numerous trials together. How much more physical and emotional strain we would face was a mystery. How much more spiritual pain we would suffer was unknown. Yet I did know that the Lord had provided each of us for the encouragement of the other, and Himself for the sustenance of us all.

Thoroughly exhausted, I collapsed into bed. The morrow and its challenges would arrive all too soon.

10
The True Liberator

There were two major reasons for which Terry and I sought out the commandant on Wednesday morning. First of all, we wanted to inquire about the possible return of the Coates and Glenys from Katoka. Secondly, we wished to obtain the official word on the handling of wounded prisoners. Our two Zairian soldiers were still alive but we desired assurances for their future.

The rebel that brought us into town raced at breakneck speeds along washboard roads while we clung desperately to the seats and door handles. On the way we whizzed past Terry's Chevy pickup which had already broken down and been abandoned by the Katangese. It was not hard to imagine why the vehicles were expiring so quickly.

As we drove through Kasaji, we found it less ravaged than expected. The buildings were pockmarked but erect, and only a few were irreparably damaged. There were no corpses in the main street, but we knew they were somewhere—the stench of rotting human flesh filled the air. We finally arrived at the Katangese headquarters only to learn that the commandant had gone to the front lines. However, a friendly officer named Roger promised to relay the message of our visit and then he invited himself over to see us that night. After the customary round of handshakes, we took our leave.

Early that afternoon I heard that the commandant was at the Fisher's. Pleasantly surprised that he should pass by so soon, I hastened over to meet him.

"David," Terry called out as I walked up the driveway, "I'd like you to meet Major Mufu." The commandant was of medium height but had a sleek powerful build. His boots were shiny and his field cap shaded a pair of intense eyes.

"Good afternoon, Doctor," he said in well-articulated French. "I hear you've been busy."

"That's right, Major," I replied. "Too busy. We're having trouble coping with the growing number of casualties. It wouldn't be as bad if all our staff were here, but as you know, Dr. Coates and his wife are at Katoka and so is one of our nurses. We would really appreciate their safe return if you could possibly arrange it."

"I understand your difficulties," he began, "but the roads are far too unsafe right now. There are still hundreds of enemy soldiers in the bush." I was crestfallen. Then he added, "However, in 48 hours things may change. Speak to me again on Friday."

"Thank you, Major," I said delightedly. "We'll gladly wait until you judge it safe."

To think that Major Mufu would actually consider our proposal was a breakthrough. I liked the man—he listened and he made sense!

"One more thing, Major," I asked. "What about prisoners?"

"We take prisoners," he replied.

"Some of your men are less certain of that. A couple of my patients are being threatened and I've heard rumors of executions." I had understated the case but even then I wondered if I had said too much.

"Prisoners will be treated fairly," he began in the same even-tempered tone. "There will be no executions. That is what I will continue to tell my men. However, you must have patience. Some of the men are very excited right now but soon they will calm down. You see, we are not against the people. We are for the people. We ourselves are Congolese! We are not Cubans or Angolans as Mobutu claims on your radio. We are not even Katangese, so don't call us by that name. We are Congolese."

His voice grew soft but passionate. "This country is our home, the place of our birth but we have been forced from it by the oppression of Mobutu. Now we have returned to liberate our people from tyranny and injustice. All of Congo will again be free. One day even our prisoners will share in the freedom and equality of a liberated Congo."

It was time for Mufu to leave. He told us to contact him if we had any other problems, then he sped off in his flaming orange Renault.

Terry and I were both impressed by the major. At least there seemed to be a man of reason and authority to whom we could appeal and expect a fair answer. We walked past the garage and I suddenly spotted Terry's Chevy.

"The pickup!" I exclaimed. "It's back!"

"That's right," Terry beamed. "Mufu let me tow it home. Much longer though, and it would have been beyond repair."

"Why? What's wrong with it?" I asked.

"The battery is stolen, the cables are cut and the gears are scrambled."

"Oh no! Do you have any spare parts?"

"I think so," he said with a flicker of a smile.

"And what about the problem with the gears?"

"Oh, that's happened many times," Terry replied. "I could fix them in a few minutes if I wanted to, but for now the pickup is staying in the garage." There was a twinkle in his eye.

Mufu was not the only visitor to the Fisher's that afternoon. A burly Katangese officer drove his army truck into the mission asking, "Where's my grandmother?" Fifty years before, Grannie Fisher had raised a little orphan girl. She grew up to marry a believer who became one of the most respected church leaders in the south. Joseph was born the last of their many children, and although he had been a rebellious son, he hadn't forgotten the hands that clothed and fed both him and his mother. Thus the black guerilla was reunited with his white grandmother. Grannie gave him a Bible and an earful as well, but the latter conversation was never disclosed.

The rebels we had encountered thus far were so different. Some were friendly and loved to talk with us while others seemed hostile and suspicious of our every move. In keeping with the word from the top, however, the vast majority accepted us as potential contributors to the new state, and some even attempted to gain our support. It was in this connection that Roger and three comrades arrived after supper.

Heavy boots scuffing on the cement walk alerted us to the four armed and rugged figures now at our front door. I had forgotten Roger's promise, so with due alarm we opened to their banging. What a relief to see Roger's smile!

"Come on in," Anne said. "Come right in." The Katangese tramped in with rifles slung over their shoulders and cardboard boxes in their arms. On their service caps were scribbled their names: Roger; Alberto; Dangereux, meaning "the dangerous one"; and Vaincre ou Mourir, meaning "conquer or die." A nice lot to have over for tea!

"You can put your guns in the corner if you like," Hazel offered. They all agreed except for M. Vaincre ou Mourir who clutched his rifle and sat sullenly behind a pair of dark sunglasses. It struck me that the friendly Roger had probably coerced him to come.

"Well," Roger began, "we've come tonight on behalf of the FNLC to give greetings to our camarades at the Garenganze[1] mission." It was so official. "We also want to give you some gifts for your personal use." He opened up the boxes to reveal army biscuits, Carnation milk and canned meat. Some of it, no doubt, was from the raided shops at Kisenge and Dilolo.

"Oh. Thank you so much," Anne said, "but we couldn't accept it. We have plenty of food."

"But I insist," he answered firmly. "It is General Mbumba's wish that we give such gifts to our friends."

"We will accept them gratefully, Roger," Hazel said. "I can share the food with some of our patients."

"But you must not! It is for you. We have already taken care of the sick camarades at the hospital. This is for your own personal use." He was becoming angry so we didn't argue further but thanked him profusely. After all, we could still distribute the food as needed.

For the next half hour, we listened to the glories of the revolution. It was much the same patter that we had heard before, but we nodded at the appropriate junctures and thus endured the dissertation. The recurring theme was that General Nathanael Mbumba was the victorious liberator of the Congolese people. As their discourse began to wind down, I seized the opportunity to talk about another liberator.

"The world has seen many liberators throughout history. Very often the lands that they free, however, become enslaved once more, sometimes even in their own lifetime. In fact, many nations have been liberated a dozen times or more. Why? Why is once not good enough? I'll tell you why. Liberators can change the system. They can put bread on the table and clothes on the back. They can even provide equality in education, in justice, and in jobs, but there's one thing they cannot change—the heart of man. That's where man is bound. That's where he needs help most but gets it least. Only one Liberator I know has ever been able to change man's heart, and His name is Jesus Christ." Detecting no animosity, I decided to carry on.

"You see, if a man's heart is changed so that he is no longer caught up in himself but can concentrate on serving others, then he can revolutionize the system from within and preserve its transformation because he himself is transformed. Jesus Christ can change hearts and He's been doing it for hundreds of years. You soldiers may free a country but who is going to free the hearts of the people? Who is going to free your hearts? You too need to ask Christ to save you from yourself and your sin. That's the message you need to carry across the country: Jesus Christ is the Liberator of the heart of man!" There was silence for close to a minute while they sat there thinking. I prayed that they would understand.

Then Anne suggested brightly, "Shall we sing something?" Roger said, "Yes. Let's sing the one that goes," and he hummed a few shaky bars of "What a Friend We Have in Jesus." I pounded it out at the piano while we lustily sang all the verses.

After some more songs and some prayer with them, it was time to go. They all seemed appreciative of the evening except for the sulking M. Vaincre ou Mourir. I shook his hand vigorously and asked, "Camarade, what is your real name?"

"Vaincre ou Mourir," he retorted.

"Camarade," I said, "you wouldn't *vaincre ou mourir* me, would you?" The corners of his mouth twisted up ever so slightly for a split second.

"Good night," was his only reply but I exulted in having seen the makings of a smile on his face. How we prayed that night for these and other Katangese soldiers who would hear again and again the life-changing message of the gospel! We were hostages of a rebel regime in a war-torn land, but like the apostle Paul in Caesar's Rome, we determined to share our faith with soldiers at every available opportunity.

Most of Thursday was spent in the operating theater. A soldier was brought in with shrapnel wounds. An old man limped in complaining that he hadn't walked well for four days—a bullet was lodged in his right knee. A young lad was carried in with a terrible injury to his thigh: a rebel had shot him because he didn't like the Banjo Boy making music during wartime.

When I finally emerged from the theater I encountered three military nurses named Little Henri, Roberto and Augusto. They introduced themselves as the new additions to the hospital staff, then told me to give each of them a house! I assured them we had no such accommodation to offer but they tenaciously clung to me. Finally I compromised and showed them three small rooms at the back of the isolation ward.

"That's not good enough, Camarade Doctor. We must also have quarters for the new commandant of the company, for the commandant of the battalion and the political commissar." I was beginning to see the not-so-thin edge of the wedge. The Katangese were planning to move into the hospital making our mission their headquarters. This violated the Geneva Convention, but after all, what did international law mean to the guerillas? I longed even more for Peter's return, and that night in my diary I wrote the rather succinct comment, "Need Peter, pronto."

Friday was the eleventh day since the invasion of Shaba province and the fifth since the battle at Kasaji. Life under the occupying forces was slowing down to a more tolerable pace. Many of the local people were trickling back from the fields to their homes, while others were checking out the situation before deciding on a return. The dispensary attendance was climbing steadily especially as the people heard rumors of free medical treatment. The guns were mostly silent except for an occasional *pop*, but we didn't even notice these any longer. Uppermost in our minds was a special prayer we had for that Friday: the return of the Coates and Glenys from Katoka. To that end we hoped that Mufu would appear early so that we could remind him of our request.

However, just when the conflict seemed to be drifting too far afield to affect us, we were jolted back to reality. The war was still near. A patrol of Katangese soldiers was ambushed a few miles outside of Kasaji. Several had been killed instantly and the rest escaped back to the hospital transporting three of the worst casualties we had seen so far.

Then, before the morning was over, in staggered another wounded Katangese. He had been shot in Kasaji itself while investigating suspicious movement in a certain hole. As he peered downward he saw a Zairian aiming his rifle upward. He dove away but not before a bullet ripped open his buttock. This gangling six-footer screamed and fought like a four-year-old through each stitch, but the Buttock Man, as we called him, became one of our most likable patients.

Major Mufu didn't show up until late afternoon, and when he did he brought very surprising news: "I'm moving my headquarters closer to the front. I leave Kasaji tonight."

"What? You've just got here," I protested.

He laughed. "If I stayed here that would mean I was unsuccessful. No, we will advance despite our problems of today."

"Then who will take your place?" I asked.

"A new commandant—Major Mujinga."

"And what about Doctor Coates?" I prodded.

"An officer may bring him back before dark. If not, ask Mujinga for new arrangements. Good-bye, Doctor David."

"Good-bye, Major Mufu," I replied shaking his hand. "I hope I don't see you at my hospital as a patient." He chuckled and nodded in agreement. It crossed my mind to pray with him, but I hesitated and he was gone.

Mufu had proved to be an approachable man and we knew it would be difficult for the next commandant to match his sense of fairness. I appreciated his friendliness, whatever the motive, but sorrowed that his business was war and death. He too needed to discover the Liberator.

Since the afternoon had been quiet, I decided to venture out in the early evening. I walked over to the McKenzie's whom I found busily engaged in one of the Kasaji missionaries' favorite pastimes: Scrabble. It was a refreshing diversion from the affairs of the day and they gladly made room for me at the game table. However, we felt a little forgotten that night. Darkness came but not the expected Coates and Glenys. Had Mufu's officer omitted the task assigned him? Had Mufu ever assigned the task? Worse still, had there been another ambush? We listened to the news but it seemed as if the BBC had also overlooked us. Zaire was not even mentioned.

Suddenly, at 9:45 P.M. we were all startled by a sharp rap at the front door. A drunken rebel had attempted to break into Hazel and Anne's two nights previously and into the maternity the night before. Was this the same troublemaker? Harold cautiously opened the door.

"Hello! Do you have the keys to the operating theater? The orderlies have just called me about a chest wound." It was Peter.

11
Stench of Death

The excited reception given the Coates and Glenys resembled the sort of welcome accorded those just released after years in captivity. Actually, we had been separated scarcely 12 days, but what days they had been for us! The Katangese takeover at undefended Katoka had been less dramatic, but there had been a few tense moments when William Rew's hunting rifle was discovered during a house search. After the initial seizure of transmitters, vehicles and gasoline, however, the Katoka folk were mostly left alone while the rebels marched for Kasaji.

It was during our happy breakfast reunion on Saturday morning that Major Mufu arrived unexpectedly. "So, the other doctor is finally here," he said with a broad smile.

"Yes. We're very grateful, Major," I replied.

"Good!" he exclaimed, then pointing back towards his car he added, "I have brought you a camarade with an injured ankle. Will you attend to him?"

"Certainly—but when do you go to the front? I thought you had already left."

"I'm leaving now," he answered, extending his hand.

"One more thing, Major," I gulped. "I'd like to pray with you now." He was as baffled at my suggestion as I was surprised at myself for making it. Without stopping for him to recover, I began to pray for the poor people of the Congo caught up in the war and for Mufu that somehow he would find God in the midst of the conflict. When I had finished, I looked at him. He stood there for a moment almost reverently.

"Major, when you are at the front you should pray too."

"Thank you, Doctor, but I have no time to pray. I have no time to eat or to sleep. I am a man of war and I live for nothing else. Good-bye." I was impressed by his strength of commitment though saddened by its object. As his car sped off, I wondered if we'd ever meet again.

After breakfast, many of the Kasaji families came over for a time of prayer and thanksgiving. Then the lepers lined up outside clapping their deformed hands and bowing their crippled frames while Ruth greeted each one in turn. The hospital staff and patients responded with equal devotion when Peter and Glenys appeared on the wards. That day was a happy one for the mission station

Peter was soon embroiled in controversy with the soldiers. When the Katangese demanded more accommodation for their men, Peter insisted that hospitals were to maintain their neutrality in time of war and should not be used as barracks. His arguments were brushed aside. Five hospital rooms, each with three beds, were taken—six beds for military patients and nine for sentries! An African orderlies' home and two local public schools were seized for the troops while the mission guest house next door to Fisher's became the officers' residence. The Katangese were settling in.

Peter was also introduced to some of our drunken rebels. One of them tottered to our back door and insisted on inspecting the house.

"I am the commandant of the technical services. It is my responsibility as commandant to search all the buildings for transmitters. Other commandants are responsible for other things but I am the commandant of the technical services. Therefore I am responsible to search your house because I am the commandant . . . " On and on he raved in his befuddled state, swaying to and fro in the breeze, and yet we had to take him seriously—a pistol sat on his right hip. No amount of reasoning or of ingenious argumentation could deter the megalomaniac from his resolve to investigate the premises. For 45 minutes the tension heightened until finally two unknown Katangese happened by and hauled him off.

The Coates were also subjected to many new noises that violated the stillness of the night. Besides the revvings of vehicles and the shouts from the barracks, there were the muffled conversations of Katangese wandering by the house. Then Saturday at midnight we were aroused by loud knocking at the door and the urgent plea to see four casualties just arrived from the front lines.

On Sunday evening ear-splitting gunfire broke out behind the house. I found Peter and Ruth lying on the bathroom floor and remembered how under similar circumstances I had flung myself to the ground just a few days before. The shooting was just one more facet of the new Kasaji life, and like the rest of us, the Coates soon adapted.

The return of the Kasaji missionaries had a settling effect on the whole community. People were already moving back from the bush but now it seemed that the process was accelerated. However, the increased population was just what the Katangese wanted. Military jeeps loaded with joy-riding adolescents sped along the roadways. Rebels gathered young boys around them and challenged each one to handle their rifles. In this way many youths were enticed to join the growing band of eager recruits that returned to Angola for military training. Although none of our students had enlisted, the pressure on them to take up arms was intensifying. For this reason, as well as the real danger of counterattack, the teachers decided to suspend classes indefinitely and to send home all the boarders who could possibly leave.

The wisdom of this decision was confirmed the very morning that the college was closed down—Zairian jet fighters arrived without warning. Peter and I dashed out of the theater to see people scattering in every direction, many holding their hands to their heads in manifest terror. Others simply gaped while a few tremulously pointed skyward to where the three Mirage jets had been sighted. My heart pounded as I spotted one of the fighters banking at approximately 5,000 feet just south of Kasaji. Its silvery wings flashed the reflected sunlight; then it disappeared behind some cumulus. Was aerial bombardment to begin?

There was no place to hide. The tin roofs of the mission buildings provided unmistakable targets for the pilots. But they wouldn't bomb a hospital—or would they? We prayed for protection and clung to the hospital wall. For an interminable five minutes the hum and whirr of the predators' planes conjured up visions of pockmarked landscape, smoking ruins and torn bodies. Then a single Mirage fighter swooped down from the clouds for a final intimidating pass over the mission. Only after it had streaked by did the deafening roar of its descent assault our ears. The planes meted out no punishment this trip, but we realized that should they return with a vengeance, there would be no chance to seek cover.

The effect of this aerial reconnaissance mission on the community was cataclysmic. Once more the people charged madly into the bush, this time without thought of home or provision. Meanwhile, the rebels roamed the villages discouraging the exodus with their claims that the jets were Katangese. We didn't believe them for a moment. Neither did one perturbed guerilla who glowered at me and murmured, "This must not continue," as if I had summoned the Mirages.

One of the commandants told us that sophisticated weaponry would soon arrive and that no plane would dare fly over us again. He also promised to relay a message to Echoes of Service (our British-based missionary service agency) indicating that we were safe. The Katangese clearly wanted to make us happy. Our presence at Kasaji was an important stabilizing factor and would draw the people back.

That evening the radio broadcasts startled us. Zaire claimed to have bombarded rebel-held Dilolo and recaptured Kasaji with great losses to the Katangese! The latter story was a lie but was the other true? Was Dilolo actually bombed, and if so would we be next? In my diary I wrote:

"The Lord is teaching us how much we need to rely on Him. . . . Every day or every other day there is a crisis: yesterday the gun-wielding drunk; today the planes; tomorrow, who knows? Everything must be committed to Him—every moment, every plan, every feeling, every step. . . . ''

On Tuesday, March 22, the newly arrived FNLC commissar began to wield his political clout. Kabeya was his name and he was a short, mustachioed man with a cavalier, roughshod manner. He ''canceled'' everything that afternoon, including the hospital, in order to stage a socialist rally. Most of the people had trickled back within hours of the previous day's aerial scare and he wanted to restore their confidence in the new regime.

Hundreds were assembled at the hospital as he began, ''I speak to you on behalf of the FNLC which has liberated you from Mobutu's tyranny, and set you free from lackey imperialism.'' A few lonely cheers were heard from the audience.

''In many ways we have already shown you the kindness of our hearts. Dear brothers, we have shared with you biscuits and canned milk. Are you thankful?'' A few more cheers from the onlookers.

''And that's not all we have given you! Remember the fresh beef.'' Even more cheers. A few wise heads turned to look at the mission's thinned-out herd of cattle.

''And then there were the free car rides. Is not this the truth?'' By now the crowd was loosening up and soon he would have their plaudits even without the cues.

''Who has made your money good for nothing, your *makuta* worthless?'' Kabeya shouted. ''Mobutu,'' Kabeya replied, prompting the people.

''Who has taken your copper and given you dust?''

''Mobutu!'' the crowd answered.

''Who has sent soldiers to harass you?''

''Mobutu!!''

''Who has sent thieves to tax you?''

''Mobutu!!!''

And so the rally reached fever pitch, led on by a master of African rhetoric to a cadence that was irresistible. Sweat poured from Kabeya's brow and his voice became hoarse, but on he raved cataloguing the many grievances of the people. Finally he painted a glowing picture of the new society, citing Angola as the prototype.

''In the new society we will all be equal. There will be no distinction of race or color or tongue. No worker will be more important to the state than his neighbor. There will be equality in opportunity and in distribution of wealth. We will all have food to eat and food to spare! Each one will wear good clothes and have fine homes! Every child will receive the best education and we will drive our own cars! All these benefits will not come right away but we must be patient. The struggle may be long, but victory is certain!''

The throng was in a frenzy and many women were dancing jubilantly as Kabeya capped his two-hour performance with another promise. ''To prove the generosity of our hearts and the good intentions of the new socialist state, I will tell you one more thing. From now on all medical care at Kasaji Hospital will be free!'' With that the political commissar was hoisted high in the air to the delirious cheering of an intoxicated crowd and was marched triumphantly around the mission.

His generosity was overwhelming. It was easy for him to be generous when what he was giving away belonged to somebody else. Our small hospital fees were used solely for staff salaries, and without these receipts the Africans were the ones who would suffer. The FNLC had promised to pay them but as one orderly told Peter, ''*Munganga*, the next wage you give us will be our last. The orderlies in Angola have not been paid since the revolution two years ago.''

Harold elaborated on one of Kabeya's points. ''He's right that under socialism everyone is equal—it's just that some are more equal than others!'' How true! The more equal ones cruised around in our vehicles. The more equal ones slept on the stolen beds and mattresses. The more equal ones had taken possession of the guest house. The chronicle of Katangese socialism had other highlights: six of our 20 cattle slaughtered and more of them demanded each day (who would supply the milk for the babies in our nursery?); numerous medical supplies taken for the war effort; Harold's tools stolen and then threats issued when he couldn't complete a job; the Coates's home ransacked; a hundred changes of lepers' clothing pirated; hospital pillows, blankets, beds and mattresses filched; the midwives harassed by would-be molesters; chickens stolen, firewood taken, hospital quarters appropriated—the record was endless after only 10 days of occupation. What made it even more ludicrous was the rebels' insistence that we fill out bills to the new state. All accounts, they claimed, would be paid in full from the FNLC's limitless resources.

Nevertheless Kabeya's rally had worked. The crowd saw only the blessings of the new society and not the rocky road to it. The people would forget the danger of the moment—that is, as long as the planes did not come back again.

But come again they did, the very next day! Two Mirage fighters approached from the east and shot by Kasaji at high altitude. Fifteen minutes later the jets swept by again, returning from their bombardment of Kisenge and Dilolo. Even though the aircraft had not made any menacing moves towards us, once more the morale of the community was shattered. Once more the civilians beat a hasty retreat into the bush, and once more the soldiers tried to obstruct their flight.

Meanwhile, the hospital work carried on as usual. More war victims arrived including another injured Zairian soldier. As we helped him from the pickup, several Katangese cursed and threatened him. We rushed him into the x-ray block before more harm came his way.

Finda was terrified. He had been crawling in the bush for seven days without medical help. His eyes were crazed and his speech was rambling. He looked blankly around the room and, despite his severe injury, he did not complain of pain. I thought he was half-mad.

"Look here, David," Peter said while uncovering his badly shot-up right knee. The wound was enormous but surprisingly clean.

"Watch this." Peter used a dropper to fill the gaping wound with fluid. Within a few moments there was a stirring of the waters and some little creatures surfaced, ostensibly for air. Peter plucked a couple of them out with his tweezers and lifted them up for us to see. "Maggots," he announced, "and plenty of them!" No wonder the injury site was so clean!

Finda's fracture necessitated rather elaborate homemade traction. We set it up and provided him with a cook, but we couldn't eliminate the abuse that he and the other two prisoners would receive at the hands of angry Katangese. Apparently they hadn't heard Mufu's call for mercy.

Nor was mercy extended to another half dozen FAZ (*Force Armée Zairoise*) soldiers who were captured that day. Their lot was death by shooting in a mass execution 100 yards from our house. The bodies were left in the sun all day as a warning to the populace not to aid the para-commandos who were still on the loose. At dusk several civilians were drafted to bury the dead. Life was worth less than a Zairian *makuta*.

Reports from the Africans continued to describe a stench that choked Kasaji town. Twelve days had passed since the battle, yet many of the dead still lay where they had fallen. Action was needed to forestall an epidemic, but none of us had felt free or safe to wander off the mission station.

Then on Friday, March 25, the opportunity came.

Peter proposed I take the day off—my first in three weeks. It was a welcome suggestion, especially as I had contracted a severe thumb infection from the war wounds and this condition had resisted both antibiotics and minor surgery. The constant ache was partially relieved by assuming a Napoleonic posture—fist on chest and pulsating thumb pointing skyward—but hospital duties were still very awkward if not impossible. I gladly took up Peter's offer.

The prospect of visiting Kasaji dulled the pain and soon Walter and I were bicycling down the main highway. At least one heart was thump-thumping with mounting excitement.

"Did you hear the latest news?" Walter asked.

"No," I replied. "What happened?"

"The students say that Mutshatsha has fallen to the Katangese!"

"Whew!! Another town! Do you think it's true, Walter?"

"I don't know. We'll have to catch BBC tonight."

The rebels seemed unstoppable. If Mutshatsha had indeed been captured, then Kolwezi was next. Likasi and Lubumbashi weren't far off, and according to the rebels all three cities were infiltrated by scores of heavily armed comrades. Was it possible that Shaba or indeed all of Zaire could soon capitulate? The Katangese thought so!

We pedaled on without seeing a soul. All we could hear were sand and pebbles spinning off the tires and our own puffing marking time like a metronome. Deserted homes lined the road but nothing else betrayed the presence of war.

Our first stop was the roads department's offices on the outskirts of Kasaji. The Zairian army had converted this place into a prison at the start of the war and here our ex-Katangese gendarme had been held. An abandoned lorry occupied the driveway along with a score of green metal helmets, hundreds of mortar shell casings and dozens of army boots. A two-foot diameter hole was punched through the front brick wall of the building and its tin roof looked like a sieve.

I surveyed the scene trying to envision the drama that had been enacted here almost a fortnight ago. Walter walked inside, then quickly came back out holding his nose.

"Don't go in there, David," he warned. Twenty feet from the room I picked up the smell. Inside was a naked blackened corpse leaning against the wall. I backed off with loathing! On the way to our bikes we recognized the smell again and followed our noses to another body lying face up in some bushes. This soldier was in full battle dress and had died where he had fallen. The swarming flies and maggots had obviously done their work as had the lone vulture overhead—the flesh was picked clean exposing his rib cage.

We mounted our cycles and sat there in silent horror. It seemed so unreal, even with the evidence before us. The problem was simply that neither of us wanted to believe our senses. These things couldn't happen. But they did.

"Shall we call it quits, Walter?"

"No. Let's turn up the Sandoa Road." We veered onto this secondary highway and stopped in front of a shop. This was where the bodies were reportedly piled two and three deep. Hundreds of pieces of army equipment littered the ground—blankets and helmets and shirts and pants and boots. Strewn amongst them were countless empty beer bottles while one lonely tripod without its artillery piece stood guard over the whole mess.

The same scene greeted us for 40 and 50 yards up the Sandoa Road. Then we came across a badly damaged building. The roof had collapsed and the inside had been gutted by multiple explosions. More than 30 sooty helmets were scattered on the floor. "The local pub," Walter muttered. "Zairian troops were in here drinking when the Katangese tossed in a few grenades." I shuddered.

"The name of the bar in Ndembu is *Uhwimino Wetu,*" he continued.

"Which means . . . ."

"Which means 'our resting place.'" The name was only too appropriate. We looked at each other and then once more at the house of drunkenness and death before we took our leave.

It was a short run from the ravaged pub to the center of town. Downtown Kasaji at the best of times was not very impressive and on this occasion there was even less to see than usual. A handful of civilians, a few vehicles and half a dozen rebels were about, all standing outside one shop.

One friendly Katangese waved us over and asked us to see the new town dispensary. As we entered the dark room a familiar voice called out, "*Jambo,* Camarade Doctor." I peered through the shadows and to my amazement spotted Augusto, our old military nurse. His contribution to our hospital had been negligible and we hadn't even noticed his departure. Now he had obviously set up his own practice.

"I treat 3,000 people with my medicines," he boasted in half-drunken tones. "I know all about this place. I'm the commandant of all this." His hand swept round his dingy dispensary: two tables sparsely populated by four or five different drugs; two soldiers reclining on some old couches with three giggling women; a couple of old chairs; and a doting band of civilians. This was Augusto's empire.

There was no point in prolonging our visit. We turned to leave but Augusto called out, "Doctor, I will come by the hospital pharmacy later to replenish my stock of drugs."

"Sorry, Augusto, but that's impossible. Thanks anyway."

The whole situation was too pitiable to be funny. Was this the sort of fellow who would have responsibilities in the new regime? If so, we were in trouble. Or perhaps the authorities recognized his weaknesses and wanted to keep him at Kasaji away from the front lines. In that case we were still in trouble. Whatever the situation, I was happy to be gone.

So far our expedition had indicated that there were fewer burials to arrange than we had anticipated. Mufu had interred about 60 Zairian soldiers but it had been our impression that many more had been left unattended. Apparently we were wrong. We decided to head home.

On our way, however, we met some African boys who knew what we were looking for. We carefully followed them down a back path watching out for unexploded grenades. Just before we arrived, our guides ran off squeezing their noses and holding their breaths at the overpowering stench. In front of us sat an open mortuary. Here five made a last stand around an anthill in a peanut field. There two fell by a warehouse. Here one dropped on a side path and there two more lay by a well. These back fields were blemished by scores more, most of them Zairian soldiers. Many still bore their death grimace. All were in advanced stages of decay and needed prompt interment.

Our cycle home was necessarily solemn. All the way I struggled to maintain my composure and only succeeded by forcing myself to make plans for the mass burial.

Early Sunday morning I returned to town with half a dozen of Kasaji's public hygiene workers. It soon became clear that digging proper graves would be difficult. The ground was hard, the stench was strong, the sun was hot and the bodies were numerous. However, the men moved from site to site as directed and soon a score had been interred.

While the workers were busy behind the offices of Kasaji's Cotton Company, I entered the premises and browsed around. The building had been the makeshift command post of the Zairian army. Now it was in shambles. Plaster from the ceiling and glass from the windows covered the floor. Craters the size of tennis balls were gouged in the walls. A lone helmet sat in a corner amidst a pile of spent cartridges. On the top of a blackboard was printed *Nos Forces Effectifs* and underneath a list of all the FAZ battalions and where they were to be posted. This was the foiled Zairian battle plan.

It was almost 10 A.M. and I wanted to return to the mission for the Sunday morning services. I left the men with some words of encouragement then headed back. On the way home a flood of grief suddenly overtook me and I began to weep. The wind licked the tears from my cheeks, but a deep inner sobbing would not be soothed. With my heart I cried, yet with my mind I wondered why. Was it a fear of death or of the unknown finally surfacing? No. Suffering and death would only expedite my release to be with the Lord. Was it a longing to be far away from all the turmoil and pain? No. I was absolutely convinced that this time and this place were God's best for me.

What was it then? It was a groan—a groan which nature shared with me at that moment. It was a lament—a lament which had fallen from countless lips since time began. It was a cry—a cry from me to my God against the wickedness and depravity of my race.

But the scene changed in my mind's eye and I heard another groan, another lament, another cry. It was that of Christ as He died to save me from the penalty of my wickedness and my depravity. His body, unlike those I had left behind, had not met a senseless end. His death had secured my pardon and His resurrection had filled my life with hope and purpose.

Tears of thankfulness and joy welled up as I slipped into the Communion service with a fresh appreciation of the work of Jesus Christ.

The Kasaji family

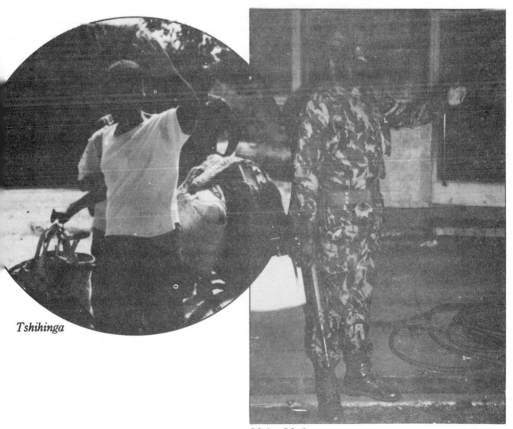

Tshihinga

Major Mufu

African village adjacent to mission

Hazel MacFarlane and ex-Katangese gendarme moments before fighting broke out around homes

Grannie Fisher

*FAZ corpse with
death grimace*

*The Kinshasa Boy and Dr.
Dawson the day before the
former's execution*

*Katangese take girls' car
soon after battle finishes*

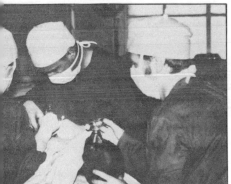

*Dr. Coates, Dr. Dawson and
Nurse Glenys Gillingham at
surgery*

LE CAMARADE NATHANAEL MBUMBA

Président du Front de Libération Nationale Congolais, Lt.
Général et Commandant en Chef des Forces Armées Populaires
du Congo - Kinshasa.

*FNLC poster of the Liberator, President
Nathanael Mbumba*

*Rebel soldiers strolling
outside operating theater*

*Refugees fleeing toward
Angolan border
as battlefront sweeps
back towards Kasaji*

rold, Peter and Robert loading trailer before flight to Angola

Leaving the bishop's palace on the way to Luanda flight

12
"Only His Daily Mercies"

By the end of March the Katangese army had rolled across one-third of Shaba province. Mutshatsha had fallen and the next target was Kolwezi, the heart of Zaire's copper industry. Fear had already gripped the mining center: the army's command post was relocated 60 miles east of the city; journalists withdrew to Kinshasa; and the U.S. evacuated its citizens. President Mobutu was infuriated. He denounced Cuban involvement, arranged pro-government rallies, and shuffled the commanders of his armed forces; yet the rebels surged on. Radio newscasts clearly gave the impression that Mobutu's vast empire was perilously close to disintegration.

Despite the growing success of the Katangese, living with them did not become any easier. We were constantly battling over old issues such as the commandeering of drugs, the occupation of hospital rooms, and the theft of mattresses and beds. In addition, many new problems also arose and these further taxed our already strained relationship.

First of all, the rebels repeatedly ignored our simple request to remove some vehicles from the vicinity of the Coates's house. A captured FAZ tank was parked in front, a Petro Zaire fuel carrier at the side, and a loaded ammunition truck behind. Not only would the vehicles be spotted by reconnaissance aircraft and thus confirm the Katangese presence on the mission, they also constituted a significant "health hazard" in the event of attack.

Only after three Mirages buzzed us on March 28 were the rebels moved to action—but not of the type we expected. They did tow away the tank but they also charged us with using a hidden transmitter to communicate with the enemy. When another house search turned up nothing, they reminded us that swift retribution would fall on all traitors.

The next battle came when the Katangese accused us of withholding optimal therapy from their wounded soldiers. The idea was preposterous!

We had treated more than 40 rebels and most of them had already returned to the front. Nevertheless, Little Henri and Edouard, the head army nurse, marched me away from the operating theater and up to the soldiers' ward. I decided to take a hard stand on this issue.

"Why didn't you give this patient tetracycline?" asked Little Henri.

"Because we have none left. Your last requisition finished it off."

"You're hiding it!" charged Edouard.

"What?" I exclaimed. "I'm telling you the truth. Are you calling me a liar?" Edouard said nothing.

"Then what about him?" continued Little Henri pointing to the Buttock Man. "Look at his wound. It's not better yet."

I smiled and put my hand on the back of the patient's neck. "Our friend knows why. Instead of resting he frolics all day with the girls. Besides, he refuses to let us clean the wound because it's too painful. Any other complaints?"

"Yes," interjected Edouard. "Henri says that you have not changed this man's dressing for four days."

I picked up his hospital chart. "Read this, Camarade. He only came in two days ago."

"Then the chart is wrong," he argued.

I was angered at their false accusations. "You waste my time with your petty complaints! I already have more than I can handle with those who are really sick and want to get better." Then I had an idea. "I came with you up here, now you follow me. Come on!"

I led them to the operating theater where a recent war victim was still on the table. The patient had been in the bush for days before seeking help and his grossly infected wound emanated a stench like that which had gripped Kasaji.

I showed the Katangese the poor fellow's leg; then, to shock them, I boldly ordered, "Smell it!" Edouard refused but both Little Henri and the Buttock Man obeyed. Their contorted faces turned away in disgust. We walked outside.

"You've been complaining about the way I look after patients, Henri. Would you like to treat that man?"

"No," he answered grimly.

"Fine. I have my job. You have yours. If you don't like the way I do my job, do it yourself or else send your soldiers to Kisenge or back to Angola."

"Maybe we will," replied Edouard, mellowed but still defiant.

"As for you," I said smiling at the Buttock Man, "no more women!" He laughed heartily and we all shook hands. This was typically African— fight like dogs then finish by shaking hands. The affair, however, was far from finished.

Another real point of tension during those days was the handling of the three wounded Zairian soldiers. They were ready-made whipping boys for any disgruntled rebels and they regularly took verbal abuse. Although they never complained, we discovered that they were frequently slapped about and beaten with rifle butts. When we protested, the commandants claimed ignorance. Peter and I didn't know what to do other than keep in touch with our orderlies and appear on the scene when trouble was brewing.

One morning Peter was in theater while I was conducting rounds with Norma and the African staff. We had finished the women's ward and had just examined the man with the gun blast to the forehead—he was smiling and thankful. We proceeded to the next room and found the first bed empty. This belonged to the Kinshasa Boy.

"Where is he?" I inquired. The orderly didn't know so he asked a relative of the neighboring patient. The response was animated, and the longer the explanation grew, the more worried I became.

"He left in the middle of the night," reported the orderly.

"What do you mean?" I responded. "He can hardly walk!"

"The Katangese took him," he replied. "They said that they would bring him to another hospital where he would get better treatment."

"I don't believe it. In the middle of the night?"

Then a question flashed through my mind. What about the other prisoners? I raced towards the other men's ward. Had Hazel's prediction been right? Had the rebels carried out their promised vengeance?

I dashed in to find Finda lying peacefully in bed, but the truck driver was gone. That didn't make sense! Why one and not the other? The orderly arrived on my heels and began to quiz Finda.

"The same story," he sighed. "Some soldiers came in the middle of the night saying they would take them to a better hospital. The truck driver went but they couldn't unloose Finda's leg from the traction apparatus. They promised to return for him tonight."

I was crushed. I knew just what type of treatment the Katangese had in mind. For two weeks we had fed, clothed, nursed and befriended these men. We had shared the gospel with them and had run to protect them when they were threatened. Their wounds were healing. They had begun to sit outside. They had started to smile. They knew we cared for them and this gave them hope. Now they had gone the way of their buddies—and Finda was next!

Peter was in the middle of a grafting procedure but he stopped and listened solemnly to the bad news. "Are there any other patients missing?" he asked.

"No, just the prisoners."

"Are you sure they've been shot?"

"No, but it certainly looks like it."

"I agree. Why don't you speak to the commandant? See what he says.

There's little we can do anyway. They have the guns and they'll do what they choose no matter what we say. Do you want me to come with you?''

"It's okay. I'll manage."

I was soon at the guest house. Several soldiers occupied the porch, some snoozing, some cleaning their guns and others listening to the radio. In their midst sat the commandant. This one was a jovial fellow though never very helpful.

"Jambo, Commandant.''

"Jambo sana, Doctor.''

"I have a serious problem, Commandant.''

"What is that, Doctor?''

"Two of my patients disappeared overnight. Both were prisoners. Would you know where they've gone?''

"No," he replied. "Ask the commandant of the military nurses.''

"But aren't you worried about them on the loose?'' He shrugged his shoulders.

"Actually,'' I continued, "we do have more news. Patients say your soldiers took them to Kisenge Hospital for better treatment.''

"Now that you mention it, Doctor, I think I remember hearing about it.''

"Others say they were shot.''

"Who said that?'' he flashed indignantly.

"Others,'' I replied.

"That's a lie! They were brought to Kisenge!'' It was amazing how vivid his memory had become.

"Commandant,'' I began, "no hospital can possibly operate like this— patients whisked off without the doctor being consulted. Were any medical reports dispatched with the patients for the next physician? No! Were any x-rays sent along? No! Is that what your men mean by better treatment? Your soldiers said they would take away the other prisoner tonight. Perhaps they'll decide to transfer other patients tomorrow. I want your men to know that nobody leaves the hospital without us being consulted first. Otherwise we will have to leave. We cannot work under these conditions. Thank you, Commandant.''

I dramatically turned and, without shaking hands, strode off. For a moment, I wondered if I'd get a bullet in the back for my efforts but I walked on and nothing happened. The commandant had certainly tasted my frustration and hopefully he had sensed my underlying suspicion. Perhaps Finda would be left alone. Perhaps not.

Other reports soon added substance to our fears and by the end of the day the whole community was convinced that the FAZ had been murdered. Finda was now avoided by all the Africans including the woman who had fed him. One of the rebels had warned her that she'd be shot just like the others if she had anything more to do with the prisoner.

We could do little but sorrow for the two who'd been taken. However, we decided to verify that Finda was spiritually prepared should his turn come that night. Wonderfully, Finda confessed to having become a Christian in 1964 in the northern reaches of the Congo. That evening many of us read and prayed with him before going home.

My sleep was restless. I was listening for vehicles or shouting or shooting. In the morning we went directly to Finda's bed. What a tremendous joy it was to find him alive and smiling! The threats would continue but the execution never did come.

Not all of our interaction with the rebels was this tense. We had many happy visits from some who were passing through Kasaji from the front lines. Joseph frequently stopped in at the Fisher's to talk with his adopted grandmother. One of Anne's old students named Jean Yihemba came to see her. We also met Henri, who fulfilled his promise to find and bring back some of the Coates's goods. One day Major Mujinga appeared bearing a broken down mobylette. It was Peter's. Amazingly we discovered an abandoned mobylette of the same make, and much to Peter's joy this supplied us with the parts needed for repair.

By the beginning of April we realized that the war could carry on indefinitely. Since everyone needed a little physical distraction, we decided to finish off the tennis court. Walter and I pulled out the weeds, marked out the boundaries, and put up the net. It was with quite a festive spirit that we launched our inaugural match before a cheering crowd of about 40 boys. Even Deirdre Davies and little Timothy came down for the occasion.

"You fellows make me so envious," Deirdre moaned. "I'd love to play." The problem was that her mobility was reduced—she had entered her ninth month of pregnancy.

Soon after Deirdre left, Brian arrived with Robbie and Ingrid in tow. Robbie dutifully collected wayward tennis balls while his father played against Walter. Then along came Peter for a game, and soon Glenys arrived to size up the competition. It was a happy afternoon even though Peter thumped me 6-0, 6-2. After eight years tennis had returned to Kasaji—albeit in the middle of a war.

Something else returned to Kasaji late that afternoon. A car screeched into the mission and a rebel soldier jumped out saying, "The major has been injured. Come down to the hospital right away."

Before we could ask which major he meant, he was gone and we quickly ran to the theater. There on the steps much to our amazement was our old friend Mufu, splinting his chest with a bandaged right arm.

"Greetings, Doctors," he smiled weakly. "You told me you didn't want to see me wounded, Doctor David, but here I am. Better wounded than dead."

"What happened?" I anxiously inquired. We moved into the theater and Peter examined him while he spoke.

"The day after we took Mutshatsha we were driving along one of the roads. My men should have de-mined it but didn't. There was a tremendous explosion. My three officers were all killed instantly. Their bodies were in pieces. My men found me unconscious beside the ruins of the car and brought me to the Mutshatsha hospital. When I woke up, the mines' doctor and the captured FAZ doctor both said I was lucky to be alive.

"The next morning the Zairians brought up heavy artillery from Kolwezi and mounted a vicious counterattack, the only time they've ever fought us. I could hardly walk but left my bed to lead the troops. Ninety minutes later the FAZ retreated." He paused for a moment then solemnly continued.

"When I finally came back to the ward I discovered that there had been a direct hit where I had been lying. That corner of the hospital was destroyed. Twice I have escaped death. God must be with me." Mufu's life had been miraculously spared, why we did not know. Only time would provide an answer.

Peter finished his examination. "Well," he said, "the burns are healing nicely, but I suspect some fractured ribs. Didn't you have any x-rays yet?"

"No. The FAZ have cut off all the power west of Kolwezi. Since the mines' doctor knew you had a generator, he wanted me to come here for the pictures."

While we processed the x-rays, Mufu freely recounted how the Katangese captured Mutshatsha.

"Fourteen miles west of Mutshatsha is the Mukulweji River and that's where the FAZ were waiting: four battalions each with a thousand soldiers, many new cannons, many new 125 mm mortars, several helicopters, more than 50 *camionnettes* [armored personnel carriers]. We would never have made it across the bridge.

"I instructed half of my battalion to approach the river slowly while I marched the rest of it 15 miles to the south. We crossed the river by canoe on the second day and fell upon Mutshatsha from the rear. We completely surprised the town and the troops at the bridge fled in panic." He smiled scornfully. "The Zairians are not soldiers—they are too old and too fat!"

The x-rays were ready. Peter was right. "You have three fractured ribs—six, seven and eight. No pneumothorax."

"What do I do?" the Major asked.

"Just what you've already been doing," Peter replied. "We'll strap it up again and give you a supply of tape to do it yourself."

"That's good news," said the Major, stretching his arms. "I feel better already."

Peter seized the opportunity to let Mufu know about some of our problems. He recited in detail all that had been stolen from him and then told about the beds, the drunks, the executions and the threats.

Mufu listened sympathetically, then one of his officers answered, "There are many different men in our ranks and some do not understand what we are fighting for. We are not against the people of the Congo; they are our people. We are against Mobutu and the corruption he has brought to our land. Please be patient. Wherever you are there are good people and there are bad people. Even in our army some are not so wise. Eventually they will learn. We ask you once more to be patient."

"We have been more than patient already," Peter replied. "Tell your men how to behave. Our patience is almost used up."

"It is very difficult for me because I am so far away," responded Mufu, "but I will speak with the officers here."

"Major Mufu," I said as we left the theater. "Remember how I prayed a couple of weeks ago? I'd like to do it again."

He agreed and this time took off his field cap while I prayed again for the people of the Congo and for Mufu that he would discover God even in the midst of war. Major Mufu and his officers expressed their thanks then drove off.

It was the very next morning that the Petro Zaire tanker was finally taken away from our house. We expected that Mufu had ordered its removal but he could not have envisioned what happened next. At the wheel was a drunken soldier. Crammed into the front cab were three other happy rebels. The vehicle accelerated down the washed-out road towards Kasaji. It rocketed through the town crashing over the central roundabout at the main intersection. Then the tanker knocked over a concrete pillar beside some fuel pumps before catapulting down the highway and somersaulting three times. The driver was killed instantly and the others amazingly sustained only minor injuries. There seemed to be no escape from the madness that swirled around us.

Then, just as we finished repairs on the accident victims, a patient named Lazaro dashed up the theater steps. He was still talking excitedly to Peter when four women ran into the next ward chased by a shouting, lurching rebel wielding a bottle and a rifle. Peter made certain that Lazaro was well then muttered, "Let's get out of here!"

As we rode off, Peter filled in the details. "The drunk tried to make Lazaro take some whiskey, but when he refused, the soldier began to beat him with his gun. Lazaro raced up to us, and as you saw, the rebel started after the women. It wasn't the time to reason with the rogue."

Back in the house we heard gunfire at the hospital and moments later some of the Katangese dragged off the drunk to the guest house.

The drama was not yet over. During rest hour I was painting some lines on the tennis court. Suddenly, several shots rang out behind our garage. I turned and tensed up, ready to run if necessary. Being in the center of the field, I was maximally exposed but I couldn't see or hear anything alarming. I went back to work. A minute later the firing erupted again but this time it seemed closer and the guns were now rattling away.

I fell to the tennis court and scrambled along it to the grass. Crawling and rolling while the shooting continued, I gained the road through the low cement wall around the Coates's property. I dived over the wall, scurried across the garden, then fell through the front door into the house.

"David, is that you?" called out an anxious Peter.

"It's me. I'm okay." I rushed to their room and joined them on the floor. The gunfire had stopped but I was still breathing heavily.

"What happened?" Peter asked.

"I don't know but I certainly wasn't staying out there with all that metal flying around!"

The story, we soon discovered, was rather simple. The drunk and another comrade had been arguing over a woman. When words were no longer persuasive enough they resorted to guns. However, they hadn't aimed at each other. Instead they had peppered the skies and the countryside with their bullets—and all this took place just behind our garage!

Once more some officers arrived and hauled the culprits off to be disciplined; but 10 minutes later we watched the drunk stagger past our house again, still brandishing his gun.

I wrote in my diary that night: "Each day brings me closer to the realization that our lives are precariously placed humanly speaking and that only His daily mercies keep us from schemed or haphazard harm. . . . We are up against wicked and unreasonable men controlled by a cunning and vindictive adversary. . . . We know that any drunken, hemped or mad soldier may let loose with any of his weaponry at a dare, in jest or simply without provocation. If apprehended, at worst he may be cooled down for awhile then released, weapon and all, to continue his harassment. . . . Yet we are safe in Christ, hidden in Him and we do not fear what bodily harm may be ours."

13
A Time to Live and a Time to Die

Early each morning we heard recruits washing from a tap at our back porch. Soon over a hundred young men would jog off to Kasaji as part of their morning exercise. They streamed past our homes four abreast, their bared black chests shining in the sun and their strong voices thundering revolutionary slogans. In a day or two new recruits would be brought in from recently liberated territory and the others would be trucked off to Angola. Soon they would return to the conflict, but we didn't relish the prospect of these novices wielding guns in our midst. That problem would be faced later. For the moment they brought us other troubles.

"Look at your tennis court, David," Ruth said one morning.

"You'll be proud of your contribution to the cause," Peter added with a mischievous smile.

There on the tennis court was a motley collection of recruits being taught military drill. Some of the comrades paraded with pants and shoes but no shirts, others with shirts and pants but no shoes. Two officers led the men through a march. Swinging their arms to shoulder height they goose-stepped across the court, but all the soldiers, including the instructors, were hopelessly uncoordinated.

"Imagine guerillas parading like that," I thought. It was hilarious but I had to restrain my loudest cackles for fear of being heard.

"I know more drill than that from my days in Christian Service Brigade," I told Ruth. "I think I'll give them a few tips."

"I don't think that's wise," Ruth replied seriously.

"I know. I was just joking."

"Maybe you'd better check the court for boot marks later on," Peter advised.

"Oh no!" I moaned. "That didn't even cross my mind." The joke was on me. The court had multiple mini-excavations made by overzealous feet.

A whole afternoon would be needed to repair it. I decided to take the matter to higher authorities lest my effort be ruined by another marching mob.

The new commandant at the guest house was Mufu's brother. He listened attentively to the problem then said, *"Munganga,* I will correct this situation. I will give orders to my men that they must parade elsewhere. Your tennis court will never again be used for military drill." The commandant kept his word.

Meanwhile the days wore on and we soon arrived at another of those special occasions on a mission station. It was the McKenzie's thirteenth wedding anniversary, and the Coates's household was invited over for a midday celebration. The dispensary was very busy, however, and Norma was delayed.

"It's amazing what a little socialism can do," she exclaimed when she finally arrived. "Now that medical treatment is free, twice as many people are getting sick!" She was right. We were treating up to 600 outpatients a day since socialism had come to Kasaji.

Our conversation at the meal centered on the medical work. After describing our most recent altercation with the rebels over the seizure of medical supplies, Peter said, "We have to make a fuss over everything or else before we know it there'll be nothing left. Any day some new patients may have to sleep on the floor. Sue tells me as well that all of our major drugs will be used up by the end of April. Right now we have almost no antibiotics except for sample packages and only another week's supply of aspirin and chloroquine. Nothing stops the rogues. Three more mattresses disappeared overnight and two more rebels moved in with their machine guns and rockets!" The stories were drearily familiar.

There was a short pause then Ruth said, "Let's talk about pleasant things. After all, this is an anniversary."

"Right," I contended. "Harold, tell us how you met Norma." Her eyes twinkled as Harold launched into the love story that spanned several years and several thousand miles.

Our little party carried happily on, but something was missing. That something was the presence of several precious loved ones. Mary Ann McKenzie was studying at Sakeji School in Zambia as were Jimmy and Elizabeth Coates. Annie was in Rhodesia, much farther away. But for practical purposes, they were each hopelessly cut off from their parents. The children had received absolutely no news from them, either good or bad, and the parents were in the same predicament. The only available information came over the radio and that was none too encouraging. How were the children bearing up under the strain?

What made the situation even more acute was that school would be finishing in one week. All the students would go home, but where would Mary Ann go? And what about the Coates's children who were to fly to

England with Peter and Ruth? Should the children go anyway leaving their parents behind—perhaps never to see them again? Each day we lovingly committed these families and our own to the Lord, and each day we thanked our Father for providing at Kasaji real brothers and sisters for mutual support and encouragement.

That afternoon the larger Kasaji family met for its daily prayer and fellowship time. Almost everyone would be there. Walter or Terry would wheel Grannie to our meetings at the Raymond's, and our little children would play in the garden supervised by one of the parents.

When Peter and I arrived from the hospital the others were still discussing the happenings of the morning. The quarrel that had chased me off the tennis court had been renewed resulting in the murder of two men and the proposed public execution of a third on the morrow. The one sentenced was none other than the drunk who had beaten up Lazaro!

Other news was more cheering. Terry informed us that according to the rebels, the Methodist missionaries at Kapanga and Sandoa were safe and healthy. Hazel disclosed that almost our entire stock of Christian literature had been distributed amongst the soldiers. Anne related some of her stirring conversations with the women patients. Brian had fascinating but more alarming news.

"Did you hear the radio broadcast this morning?" he asked. He pulled out a piece of paper and said, "Here, let me quote it: 'There has been no word from 21 Plymouth Brethren missionaries who have been missing in Shaba province since the outbreak of the war. Planes flying over the area have reported heavy shelling and significant damage to buildings in their towns but there has been no sign of the missionaries.' " Brian sighed. Several different Katangese officers had promised to forward messages to Britain so that our families would at least know we were alive. Apparently none of these communiqués had arrived, and this latest news bulletin would simply aggravate our relatives' worst suspicions.

Our conversation then slipped into singing and into sharing of Scriptures, both of which uplifted our hearts by pointing us to the source of our every blessing. Finally we poured all our needs, burdens and uncertainties before our ever-listening, ever-caring Father. And so it was for the Kasaji family that our faith was deepened, our hope purified and our love strengthened. I carried the following words home to my journal:

"Although I haven't written too much on the subject, I certainly often think of the folks back home. It is four weeks tomorrow that this all started and we have no confirmation that any of our messages about our well-being have been received. I imagine that everyone is praying rather fervently, and so they need to, for our safety here is never secure humanly speaking. . . .

"My plans for the Royal Victoria Hospital, youth work and camps are all shelved—of course the Lord knew all this before He sent me so really nothing is changed that He has not foreseen and approved. It's a thrill to know that the Lord is strong and good, and that He will hold me fast. I pray for the same preservation and keeping power for my family, my assembly, the kids and all my friends. God grant that I may see them again to extol Him and report on His never-failing kindness.''

Our African brothers and sisters were also feeling the increasing strain of the war. The Katangese had long run out of their gifts of food and now expected the people to supply their needs. Moreover some of the rebels treated the civilians in almost heartless fashion as evidenced by the story that one of our senior students told me.

"Last week,'' he said, "I walked into Kasaji to visit one of my friends. I went to his door and called out, 'Citoyen Kutenda, are you there?' Unknown to me, a soldier was resting in some bushes nearby. He approached pointing his rifle at me and challenged, 'What did you say?' I recognized my mistake at uttering 'citoyen' but it is a habit now for several years. I apologized but he was still very unhappy.

" 'Kneel down!' he ordered. He pointed his gun at my head from a distance of five feet and told me that I deserved my punishment. He started to count to 10. I prayed for the Lord to look after my wife and my darling baby. I even asked the Lord to forgive him for killing me. Then, 'Boom!' I slumped to the ground. I thought I was dead, but feeling no pain, I opened my eyes. There in front of me was the rebel and when I saw him I realized I was not in heaven but on earth.

" 'Stand up!' he commanded, so I stood up. 'Say camarade three times with a loud voice!' I obeyed. 'Now run as fast as you can!' he ordered. I turned and raced down the path expecting to be shot down at any moment. The shot never came but I didn't stop running until I arrived at the mission.'' I choked with emotion at this story of savagery. How could any human being torment another like this?

"Two days ago,'' he continued, "I gave some soap to the FAZ because he asked for some. One of the rebels found out and told me that they could take me away in the night just like the others. But I have no choice. Jesus says to give even to our enemies. The FAZ is not my enemy, but even if he were, I must give to him. Isn't that right, *Munganga?*''

"That's right, Katemba,'' I replied soberly. "Jesus said to love our enemies, bless them that curse us, do good to them that hate us, and pray for them who persecute us. It's hard, but we have the Lord Himself as our example.''

"And my wife,'' he sighed. "She cries every day. She is afraid for us and the baby. She wants us to flee but we have no place to go. My parents themselves were refugees from Angola and we have no real home.'' He thought for a moment then whispered, "One day we will have a home that no one can take away!''

My poor African brothers and sisters! They were "liberated" but they had no freedom to live. They found themselves not only in peril of death but in peril of life itself. Yet despite all their trials, the people had a strong faith and a keen perception of spiritual realities.

A tall African appeared at our back door early Wednesday morning April 6. He limped away with Peter, and I noticed that his left leg was all bone and no muscle. He was a polio victim.

"Peter and Harold are sending some letters to Sakeji School with this Christian fellow," Ruth explained solemnly. "We're the only ones with children and we have to tell the school what to do with them at the end of the term. Some of the folks might object so we haven't told anyone else."

"I understand, Ruth," I replied. I wandered outside where Peter was delivering last minute instructions to the courier. I watched the cyclist's muscular right leg power him off on his important mission. Peter's eyes followed him until he disappeared from view.

"He's going to cross into Angola and then cut into Zambia," Peter stated, anticipating my question. "There should be no problem. He tells me that the Africans are freely crossing the frontier every day."

"How long will it take?"

"He should be there in two to three days and back here the middle of next week. Just pray that all goes smoothly."

"I certainly will. This could be our first contact with the outside world."

Thursday was a quiet day. The rebels had not yet attacked Kolwezi although they claimed that the city was being encircled. They had also opened up a new front by heading north to the Zairian military base at Kamina. On the way, however, they seemed to be having trouble capturing a village called Kafankumba. Meanwhile, Kasaji was almost deserted by the military.

The day passed quickly and in the evening Peter showed some films of Victoria Falls. Since the morrow would be Good Friday, we read the beginning of the Easter narrative before retiring for the night. It was good to fall asleep early.

Knock! Knock! Knock! Knock! "I'm coming, I'm coming," called Peter as he staggered towards the door. It was midnight. "What's the matter?"

"*Munganga,* there are three wounded soldiers at the theater," replied the orderly, "and their officer is very mad."

"I'll be right down." I heard this conversation but wasn't sure if I was dreaming or not.

"David," Peter muttered, "I think both of us should go." Obviously I wasn't dreaming.

I dressed hurriedly and stepped outside with Peter into the crisp night air. As we strode towards the hospital, we took deep breaths in order to shake off our drowsiness.

"The orderly said that the officer was mad," Peter murmured. "We don't need another row at this time of night." There was an illustrious gathering on the steps of the theater: Edouard the head army nurse, Kabeya the political commissar, and a third rebel named Alexis. We hadn't met him before but he was supposed to be the medical officer in charge of the whole battalion.

We darted past all three into the theater as Alexis muttered something about us coming late. Two of the wounded guerillas had sustained shrapnel injuries to the legs. The third had been shot through the right chest, and both lung tissue and ribs were exposed through a hole two inches in diameter. We were still assessing the extent of the injury when Alexis made his appearance inside.

"Just give them first aid!" he barked. "I'm evacuating all of them to Kisenge Hospital tonight!" It was obviously Alexis who was the angry officer. His tirade, however, was only beginning. We bandaged up the wounded while he expounded on the manner in which patients should be treated.

"I trained at Kimpese for several years," he claimed. Kimpese was a prestigious paramedic institution near Kinshasa. "Then I carried on my studies overseas before practicing medicine in three countries. I know how to treat patients and I know who is not treating patients as they should. I am taking my men to Kisenge tonight because your treatment is so poor!" His stinging denunciation cut us through like a knife.

"Edouard tells me that the soldiers' wounds are all infected. There is no reason for this!" he shouted. "You are supposed to have a sterile operating theater, but here you have none."

"It's as sterile as can be expected," Peter retorted.

"No, it isn't! Don't argue with me! I've studied in Kimpese and overseas and I should know. What's more, even the civilians' wounds are infected. You have no love for the injured!"

We had finished the first aid and had moved to a side room. Peter and I leaned against a counter while Alexis paced in front of us. At the door stood Kabeya enjoying the roast.

Alexis' voice grew more and more threatening with each charge. "What's more, I know what you do with your good medicines. You keep on saying that you have none but you have plenty! You hide them from us! You withhold the good medicines from the soldiers!"

"If you have *makutas*," chimed Kabeya, rubbing his thumb against his forefingers, "then you get good medicines."

"That's not true," I argued. "Good medicines are dispensed according to need not according to money. Why don't . . . ."

''Be quiet!'' he bellowed. Peter's hand inched along the counter's edge to mine and squeezed it as if to tell me the same thing.

''I am from Kimpese!'' Alexis thundered. I spotted the pistol on his right hip.

''You have infected our soldiers! You have withheld good medicines from them! You have shown no love to them!'' He paused and his voice dropped ominously to a fiendish growl.

''When I catch your orderlies maltreating my men I will shoot them and ask questions later! As for you, if I find either of you not doing the best for my soldiers, I will shoot you without warning!'' His hand drifted to his pistol and sat there.

Would his fury be unleashed before morning?

14
Easter Peace

"I am from Kimpese," Alexis bellowed yet again, "and I will tolerate nothing but the best—the best medicines, the best operating theater, the best orderlies, the best doctors." We now grunted approval at everything he said.

"The soldiers of the liberation army deserve the best of everything. If they don't receive it . . . ." His scathing condemnations continued while we stood there nodding assent and praying for deliverance.

After what seemed like an interminable length of time, the political commissar interrupted and asked Alexis to step outside. Peter and I breathed more easily and moved back into the theater to clean up.

"Nasty fellow, that one," Peter muttered.

"Generous tonight, aren't you?" I replied. "He only threatened to kill us!" We worked quietly for several minutes hoping that the rebels' transport would soon arrive.

When we finally emerged, Alexis the Great was much more subdued but he hadn't finished his venomous attacks. Pretending that we had not arrived, he and Kabeya continued their discourse.

"Mr. Kennedy escaped from Kafankumba in his plane this morning," Alexis remarked, in obvious reference to Ken Enright. "How did he know when to flee?"

"He must have received a message from inside liberated territory," Kabeya answered in grave tones.

"But who could have done it?" Alexis queried as the charade continued.

"We must be vigilant, Camarade," warned Kabeya, "because enemies still lurk amongst us—right here!" He cast a dagger-filled glance at us, then once more riveted his eyes on his colleague.

"Vigilant, Camarade, we must be vigilant!" Both Peter and I shook our heads in approval.

Soon their conversation switched to the usual subjects: the corruption of Mobutu, the suffering of the Congolese people, and the glories of the revolution.

"In Angola," Kabeya boasted, "everyone must have an education. Even old men and old women are in school from 6 A.M. to 9 A.M. learning how to read and write. But school is not important now," he frowned. "We don't need students, we need soldiers. Who will replace these wounded boys?" he asked, pointing to the injured rebels. "We will fight one year, two years, five years, however long it takes to win the struggle. When all is finished we will need students, but not now."

Alexis impatiently looked towards the highway for any signs of the expected vehicle. The man from Kimpese had exhausted himself with nearly two hours of rhetoric at the end of an already long day. His eyes still flashed, yet he spoke more reflectively. "Congo is my home even though I have not lived here for 15 years. I have struggled in Angola for too long and now that I am home, I will never leave again." A pair of headlights veered onto the dispensary road.

"I will stay in Congo until I die and no one will stop me—not Mobutu, not France, not the CIA," he glowered at us as he stepped into the Land Rover, "not any one!" The wounded were helped aboard and the vehicle sped off into the darkness.

Four of us drifted into a circle in front of the theater—Peter, our orderly Moise, the night watchman and I. We were quivering in the wake of this terrifying experience. Moise hung his head. "It is so difficult," he sighed. "They know everything but they know nothing. It is so hard to carry on."

"But we must," Peter replied softly. "Our patients need us and the Lord has not abandoned us. We are staying because this is His work and it is not finished."

"I am staying too," Moise muttered through clenched teeth.

It was 2:15 A.M. We plodded home with heavy hearts. The false accusations and the stinging abuse were still ringing in our ears. The denunciations and the insults, the ridicule and the death threat—our minds replayed each one while we trudged along.

I slipped into bed but I couldn't sleep. I suffered through each scowl, each glare and each snicker. I relived each rebuff, each insult and each slur as I tossed and turned.

Finally, when I thought it would never end, I was seized by one grand realization. Today was Good Friday! This was the exact time when Jesus Himself endured the ultimate abuse and degradation at the hands of wicked men! If I could be in such mental anguish for what little had been done to me, how much more agonizing had it been for Christ who undeservedly bore my sin and that of the whole world.

Reverence and peace flooded my being. My midnight ordeal had become a blessing, for through it I had entered into a deeper appreciation of the sufferings of Christ.

Remembering Paul's words in Philippians 3, I wrote: "Suffering goes along with His resurrection power and becoming like Him in death may yet be my privilege."

Good Friday was not a holiday—such was the law of Mobutu's Zaire. Rounds brought me to the soldiers' ward at the usual time.

"*Jambo*, Camarades," I boomed.

"*Jambo sana*, Doctor," they chorused. Jean Yihemba smiled appreciatively when I told him that his injury was healing well. He was a very pleasant officer and an excellent buffer between us and any hostile soldiers.

I examined the next patient, my every move studied by two new military nurses named Alphonse and Roberto. I discovered that they had changed the soldier's dressings quite on their own. That was a vast improvement over Little Henri and Edouard.

Two suspicious-looking characters occupied the next couple of beds and I soon established that their complaints were feigned. Being ill had certain advantages. These rebels would enjoy vacation from military duty as well as comfortable slumber in our hospital beds. They were the first malingerers we had encountered amongst the Katangese but several others would soon present themselves. Was this a sign of the changing fortunes of the FNLC?

While I was leaving the ward, I beckoned Jean Yihemba to follow. "Jean," I inquired, "who is Alexis?" Our friend was taken aback at my candid approach but furnished the answer.

"He is commandant of the nurses in the Third Tiger Battalion."

"Did he ever go to Kimpese?"

"Oh yes, he was there," Jean affirmed. "He trained at Kimpese many years ago but," his voice dropped to a whisper, "he failed the course!" Poor Alexis the Great! He probably never forgave the medical instructors who had dismissed him from the program. Only prayer could change his hateful attitude towards us.

The news that day was far from comforting. Two more nations had joined Belgium, France and the U.S. in forwarding aid to Mobutu's troubled empire: China had promised to ship 30 tons of goods and Morocco pledged 3,000 crack infantry. How many more countries would be dragged into the escalating conflict? The Katangese, however, were not backing off as evidenced by the trucks and trains we heard roaring through Kasaji each evening. Where and when would be the point of collision?

Saturday morning a soldier with a toothless grin asked us for a bar of soap. Ruth gave him one, little realizing how valuable that act of kindness would be.

On arriving at the dispensary we learned that Alexis had ordered a general staff meeting for that afternoon in order to outline the new hospital regulations. Tshihinga was fearful of the confrontation. "I have already started to pray and will not stop until that meeting is over," he solemnly vowed. Such were our sentiments as well.

In mid-morning a rebel was brought in from the front at Kafankumba. The flesh between his thumb and index finger had been blasted away while he was cleaning his gun. I worked on him for some time then casually asked, "Camarade, how goes the fighting?"

"Slowly."

"I hear there are marshes around Kafankumba," I prompted.

"And 700 para-commandos in the town—flown there by Mr. Kennedy." I knew that was impossible because Ken only had a four-seater. "We will capture Kafankumba anyway," he muttered, "and then on to Kamina."

I gently bandaged his hand then told his waiting buddies that I was keeping him in the hospital.

"Oh, Doctor," one of them interjected, "this is for you." He handed me a piece of paper requisitioning more drugs for the Kafankumba front. I reluctantly wrote a note scaling down the quantities and sent the soldiers to the dispensary. With my work all done I returned home.

"*Mwani Vude,*" greeted Harold as I entered our living room. "Just getting away from the rat race," he said explaining his presence.

"Are they bothering you again?"

"They haven't stopped! For four weeks now I fix it when the camarades say 'Fix it!' and I hurry when the camarades say 'Hurry!' I don't mind the work, but not at gunpoint."

Harold had spent hours repairing Katangese vehicles. He had been pulled from his mission responsibilities, from his meals, and even from his bed to patch up their jalopies. His bad leg ached from overwork and he dragged it painfully when he walked. Many rebels had cursed him but none ever thanked him except for Mufu. Long ago, the major had commanded Harold to save his leg by driving his hitherto hidden motorcycle.

"Anyway," Harold continued, "after a little rest I'll go back to the camarades."

"Alexis has called for a general meeting of the medical staff this afternoon," I told him. "He's going to explain all the new hospital regulations. I'm afraid of another harangue by Alexis but this time in front of everyone."

"I'll pray about that," said Harold. "The Lord can change him."

At 1:20 P.M. Alexis's white Volkswagen rattled along the dispensary road. "He's early," Peter announced surprisedly. We rode down after them and parked the mobylette by their car. Alexis stepped out from the OPD and greeted us warmly. I was surprised.

Together we went inside and set up the seats while others gathered. Alexis positioned himself at one end of the head bench and invited Edouard, Peter and me to join him at the front.

"Where are the women?" he inquired, checking his watch.

"Do you want them too?" Peter asked. We had hoped to spare the girls from the proceedings.

"Of course," he replied. "Somebody bring them. I don't want to say everything twice." He was firm but not harsh, and as the minutes ticked away I sensed that somehow Alexis was different.

"Shall we start?" he asked while Norma took a seat beside Peter. He slowly scanned his audience of orderlies, midwives, laundrymen, janitors, rebels and missionaries. Then lighting a cigarette, he spoke.

"This hospital is now a state hospital. It will no longer be a mission hospital. All the staff will be state employees and thus paid by the government." After each statement he paused briefly to let us reflect on the new policies.

"More doctors will come. There is too much work here for even two doctors." I wondered where he'd ever recruit the physicians.

"The man in charge of the hospital will be the doctor. Right now that means Doctor Peter and Doctor David." This was amazing! I expected him to say that he was in control.

"The military nurses will work here but they will be under the doctor's supervision." Peter and I glanced at each other. So far, the content and manner of his speech had been remarkably subdued, almost conciliatory. Even if he couldn't enforce what he promised, it sounded better than we had hoped for.

"No bribery or corruption will be tolerated. That is Mobutism. Offenders will be shot at the flag." He rolled his cigarette and studied the falling ashes.

"There will be no favoritism or tribalism. That is Mobutism. No relative will be allowed special privileges for the line-up, for medication, or for anything else."

He continued his slow reasoned delivery for about 20 minutes then asked for questions. Some inquired about salaries, about hiring new staff, and about medical supplies. To each he gave a civil response.

"What about the soldiers who push in line and expect immediate treatment?" someone bravely asked.

"The soldiers must wait their turn like anybody else." All the orderlies smiled approvingly.

After he had fielded a dozen or more questions, he again drummed out the ideology of the FNLC. This time, however he added something new.

"Don't be afraid of the Moroccans and the Chinese," he snarled. "This land is our home and no Moroccans will force us from our rightful heritage.

We will slaughter them as gladly as we slaughtered the FAZ—even more so, since they are invaders. With foreigners coming,'' he said bitterly, ''this conflict may become a second Viet Nam, but this is our home and we will win.'' I shivered at his reference to Viet Nam, but I knew that he was right. This struggle had the potential to engulf both East and West in a deathly conflagration. It just depended on how far the distant powers were prepared to go.

Alexis wished to emphasize, however, that the Soviets were not involved in the war. ''Look at my gun,'' he said while he displayed its markings. ''These are not Russian weapons. They were given to us by the Portuguese when they left Angola. Here Doctor David, take it,'' he ordered. ''Tell me what type it is.''

I held the gun for a moment then handed it right back.

''I honestly have no idea,'' I declared. ''I only know the types of stethoscopes.'' The crowd laughed heartily as did Alexis, and the latter decided that this was the appropriate way to end the session.

''If you have any questions or problems,'' he advised the people, ''speak to me. Now you can go.'' The whole meeting had taken less than an hour and was conducted soberly and respectfully by the medical officer. He bore no resemblance to the arrogant man who the other night had threatened to shoot us without warning. We praised God for answered prayer!

''One more thing,'' Alexis told Peter. ''I want to inspect the pharmacy.'' No soldiers had ever been permitted inside the pharmacy but we could no longer bar it from their perusal. The two Katangese entered our stockroom with conspicuous delight. Alexis the Great strode from shelf to shelf like a general reviewing his troops. Peter underscored our predicament by pointing out the almost empty antibiotic counter.

''Perhaps you can hasten the transport of your drugs from Angola,'' Peter recommended. ''As you see our situation is desperate.''

''Yes, yes. We'll arrange that,'' Alexis insisted. ''We have so many drugs in Angola. Too many!'' Edouard murmured in agreement. We parted company most courteously and they drove off.

''Well, Peter, our problems aren't solved but we have much to be thankful for.''

''Yes. He was most civil, wasn't he? I hardly recognized the man. Well, a lot of people were praying.'' We both gazed up the dispensary road at the many buildings which comprised the mission complex. This was our home. Its future enshrouded with uncertainty, the mission was still our home and the troubles had made it even more precious.

''Whoops!'' Peter yelped, checking his watch. ''If we don't hurry we'll be late for tea—and that wouldn't do!'' He mounted his mobylette.

''Quite!'' I replied in my thickest English accent. ''A spot of tea would be most delightful just about now.''

"I should make you walk," Peter retorted. "Hop on. Your glass of water is waiting!"

Late that afternoon Peter was accosted by two soldiers behind the house. Since they were giving him a hard time, I sauntered over and greeted them warmly. One rebel sported a bushy black beard while the other I recognized as Major Mujinga

"They're drunk," Peter muttered. Blackbeard was the more vociferous of the two. He was preaching FNLC doctrine with a fervor. He denounced the foreign powers for interfering in the struggle and promised vicious treatment of all alien soldiers. Then he complained that we too were fighting against the Katangese because we had withheld drugs from the front.

"But I sent a large quantity of drugs to Kafankumba just this morning," I disputed. Peter didn't know about this.

"They had none yesterday," Blackbeard snapped.

"That's why we shipped them some today," I replied. Their whole attitude began to change with this piece of news. Within minutes they were thanking us for our contribution.

Blackbeard and Major Mujinga had been pacified for the moment but we knew that as more nations entered the conflict, our troubles would be aggravated. That evening Egypt declared its support for Mobutu and my diary reflected our dilemma:

"The situation seems to be more serious now. If foreigners come in, as they are, they may be enough to turn the tide. Another battle at Kasaji would be inevitable but this time much fiercer. We probably would have to leave, but how?

" . . . Again we are brought to the realization that we must live a day at a time. We have no concept of what may come to pass—thank the Lord for that—but are living each moment content to be in His will knowing that He cares."

It was only 7 A.M. but music was drifting across the mission station. It was Anne's piano raising the joyous strains of that jubilant hymn, "He Arose." This was Resurrection Sunday and Anne was proclaiming through her opened windows that Jesus had risen from the dead ever to live with His saints. Jesus was alive.

Easter Sunday, April 10, was a happy and a quiet day. Oh, there was an obstetrical emergency and there were a couple of minor problems with the soldiers, but gone was the commotion of recent days. On rounds we greeted each patient with the declaration that Jesus was alive, and at the leper assembly we celebrated the Lord's Supper with a wondrous sense of His risen presence.

Sunday was also Ruth's birthday. Several families joined us for the noon meal. Everyone dressed up and I took a number of pictures. Anne gave out homemade Easter cards and we sang around the piano. It was such a relaxing time.

In the afternoon we took a restful snooze then strolled around the mission station. The skies were clear and it seemed that dry season had arrived prematurely. The sun's bright rays bestowed a warmth that was perfectly tempered by a gentle breeze. Some Africans chatted idly by their dwellings while others pounded manioc and still others listened to radios. Not a vehicle passed on the highway and not a soldier was to be seen. Even the guest house was empty except for one bleating goat. From a distance we watched our windmill twirl high above the well. It was an idyllic setting.

We then enjoyed a happy communal supper at the Raymond's. After Mr. Raymond thanked the Lord for His every provision, Phyllis served the food as she alone could. The little girls in long dresses and the boys in their Sunday attire had their own party on the porch supervised by Sue and Deirdre. The rest of us ate inside, entertained by Harold and Terry, both at their storytelling best. Anne and Walter cheerfully reported that some patients and students had just become Christians while Grannie updated us on her personal project—evangelizing the officers at the guest house. Our fellowship was never sweeter.

After congregating on the lawn for a photo, the Kasaji family returned inside for some joyful music. For over an hour we sang all the Easter hymns in the book. Then Mr. Raymond opened the Bible and read us the appropriate Gospel narratives.

Many of us realized that our situation was similar to that of the first Easter. The land was filled with fear and discontent. Many people were ready to follow any cause which might give hope of liberation from an unpopular regime. Men were taking up the sword and perishing by the sword. False accusations abounded and many had been scattered. The disciples were huddled in a room locked off from the outside world but never knowing whether soldiers would barge in and drag them away. They couldn't foresee much of a future nor could they fathom much of their past.

Suddenly, into their gathering walked the risen Christ, as alive as when they had first seen Him. Knowing their every fear, their every anxiety, and their every uncertainty, Jesus whispered to them, ''Peace be with you!'' The disciples were overjoyed to behold Him but some of them were probably wondering what peace He was talking about. There was no peace! All was unrest and turmoil! Again Jesus said, ''Peace be with you!'' and then they understood. His peace was an inward peace, something the world could never touch nor take away. The Lord did not show them an outline of their future nor did He explain the past, but when He left they were abundantly satisfied. His presence and His peace would be sufficient for their every situation.

In a wonderful way, the same thing happened that night at Kasaji. The Lord moved amongst us and reminded us that His presence and His peace would be sufficient for our every situation. The message was exactly what we needed because the next day the jet fighters would return, this time to bomb and to destroy.

15
Terror from the Skies

Our afternoon prayer time had barely finished when an unmistakable whirr was heard overhead. "The planes!" several gasped simultaneously. Their sudden arrival startled us though in fact we were quite used to the aircraft; they had spied on us often but had never attacked. Several of us cautiously slipped outside into the yard.

"There's one," pointed Peter. A Macchi fighter swept by us and ducked into clouds south of Kasaji. Another jet banked to the northeast, red lights flashing on its wings. A split second later the first fighter was diving at the town. *Booom! Booom!* Two thunderous explosions shook the ground. Pillars of smoke and debris rose hundreds of feet. This was no reconnaissance mission—this was a bombing raid!

"Into the house!" someone shouted and we charged madly inside. A speeding head smashed the low ceiling lamp. Norma tripped and crashed to the floor. Beside me lay Peter and Ruth huddled together on this their wedding anniversary. *Boom!* Another tremor shook the house. As the planes screamed overhead, the Katangese unleashed a frenzied barrage of machine gun fire into the skies. We remained motionless and silent wondering where the next bombs would be dropped. So far the fighters had been striking at the town. Would they be merciful and spare the hospital?

Several minutes passed. The shooting stopped. The planes were gone. Slowly, carefully we picked ourselves off the floor, straightening our clothes and the furniture.

"I want to see how Brian and the children are," Deirdre trembled. "I'm going right now."

"I'll come, too" answered Sue and they both hastened home.

"Walter, let's go over to the college," I suggested. Ever on the alert, we stepped across the lawn and onto the road. A few students stood in a group staring at the heavens.

"Are you fellows alright?" Walter called out.

"Yes, Mr. Walter," they nervously replied. "Do you think the planes will come back?"

"I don't know. Just be careful," he warned.

"Kasaji must be a mess," I mumbled.

"At least they left the hospital alone," Walter replied.

I tensed up again. "Listen!" Was that another plane? "Quickly!" I shouted. We raced back across the lawn, but before we could make the house a fighter swooped out of the clouds and streaked over our heads. A chain of five deafening explosions ripped through the heart of the mission station rocking the ground underfoot. Staggering, we gained the porch and dived onto the floor, stunned by the narrow miss.

We were almost certain that the hospital had been hit. The jet had been so low and one of the rockets must have found its target. However, we began to hear cheering. What did that mean? Could the Katangese have shot down the plane?

We dared not move for many minutes but swelling shouts of triumph outside emboldened us and we abandoned our shelters. Although no one had been hurt each of us had been shaken up. Strangely enough, Grannie appeared to be the least disturbed of all.

"I just turned off my hearing aid," she explained.

On leaving the Raymond's, we encountered many jubilant Africans. They excitedly told us that the plane had indeed been shot down and that the hospital had escaped unscathed. It was incredible! Although several rockets had crashed into the station, nobody had been injured and none of the buildings had been hit! It seemed impossible! Guided by our tin roofs, the jet fighter had passed over the college, our homes and the dispensaries while firing its missiles, but somehow it had missed everything. In a miraculous way the Lord had protected us during this murderous attack. We praised Him from thankful hearts!

Peter and I hopped on a mobylette and headed for the main road. Hundreds and hundreds of people, perhaps thousands, jammed the highway, laughing and dancing and singing as they swept along towards the site of the plane crash. Soldiers were being hoisted onto shoulders and gunfire blasted skyward in celebration. A real carnival spirit reigned in the crowd.

Peter and I zigzagged through the mob listening to the many accounts of the deathblow to the plane. One said he saw a rocket detach from a missile and destroy the jet. Others attributed the hit to machine gun fire. Several individual soldiers claimed the kill. It was clear to us that no one really knew.

We were advancing at a snail's pace and beginning to wonder if we should stop when along came our friend the Toothless One, the rebel who had requested the soap. He told us that the crash was quite distant and he suggested that we turn back especially as his comrades were too trigger-happy for anyone to be safe. We thanked him and happily took his advice. On the way home we overheard even more tales, some of them very disturbing. Several of the Katangese were accusing us of having sent for the planes!

"The Garenganze have a hidden transmitter and are radioing messages to the enemy," one insisted.

"They have a direct line to Mobutu," another swore.

To argue was pointless. We pushed on to the hospital to wait for any casualties from Kasaji town. Only one civilian had been killed, but several others with shrapnel wounds were brought in. We had already gained much experience in treating this sort of injury. Fluoroscopy would give us a three-dimensional view of the metal fragments in the wound and thus facilitate operative approach. We had also rediscovered that one of the most sophisticated surgical instruments for extracting bits of shrapnel was the finger. By mid-evening, we finished our surgery.

There was much time for reflection that night. Our biggest concern of course was whether the aerial strike represented a once-for-all scare tactic or whether it was the first of many in a stepped-up Zairian offensive. Only waiting would provide an answer; but in the meantime we were thankful for the Lord's protection during that day's bombardment. I went to bed with the words of a psalm-come-alive on my heart: "Thy mercy, O Lord, is in the heavens; and thy faithfulness reacheth unto the clouds" (Ps. 36:5).

By morning hundreds of villagers had already stolen into the bush. They had quickly forgotten their moments of jubilation and remembered their minutes of terror. This time, however, their flight was more calculated—they escaped in the darkness along rarely frequented back paths. The Katangese were unable to stop them.

Although the wards were full, our OPD was virtually empty for the first time since the abolition of hospital fees. Work finished early and I was able to track down the explosion sites. The first rocket had crashed into Matamba's village next to the college. The second exploded behind the Davies's house and the third beside the mortuary just before the main dispensary. A fourth rocket passed over the hospital and another one or two had landed in Tshisangama's village farther west.

Anti-personnel missiles had been used. The holes were not deep but shrapnel had caused damage over a wide radius. Six-inch-long chunks of wood were slashed from trees 70 feet from the explosions and large plate-like metal fragments were found much farther away. The damage to the mission, however, was minimal: the windows of the mortuary were blown out and the Davies's violently shaken house had released a shower of debris from its thatched grass ceiling.

"David," called out Walter as I passed by his home, "let me show you the latest from North America!'' He pulled out a segment of rocket casing and read the inscription for me. I suddenly felt sick inside. American arms had been used to attack our hospital! The very people who had donated to the support of our mission had given up taxation money that was used to destroy at the same mission. I realized that such paradoxes were common, but that didn't take away the gnawing feeling in the pit of my stomach.

I later mapped out the location of each crater. Connecting the points I visualized the flight path of the missiles. They fell along a line that stretched over the college, our homes, and the main dispensary; yet not one rocket had touched any buildings or injured the hundreds of people who were sheltered in them. God's faithfulness had certainly reached unto the clouds and even to the jet fighters that hid therein.

At lunchtime Peter asked me if the rebels had discovered the site of the plane crash.

"No," I replied, "and they won't. A whole village east of here saw two jets heading for Kolwezi after the raid. One was flying high, the other was limping along very low but it didn't seem to be in danger of falling."

"When that news gets widely known," Peter predicted, "many more of the Africans will disappear. Personally, I think they're wise. They have no reason to stay."

"Then why are we staying, Peter?" I asked, raising an issue over which we had all agonized countless times. There was a long pause.

"Well," he started slowly, "on the purely practical side, the Katangese won't let us go nor do we have the transport at the moment. The real reason for staying though is that we have a responsibility to our people—patients, hospital staff, students and local Christians. We just can't abandon them. However, if our ministry is somehow shut down, we might have to reconsider."

Ruth interjected. "You see, Peter's professional and spiritual work is centered at the hospital. If he has no drugs, no bandages, no x-rays and no beds, then he has no hospital."

"And that's rapidly becoming the case," he explained. So far I agreed. The thorny question was what would happen if some of the Kasaji folk felt their ministry was closing and others felt that theirs was still open. Should some go and others stay even though we were so interdependent? The Lord would have to make it abundantly clear both collectively and individually.

"Suppose we were all meant to leave, Peter," I speculated. "How would we?"

"I've been thinking about that." He took another sip of tea then scribbled on a piece of paper. "We're 23 in all. With half an hour's work Terry's van could be running and could carry about 10. The McKenzie's Land Rover looks a sorry mess with its engine sitting on the ground, but Harold's been repairing it on the sly. He'll need four hours' warning and he can take eight or nine of us. Glenys's mobylette is hidden and the commandant just returned Terry's. Those two plus Harold's and mine give us four more places. I could drive the tractor and, by my calculation, that makes approximately 23.'' Peter put down his pen and finished his tea.

I was astonished at the number of potentially available vehicles. That Peter had worked out some contingency plans was no great surprise, but the whole thing seemed so fanciful. The present reality was that we were hostages of the new regime, cut off from the outside world and under threat of aerial attack at any moment.

Late that afternoon, however, the outside world came to us. The Sakeji courier arrived! For the Coates his successful trip was a relief and meant that the children would fly to England in a few days. With them would go a few discrete messages and very soon all our families would know that we had been alive as of early April.

But the Sakeji courier was the source of even greater rejoicing. Many friends and relatives had wisely posted their Kasaji mail to Sakeji School in the hope of just such a communication. The result was that there were letters for every family and every adult of the mission—everyone but me. My last piece of news was dated February 11, more than two months previously. Those back home had written but their mail was probably trapped somewhere in Zaire itself. Oh, if only I could see what was in a couple of the letters, any letter! The martyr in me waxed most self-pitying—and then I remembered my good friend Frederick Stanley Arnot. I had read in his biography that he went six months and more in Central Africa without a single piece of mail. Grannie Fisher herself may have gone longer for all I knew! I thought less of myself and began to rejoice with those that had been blessed with news.

Just at this moment Ruth came into my room and handed me her letters. ''You're part of the family,'' she said. ''Read our mail!'' Sweet Ruth! I knew that she herself was aching—aching to embrace her children again but knowing that they would soon be thousands of miles away. I determined that evening to work harder at the hospital so that Peter could spend more time at home with her.

Wednesday and Thursday were very quiet days. We waited for news from Kafankumba but the same story came back—it would be captured tomorrow. We waited for news about Kolwezi but there was none. We waited for the planes, not wishing to see them of course, but expecting them anyway. Thankfully, they never showed up. We waited for drugs from Angola, for Mufu, for wounded, for anyone who could tell us anything, but all was quiet. The OPD had few patients although the rest of the hospital was still near capacity. One new case was a young man with a grapefruit-sized knee mass. Our diagnosis was sarcoma and we booked an amputation for Saturday morning.

The only ward which had more activity than usual was that of the soldiers. More malingerers had themselves hospitalized—sprained fingers, sore feet, irritated throats—anything would do. I kept on turfing them out but others would sneak in.

One fellow repeatedly pestered me about an aching scar from an old hernia repair. After numerous negative examinations I became convinced that he was faking it and I discovered a remedy. An orderly smeared the whole region with a black, greasy, foul-smelling potion. The Hernia Man did not return.

Kabeya attempted to have another socialist rally at the hospital to boost sagging morale but it was totally unsuccessful. The rebels could round up just a handful, and even under duress the people were less than enthusiastic. The political commissar told them that the FNLC had their own planes—Migs—and that reinforcements including heavy artillery would soon come from Angola. His diatribe continued unabated and then he closed by castigating the group for wanting to leave because of the planes. It was obvious though, that the real objects of his wrath had already fled and that he was simply antagonizing those who, if anything, were sympathetic.

I profited by the lack of work to accompany Walter to Kasaji and on our trip we made three observations. First of all, there were many people who still lived in town. Secondly, there was no more stench—the gravediggers had buried over a hundred corpses. Finally, the aerial strike had been rather unimpressive, if not comical. The craters were waist deep but all the bombs had missed the rebel headquarters and other strategic points by more than half a mile. In comparison the attack at the mission had been dreadfully close, especially to such things as the drums of gasoline we had concealed in our garage.

"If the planes come back and hit anything near us it would be rather messy," Peter told us. "I'd like to pump the petrol into our underground tank. Come tonight at nine o'clock and be sure to wear dark clothes." The enterprise was dangerous but necessary. We didn't want the Katangese to know either that we had hidden some gas or that we had a storage depot.

At 9 P.M. we slipped into the garage, shut the door and put on the light. Clad in a long black raincoat, Peter pointed out each of the three barrels and then we eased the first one to the entryway. Peter put the lights out, opened the door and then Walter and I carefully lowered the drum on its side. All was quiet. We waited until our eyes adjusted to the blackness then carefully rolled our cargo towards the tank.

Each time the barrel hit a stone it sounded like a gunshot. No one else seemed to hear it, however, and we rapidly covered the distance. Peter attached a hose to the drum and led it to the underground tank. After a mouthful or two of gas, we got the flow going but then it stopped and wouldn't be restarted. We resorted to a hand pump which Peter had brought along. It was noisy but we had no choice. The first barrel was emptied and the second was brought.

"Shh!" Peter whispered. A lone figure carrying a flashlight appeared on the dispensary road.

"It's a soldier!" I breathed. He strolled along whistling a tune while the flashlight's beam swung back and forth. He came to a cutoff in the road. Would he go straight ahead or would he take the path that led directly to us? There was a moment of hesitation. He finally passed by and out of earshot.

"Let's get this finished!" Peter muttered. Each one in turn pumped as fast as the noise would allow and the job was soon complete.

We entered the house dripping with perspiration. "I never want to do that again," I sighed.

"Neither do I," Walter echoed.

The terror of those moments, however, was nothing compared to what would happen on the morrow.

16
"We Will Eat You!"

Friday, April 15, started off like any other day. Rounds were quick and there were only a few cases in OPD. We finished everything by 10 A.M. and returned home for morning break. Peter and Ruth sat down to do some hospital paperwork while I was reading in my room. It was so good to relax and catch up on some studying.

Suddenly a fighter screamed over our roof. We dropped to the floor and scrambled into the washroom but not before a mighty explosion rocked the house to its foundations. We held onto the walls, each other, and our breath while we waited wide-eyed for the next blast. Another screech overhead! *Boom!* The building trembled again. Our ears ached and our hearts pounded as we whispered, "Lord, protect the mission!" Minutes passed. We listened for the predators but heard nothing. We kept on listening. No more planes. Finally we vacated our shelter.

Several gigantic mushrooms of smoke towered hundreds of feet over Kasaji town. That meant that the explosions were over a mile away. I dared not imagine the effects had they been much closer!

Apparently, two Mirages had circled down from the north flying low over the mission. Each one dived even lower as it approached Kasaji, then sat on its tail to unload its bombs. Once more no strategic targets were hit but again someone was killed. The FAZ, however, were dropping much more powerful explosives and many eyewitnesses quivered in fear as they described the size of the craters left behind.

In some ways the aerial strike brought relief. We had been continuously on edge expecting it, and now that it was over we could carry out our responsibilities with a little less tension. We doubted that they would attack us more than once a day so we looked forward to the calm after the storm. Today, however, there was to be no calm after the storm. Mr. and Mrs. Raymond had come over for lunch and we were about to eat when we received a frantic phone call from Anne. "The soldiers are at Terry's place and have forced them all outside!" she exclaimed.

"We'll be right there," Peter promised.

Peter, Mr. Raymond and I hopped onto our vehicles and raced over. Blackbeard, the rebel captain, was pacing back and forth in front of the three Fishers.

"I want all the missionaries here right now," he screamed, "man, woman and child!" I went home to get the ladies and by the time I returned everyone was there except for the malarial-stricken Walter. He was so sick that we weren't going to disturb him and we chanced that the soldiers would not discover his absence.

Blackbeard was furious. Several young rebels herded us together beside the house while a raving Blackbeard stomped to and fro brandishing his machine gun. "You have caused the bombing," he shouted wildly. "You have spoken to the enemy! You have told them where to bomb! You are traitors!" I watched his weapon closely. He was crazed and I half-expected him to lower his gun and blaze away at us.

"You have a hidden transmitter," he ranted, "and we will find it if it takes days!"

"The transmitter was taken from my house long ago," Terry protested, "and our old ones were given to your men at the same time!"

"We know your ways!" retorted the rebel captain. "You are using another one some place!"

One young Katangese suggested, "It may even be that," and he reached out to grab Grannie's hearing aid.

"You are all coming to Kasaji for interrogation," glowered Blackbeard. "You will tell us why you sent for the bombers."

"Yes, you will live with us there, and if a bomb comes you will be killed with us," shouted another Katangese.

"We may be killed here, too," Peter reminded them. "A rocket exploded just behind one of our families' homes, and all the children were inside. Do you think we are sending for the FAZ to bomb us? Do you think we want to die?" Blackbeard could not see the logic and remained adamant in his charges of conspiracy.

The rebels, however, were obviously divided over these strong accusations. There were some such as Mufu's brother and, strangely enough, Alexis the Great who attempted to calm the troubled waters. When Blackbeard was raging his most violent, Alexis whispered to Peter and me, "Don't worry. Nothing will happen." Then he and Mufu's brother tried to reason with the madman while a number of us stood in a circle and prayed.

"I am a hero, a Congolese hero!" Blackbeard bellowed beating his breast. "You are British colonialists," he mouthed contemptuously, "and you are all coming to Kasaji." While the rebel captain continued to wave his gun at us, Alexis reached over and slipped the safety catch back into position.

"Would it be possible to leave the women behind?" Mr. Raymond entreated.

"Be quiet, you old man," scoffed Blackbeard and he continued to berate the gracious Mr. Raymond. However, after some intercession by Mufu's brother, the captain relented and agreed to let the women stay behind.

The men shuffled towards the front walk. Norma clung to Harold and lovingly kissed him good-bye while tears streamed down her cheeks. Brian and Colin gazed at their children and cheerfully promised their wives they'd be back soon. Then Peter spoke up and asked that the fathers be exempt too.

"No!" the rebel captain thundered. On our minds, of course, was the real possibility that Blackbeard might just kill us. What we didn't know was that much the same drama was being enacted at Kapanga in those days. On similar false charges, the rebels would take away and execute our beloved brother in the Lord, Dr. Glen Eschtruth.

We stalled on the Fisher's front walk while Alexis and Mufu's brother continued to argue with our crazed antagonist. Finally, he gratuitously announced that he would give us five minutes to talk, five minutes to reveal the hiding place of the transmitter that we were using.

"There is no transmitter," Peter repeated. "Waiting will not make it appear."

Terry had been silent for a few minutes. "In my attic there's a Heath Kit for assembling a transmitter," he whispered.

"Bah, it's not assembled," Harold interjected.

"I've had it for five years and it would take a hundred hours to put together," Terry continued. "I wonder if we should tell them."

We didn't know what to do. If we were dealing with reasonable men, we could show them Terry's unassembled Heath Kit. The rebels, however, would probably consider the discovery a confirmation of their charges. What would be even worse, we decided, was not telling the rebels and then having them find the Heath Kit on their own.

"I have a package," Terry explained, "of little bits and pieces which if you worked at it for several weeks could make a transmitter."

Blackbeard's face lit up. "Where is it?" he exulted. "In my room," Terry replied.

"Bring it here," the rebel captain told his men. Within minutes a cardboard box full of knobs and wiring and transistors was placed at a triumphant Blackbeard's feet. He seemed a little disappointed that everything was so piecemeal but his countenance brightened when he browsed through the accompanying manual and spotted a picture of the end product. We wondered what reprisals lay ahead.

"I will go into Kasaji with the transmitter," he announced to us. "Don't be afraid. You can all stay at home and nothing more will happen." He smiled, shook our hands then left with his precious catch. The reversal was sudden and unexpected. It took us completely by surprise. Incredulous but thankful, we filtered into the Fisher's living room.

I felt sorry for Terry. He could never have imagined what an albatross that Heath Kit might have been. Any number of us could be likewise victimized if the rebels discovered the numerous diaries, the film, the hidden rifle, the gas depot and countless other objects.

Many of the African Christians now arrived to express their joy at our deliverance. They had prayed for us from a distance while others of their number had stood near us during the confrontation. We rejoiced at their love and concern for us. We also rejoiced that our antagonist of the previous week had been our defender today. Alexis had undergone a remarkable transformation. There was much for which to be thankful, and we prayed from overflowing hearts realizing afresh that we were completely dependent on the protection of the Lord.

At 1:15 P.M. we were returning home when the Land Rover and Blackbeard roared up. The rebel captain was much more subdued this time, but his message was unequivocal. "The major wants all of you in Kasaji right now." We could tell by his deliberate manner that there was no room for argument.

The Coates, Raymonds and the girls went off in the first set of vehicles while the Judkins, McKenzies, Terry and I followed. Barbara was allowed to stay and care for Grannie, and mercifully, the rebels forgot about the Davies and Walter.

We arrived at Kasaji and pulled through the main intersection into a courtyard behind a large shop. The area was now occupied by the rebels, their women, and our freshly slaughtered cattle. We were directed to a tin-roofed veranda where the others were already sitting facing Major Mujinga. Several Katangese brought out some chairs for us trying to make us as comfortable as possible before the harangue. Blackbeard hovered menacingly in the sidelines. What an entertaining lot!

Since Mujinga's French was poor, he was unable to work up quite the fervor of Blackbeard. Nevertheless he covered the same territory as before—why had we communicated with the enemy, where was our real transmitter, why should we turn against them when they had treated us so fairly and on and on it went. As diplomatically and as succinctly as he could, Mr. Raymond responded to each charge.

While the major was remonstrating, first David then Rachel Judkins began to cry. The two of them were usually such good children, but now they were hot and hungry and tired. Major Mujinga glanced over at them a number of times but continued to censure and threaten us.

"Do you all want to go to Dilolo and then to Angola for a fair trial?" he demanded. There was no answer. He slouched back in his chair and looked at us.

"Then tell me where the transmitter is," he ordered. Again there was no response except from the children and especially David who began to cry even louder. Several Katangese including Mujinga winced

"If you have nothing else to say, let's go to Angola," he stated and started to rise from his seat. There was no movement on our part except for the children's vocal cords. David was now bawling at the top of his lungs, but both Colin and Sue were not trying very hard to soothe him. We all knew that Africans would do almost anything to stop a baby crying. Major Mujinga reached out to comfort David but that just intensified his shrieks.

The Katangese were clearly rattled at our continued protestations of innocence but Mujinga tried once more to secure an admission of wrongdoing. He failed. Finally, after several moments of contemplation during which the children screamed their loudest, Major Mujinga made an incredible announcement.

"I trust you," he stated, "and I want you to know that we will protect you. We are interested solely in your security." He jumped to his feet. "We are all camarades," he said shaking each of our hands, "and we must all work together in this struggle!"

I obviously did not understand the Katangese mind. From traitors to trusted friends within the space of minutes was more than I could fathom. Perhaps, however, his accusations were just words. Perhaps his promises of friendship were just words. Perhaps all his words were just words. I didn't know.

"We want you to search our homes, Major, so that you will know we are telling the truth," Mr. Raymond insisted.

Blackbeard was not enjoying this turn of events. "They want you to search their homes because the transmitter is hidden outside!" he flashed.

Mujinga ignored the rebel captain and reiterated, "No, we don't need to look. We trust you." Mr. Raymond tried again but the major replied, "I will give you a letter to say you are clean."

The women and families boarded the first set of vehicles to the mission; then, as we readied to leave a hateful Blackbeard approached us. He strode to the back of the Land Rover and glared at us inside. "If the planes come back tomorrow," he sneered, "we will eat you!"

As soon as we arrived, the Africans started to visit our homes with tears of joy and thanksgiving. "We never thought we'd see you again," they cried.

Our time of prayer and praise at the Raymond's was full of meaning. Robert Raymond, who had suffered considerable abuse, read us 1 Corinthians 4:12,13: "We work hard with our own hands. When we are cursed, we bless; when we are persecuted, we endure it; when we are slandered, we answer kindly. Up to this moment we have become the scum of the earth, the refuse of this world'' *(NIV)*. I realized I had a lot to learn from this passage and from Mr. Raymond.

Many things had happened that day but one particular memory lingered into the night. I could still picture the enraged rebel captain and I could still hear that snickering voice, ''If the planes come back tomorrow, we will eat you!''

My prayer that night as I went to sleep was simply, ''Lord, keep away the planes!''

17
The Valley of Decision

It was my evening prayer, it was my morning prayer! "Lord, keep away the planes." Aerial attack was formidable enough, but now we were also haunted by the vengeful rebel captain and his savage threat.

"We've met our share of unsavory characters, but nobody quite like him," I commented.

"He's capable of anything," Peter stated.

"Of eating us?" I suggested.

"No," Peter replied. "Elimination is more the word. Well," he said rising from the breakfast table, "rebel captain or not we have lots of work to do. If we want to finish that amputation case in good time we'll have to hurry."

"Do be careful, Peter," Ruth urged.

"I will, and you stay by the house," he cautioned.

Glenys was already at the theater but the patient hadn't arrived. "I don't think he'll come," she said, "and I wouldn't blame him. Without a leg he'd be less than fit if he had to flee into the bush."

On rounds we discovered a few more empty beds. The hospital was still three-quarters full but the vacancies were unsettling reminders to the remaining patients of the ever-present danger. More disturbing were reports about the bombing in Kasaji. Moise produced a piece of shrapnel much bigger than I had ever seen, and he described fearfully large craters.

"The holes are so big, and all the bushes and trees roundabout are burnt. It is too terrible to think about," he muttered shaking his head.

Our patient with sarcoma never turned up and the OPD was even quieter than the previous day. Having so little work to do left me with plenty of time on my hands. I took some photos. I packed an emergency suitcase. I updated my diary. I read—and I continued to pray that the planes would stay away.

Blackbeard and Alexis the Great strolled by the front of the house just before noon. I wondered what they were doing on the mission at this time of day, but I didn't plan to ask. I was headed to the girls' house for lunch.

"Doctor," Alexis called out, "I want to tell you something." Reluctantly I walked over. The rebel captain stood sullenly by while Alexis spoke. "I have decided to evacuate the sick soldiers to Dilolo—not for better treatment," he stressed, "but this way they'll be closer to the border."

"Because of the planes?" I asked.

"Well, yes. Mobutu is a poor shot and may bomb places he doesn't intend to hit," Alexis replied seriously.

"I'll arrange for their records to go with them."

"Very good. Thank you, Doctor," he replied then continued his promenade with Blackbeard. I was troubled by Alexis's undisguised explanation for the departure of the soldiers. He obviously felt that more air raids were a real possibility. Did he have inside information? We didn't know, nor could we.

I enjoyed eating at the girls' house. They always managed to make something special and today was no exception. On the menu were some of Hazel's finest homemade sausages.

We thanked the Lord for the meal and for the fact that the planes hadn't come. Then, while dishing out the food, Hazel said, "I don't know how much longer my women will stay. Yesterday a couple of them were in labor during the bombing. They were terrified, and the women who saw them are even more terrified that the planes will arrive during their delivery. Well," she sighed, "at least Tshihinga's wife has had her baby."

"Yes, wasn't she a beautiful girl?" Anne enthused.

"Tshihinga is taking his wife and the four children into the bush. It's too early for her to go but I can't blame them," Hazel admitted.

"Glenys, where were you when the planes came?" I asked.

"In the pharmacy with Sue. We both scrambled underneath the shelves and looked at each other." She chuckled. "We felt so foolish. Over our heads were a tin roof and half inch thick wooden shelves. Anyway, nothing happened except that all the jars and bottles were rattled—and so were we!"

"Here, David, have the last of the sausages," Hazel urged. "It'll strengthen you for those tennis matches. How are you managing against Peter?"

"Let's just say that it's more of a contest now."

"He beat Peter for the first time yesterday," Glenys chirped up, "although we won't mention the slight irregularity." She glanced at me then studied her plate.

"Tell us, what was it?" Anne said.

"Well, it's like this. I have a fast serve but it usually hits the net. Yesterday it didn't."

"What's so irregular about that?" Anne asked.

"The net was sagging by about a foot." Everyone laughed heartily.

We finished our fruit salad then sat back and read some Scriptures together. We prayed for our African brothers, then once more asked the Lord to keep away the planes.

The dishes were cleared from the table and I was tuning in for the one o'clock news on BBC when all of a sudden Anne shouted, "The planes!" *Screech! Boom!* Before we could move the first of the bombs had shook the earth. We scrambled to the cubbyhole. *Boom!* The house trembled and the doors and windows reverberated. It was much louder then yesterday. We continued to pray. *Boom!* A third explosion rocked the mission. For an insufferably long time we agonized as the fighters circled overhead. We held our breath wondering who and when and where the next bomb would hit. Then they were gone.

Why hadn't the Lord answered our prayers in the way we thought best? Why had He allowed the planes to attack? Would the rebel captain and his men now come to kill us as they had promised? I could still hear him sneer, "If the planes come back tomorrow, we will eat you!"

We simply lay there in our shelter and cried out to God. "Lord, we don't understand why this has happened. We prayed and you answered differently. But we thank you for the way you've preserved us and we ask you still to deliver us from wicked and unreasonable men!"

When I went outside, I found Mufu's brother hiding behind an anthill. He left his refuge, however, and together we tramped through the grounds looking for any damage. There was none. All the bombs had fallen along the railway line between the mission and the town. I then headed for the hospital where Peter was already waiting for the wounded. The minutes ticked by. When would Blackbeard show up?

A jeep tore down the dispensary road. Who was it? The vehicle skidded to a halt in front of the theater—two shrapnel victims were carried out. We breathed more easily. Rapid evaluation showed that fragments had completely traversed the woman's buttock, but in the injured man they were still lodged in the leg. The hot metal had sliced through the breadth of his thigh stopping just below the opposite surface where it had singed both hair and skin. We treated these casualties, all the while expecting the rebel captain to appear.

We saw other patients too. One of our most-loved senior students was brought in raving mad, his mind completely unhinged by the bombing. Mbavu Toka, a faithful old Christian who had lingered for months in the hospital, began to deteriorate very rapidly for no apparent medical reason. The air raids were taking their toll both physically and mentally. As for us, we waited with mounting suspense for the arrival of the rebel captain.

One hour passed. Two hours, then three hours passed. Blackbeard never came! What a wonderful answer to prayer! The Lord's ways were inscrutable but that day He relieved us of the extra burden that if the planes struck, the rebels would too. Only later did we remember and triumph in the words of the psalmist David who wrote, "The Lord is my light and my salvation; whom shall I fear? . . . When the wicked, even mine enemies and my foes, came upon me to eat up my flesh, they stumbled and fell" (Ps. 27:1,2).

For the Africans, however, the situation was becoming truly desperate. Many more attempted to flee the area, but those that weren't quick didn't make it. The Katangese lined the roads and bush paths driving people back while others guarded the hospital wards. The freedom fighters were at work.

I met one of our married students who told me that he had to leave.

"Where will you go?" I asked.

"Near Kisenge."

"Do you have a home there?"

"No, but we have some friends."

"What about food?"

He shrugged his shoulders and said, "We have none."

"What if you are turned back? Where will you go?"

"Perhaps the refugee camps in Angola," he sighed. My heart melted for this young man. He was only three months away from becoming a certified teacher after six long years of specialized training; yet he and his wife and their two little ones would lose all that and everything else. Their plight was horrendous but typical of the tens of thousands of civilians caught up in this war.

"When do you leave?" I asked.

"Tonight. Hazel and Anne are looking after us."

"Good-bye. The Lord be merciful to you, my brother."

"He will." I fought back the tears while I plodded home.

When I entered the house, Ruth had some alarming news. "David, Peter's down at the hospital. The Katangese are beating up Finda!"

I raced to the men's ward where I found Peter berating one of the soldiers. The others had escaped but this pint-sized rebel had been a little too slow. I strutted up beside him at the door while Peter continued his tirade. The reason for his boldness, I presumed, was that this fellow carried neither gun nor pistol. As Peter blasted away in Swahili, I inched closer and closer to the rogue until the side of his face was about one foot from my chest. With eyes glaring and hands on hips, I towered over the runt for several minutes until Peter relented and the soldier retreated licking his wounds.

"The scoundrels!" Peter growled. "They were hitting a defenseless man with their fists and their guns. Let's go see him."

Finda was shaken but otherwise unharmed. He had been in traction for almost four weeks and he would need several more before his femur healed. Would he make it?

Dusk was settling in. How we welcomed it and the darkness that followed on its heels! This was the only time we could be sure the planes would not attack. I walked to the Judkin's in the six o'clock coolness with the happy prospect of spending a peaceful evening with several friends.

After supper, Sue put the children to bed while Colin turned on the news. "Tonight from Zaire comes a report that Moroccan troops have stabilized the defenses of Kolwezi in troubled Shaba province. Now they will spearhead a Zaire Army counteroffensive designed to push insurgent rebel forces back into Angola. President Mobutu states that the crisis in Shaba is over."

The room was quiet for several moments while we contemplated the broadcast. "So, what do you think?" Sue finally asked.

Walter spoke up. "Considering how wrong the news has been in the past, it's hard to make any solid judgment. One thing is certain. The Katangese will have their hands full with the Moroccans."

"But what about us?" Sue interjected. "What do we do?"

"What can we do?" Glenys replied. "The rebels aren't about to transport us anywhere. Besides, the hospital is over half full. We can't leave all those patients."

"What Sue means is that it's becoming increasingly difficult to cope with the children," Colin explained. "We can't leave them alone for a moment in case the planes come."

"What do I do if they are playing outside?" Sue asked. "Which one do I run for first? The planes have come and bombed before I can even reach the children."

I hadn't realized how trying the bombardment was on all the parents. They couldn't chain their little ones to the furniture and they couldn't let them run free. We had learned that the Zairians had resorted to rocket attacks and strafing at Mutshatsha, and there was no way of knowing when they would start the same with us.

"The Lord speaks to us even in such situations," Colin remarked. "Shall I tell them what Rachel said?" he asked Sue. She nodded.

"While we were scrambling for cover during the last air raid, Rachel looked up and said, 'Why are we running? Jesus will take care of us!' I know we still have to bring them to shelter, but her words spoke to us."

And they spoke to me too that night as I walked home. The war was almost six weeks old and the morrow would mark five weeks since Kasaji had fallen into rebel hands. Jesus had taken care of us all the time. During our captivity, however, an inexplicable feeling dogged my every step. I knew that I was in the Lord's hands, but somehow I felt that this was the time He would take me to be with Him. The thought did not alarm me; in fact it brought perfect peace. I had been forced to the very edge of life itself and for several weeks had been staring into the face of death; yet even in that situation I had discovered that God was sufficient for my every need. Death had no terror for me—its power had been defeated long ago. Death simply gave God one final opportunity during life to succor and prove His faithfulness before He would take care of me forever in His presence.

On this Saturday, April 16, however, a new conviction started to grow. It was the most unlikely time to occur, what with the daily bombardment, the escalating international involvement and the increasing Katangese hostility, yet occur it did. A combination of events and Scriptures and my own communion with the Lord now fueled an assurance that I would return home; there was a story to tell and a job to do, and He wanted me for both.

In my diary that night I copied and underlined a prophetical biblical promise, "But not a hair of your head will perish," and I fell off to sleep knowing that Jesus would indeed take care of me.

On Sunday morning Jimmy and Elizabeth were to leave Kitwe for London, and both Peter and Ruth were struggling with that reality over breakfast. The family would now be separated by thousands of miles. "Peter, I'll do rounds this morning," I offered. "There's no need for two of us to go."

"Would you? I'd appreciate that," he replied.

The hospital was still surprisingly well occupied. The regular wards and the maternity were over half full and the tuberculosis wards had only a few empty beds. The soldiers, of course, were gone, and with them the military nurses. One other person gone was Mbavu. He had died peacefully during the night and a mid-morning funeral was arranged. A spirit of apprehension hung over the wards, however, and there was little I could do to change the gloom on peoples' faces. They had watched a number of fellow patients flee, and if they had been able to, they would have gone as well. The planes would come again—they were certain of that. I discharged any who could conceivably go then finished my work in the OPD.

Sunday School was held for our children at the girls' house. Anne introduced them to the cubbyhole in case their class would be interrupted by aerial visitors. "Now if I tell you to come with me, we'll run into the little mouse hole and sing 'Jesus Loves Me,' " she instructed.

"Oh, Auntie Anne," Robbie said quite enchantedly, "let's have a picnic in the mouse hole."

"Oh, Auntie Anne," Rachel said quite earnestly, "I think I'll sing 'Who's Afraid of the Big Bad Wolf?' "

The Sunday School finished without incident and so did the Lord's

Supper which was held in the chapel despite its proximity to both highway and railway lines. I wheeled Grannie back to our home. All the Fishers were invited for lunch, and Terry and Barbara would join us there.

"Isn't it dreadful all my poor Africans having to live in the bush!" Grannie exclaimed, as we were making our way home. "Of course, Singleton and I did it for the longest time, but in this day and age, what a shame!"

"I hear you've given up your reading classes, Grannie."

"Yes, I have. All the women fled with their families," she explained. "Some of them were reading so jolly well, too. A pity! But as a consequence I have had plenty of time to work on my last project."

"What's that?"

"Oh dear, didn't I tell you? The Bible Society commissioned me to write headings for all the chapters in the Ndembu Old Testament. I've been at it furiously for months and I've just finished. My problem now is how to send it."

"I'm sure you'll find a way, Grannie." She laughed heartily, her whole body sharing in the mirth.

Cutting across the road in front of us were Blackbeard and Alexis at the same time and in the same place as I had spotted them the previous day. It suddenly dawned on me that they were headed for safe parts in case the planes came again. I quickened my step. Soon we were inside the friendly confines of the Coates's house.

Ruth showed us to the living room where Grannie rose from her wheel chair and hobbled to another seat. "My legs aren't that bad but I must take care of them. They're the only two I've got and I want them to last," she chuckled.

Since Ruth and Peter were busy in the kitchen, I entertained Grannie— rather Grannie entertained me. "That's the closest I've come to your tennis court, David. My, it has potential. You know when I . . . ." and her stories continued to flow with all the detail and animation of a master playwright.

"The planes!" Peter shouted. "Put Grannie under the table," he bellowed, then dashed off behind Ruth.

"Just let me take you," I exclaimed, and I half-carried, half-dragged her towards the dining room.

"Slowly," she insisted as we staggered to the table, but we crashed in one inglorious heap onto the floor. "Oh, my leg!" she moaned. A fighter screamed overhead. *Booom!* She soon forgot about her leg.

Since we were lying on concrete, I dashed to the couch for some pillows. I placed one under and one over Grannie's head like a protecting sandwich. After a few moments the terrifying whirr disappeared. Wide-eyed with excitement, Grannie peeked around the edge of the pillow and whispered, "Are they gone?" I shrugged my shoulders. She wouldn't be able to hear me if I spoke; she had turned down her hearing aid.

I crawled to the front door and was about to go outside when I heard another Mirage coming. I dived towards the table while a piercing screech electrified the air. *Boom!* Louder and closer than ever before, it sounded like lightning striking nearby. The house convulsed and bits of plaster plopped from the ceiling to the floor.

Looking out again, Grannie mouthed, "A big one," then covered herself up. Even without hearing she knew.

The Mirages were soon gone. I helped Grannie to a chair then toured the mission with Peter. All was well but I decided to locate the site of the explosion. Several recruits stood beside the primary school staring shell-shocked at the base of the dispensary road. I knew where to look.

Fifty paces from the highway was the railway line and another fifty paces brought me to my destination. I strode out of the elephant grass to witness a sight more devastating than I ever imagined. My knees almost buckled. There in the middle of a newly created 150-foot clearing plunged a crater 20 feet deep and 50 feet across. Sod was strewn in a 70-foot radius from the center of the hole and chunks of hot shrapnel jutted out here and there from the ground. The smell of freshly scorched metal and earth filled the air; the horror of what could have happened dominated the atmosphere.

I returned home, a scarce 300 yards away. It was clear that the Mirages were bombing for the railway line, but that was no consolation at all—their aim was so poor. Had they missed their target by as much in our direction, the primary school or the corner of the mission near the house would have been hit. Any of our hospital buildings would have been demolished in an instant. What I had observed was too dreadful to describe in detail back at the house. Instead, Terry accompanied me to the hole after our meal.

"Whew!" he whistled. "That's some crater. Those bombs are thousand-pounders I would guess."

Back at the mission I asked the inevitable. "What do you think we should do, Terry?"

"I know that the situation seems worse," he began "but I still think we should stay. The patients, the local Christians, the staff—we can't abandon them. Besides I really don't think Mother could make the trip, and our transport is a little thin even if Harold gets his Land Rover going." Terry paused then said, "I guess the key for all of us is to stay close to the Lord and trust Him to make the next step very plain."

News from the town had it that a warehouse as well as some siding had been destroyed at the railway station. The Zairians still hadn't hit their target, but even more people were taking to the bush and fewer soldiers were around to hinder them. Hazel was heartbroken. Most of her patients came to say good-bye.

"Take this," they sobbed handing her money even though payments were illegal. "This is all we can afford but we want you to have it. You've taken such good care of us."

Others moaned, "We have to leave. They will take you and kill you and we won't have you with us anyway."

Despite the maternity exodus, the tuberculosis patients and the regular ward patients were still there late in the afternoon. Some were in traction; some were recovering post operatively. Some had impending skin grafts; some had infected war wounds. Some were too debilitated to move; some had nowhere to go. Their families waited on them and our evening staff showed up as usual to medicate them, but all in all it was a pitiable situation. Even Mufu's brother seemed a little restless when I talked with him just before supper, but with great bravado he promised, "I will protect you. Don't worry about the planes or about the news. I will stay with you and look after you to the end!"

The evening radio broadcasts carried Mobutu's claims of pushing the Katangese back 12 miles, but such information was hard to interpret. There was much speculation but few hard facts, and we asked the Lord to make His way for us clear in the midst of confusion. We retired early.

My sleep was troubled, however, and from three o'clock on I tossed and turned. I heard noise and I thought I heard trains, but everything was inseparably incorporated into my dreams.

Then at 6 A.M., there was a knock at the door. While Peter went to answer it I foggily peered out the window. Hundreds of little figures with sacks on their heads were scurrying along the highway. I blinked and looked again. The same sight greeted my eyes. I jumped out of bed at the same time as Peter bolted back down the hallway.

"The orderlies are all fleeing! They say the hospital is empty and all the villages are deserted. The Katangese are in full retreat to Kasaji where they will make a stand. I think it's time to go!"

18
The Refugee Trail

A quick tour of the mission confirmed the orderlies' report. Rebel soldiers swarmed around the property scrounging for food. Some huddled beside fires cooking chickens already snatched from us, while others cleaned their weapons or rested on the grass. Famished and fatigued, they looked like an army in retreat.

Walter was outside when I arrived at his place. "All the students have fled except for one who's sick," he exclaimed, "and the village across the way is completely deserted. Looks like this is it!"

I scooted past shelters where patients' relatives usually slept and prepared meals—all were barren. A lonely General Mbumba stared down on an empty dispensary from his tattered time-worn poster. The tuberculosis camp was abandoned. The maternity was abandoned. I ran from ward to empty ward finding beds stripped and traction unharnessed. In all the hospital there were only two patients—Finda who happily awaited the FAZ, and an African chief who would go to Kalene Hospital. I skirted the orderlies' homes—forsaken. I raced up the dispensary road—deserted. The people—our reason for staying—had taken flight.

By the time I arrived home, Peter had already conferred with the McKenzies, the Fishers and the girls. "Some aren't packed yet, but everybody feels we should leave," Peter disclosed.

"The others are already preparing to go," I said. Without general discussion or lengthy communal prayer, there was a uniform conviction on a hitherto thorny issue. It was perfectly clear that the Lord had brought us along different paths to a united decision.

We sat down to a hasty breakfast.

"Peter, is Harold going to repair the Land Rover?"

"No. There's not enough time," he replied. "We must get away before the planes show up. With all the Katangese here, the Zairians are likely to rocket and strafe the mission."

FLIGHT FROM KASAJI

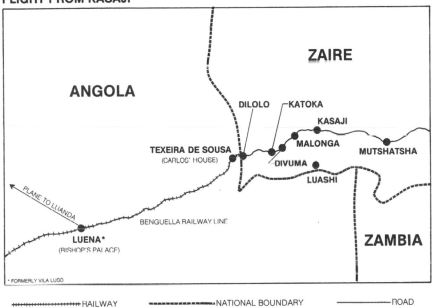

Diagram 4

"Can we manage without the Land Rover?" I asked incredulously.

"We'll have to. We'll double up on the bikes and squeeze the rest into Terry's pickup. He's unscrambling the gears now." It was a miracle that we had any transport at all—Terry's van rescued from the highway, Peter's mobylette returned broken, Glenys' and Harold's bikes hidden and the Fisher's brought back inexplicably, the tractor and the trailer never seized—each vehicle in itself was a provision from the Lord.

"There goes Mufu's brother," I said pointing out the window as he marched past us towards the highway. "He was going to protect us to the end."

"There's only One who'll protect us," Ruth breathed softly.

"Let me check the verse on the daily calendar," I suggested. I retrieved it and softly read the words of Jesus as recorded by John: "My peace I give unto you . . . Let not your heart be troubled, neither let it be afraid."

Tears filled Ruth's eyes. "The words of another passage keep coming to me: 'My grace is sufficient for thee: for my strength is made perfect in weakness.' " Unable to contain herself, Ruth rose from the table and walked to the refrigerator. "And I know how weak I am," she wept. "but I know how strong He is."

We finished eating then prayed before Peter commissioned me to report to all the homes. "Tell them to bring their baggage here as soon as possible. I want to leave by 9 A.M." That gave us 90 minutes to close up what had been a lifework for so many.

The Davies and the Judkins were almost ready. "David," Sue asked, "which way are we going? Through Luashi or Mutshatsha?"

"Neither. We can't go south because that border with Angola is closed. We can't go east because of the fighting nor north for the same reason. We have to go west."

"To Angola?" she gasped. "They'd never let us in!"

"The Katangese are getting in so there's a way. In any case our job now is to take off as soon as we can."

"Give us half an hour," Sue replied rushing inside.

Several Katangese were reclining on the grass beside Raymond's and a couple of them were just leaving the back door with some food that Phyllis had given them. "Oh, David, do come in," she said. "What's the news?"

"Peter wants your baggage at his place right away."

"Yes, and then what?" Phyllis asked.

"Both you and Mr. Raymond will be in the van with the families and the Fishers and a few others," I explained. "Anne, Walter, Harold and I will be riding the bikes."

"Is there enough room for everybody?"

"No," I replied, "but it'll have to do."

"David, you need a hat for the sun," Walter warned. "This is no time for a case of sunstroke."

"Yes, of course," Phyllis agreed. "Here, take Robert's hat. He has another one." It was a green, wide-brimmed, army-type hat and it fit perfectly. I felt like a trooper.

"See you soon, Camarade," Walter called as I sped off.

My next stop was Fisher's garage where Terry and Harold were working on the van. "How are things going?" I asked.

"We're getting there," Terry answered.

"Listen. Do you both know about the luggage?"

"Ours is already over there," Harold replied.

"Barbara is still putting ours together," Terry explained. "What with Mother's paintings and all, we'll be a bit longer."

"That's fine," I replied. "Do you have any more news on the retreat?"

Terry nodded. "The planes did it. They caught the Katangese on savanna outside of Kolwezi. With nowhere to hide, the rebels were bombed and strafed every day until they finally retreated. They plan to regroup here and hold the town."

"What about the civilians, Terry?"

"One of the commandants told me that they've evacuated as many villagers as possible from Mutshatsha westward because of the expected bloodshed. It was he who said that we should go too.''

"I hope the other thousand commandants we meet up with feel the same way,'' Harold mumbled.

At the girls' house I unexpectedly found Safi and her two children. They had fled the hospital but Hazel had already arranged for one of the local Christian families to take care of them. Poor Safi! Six weeks ago she had been a healthy woman with a husband and a home. Now she was maimed, a widow and a refugee.

Peter was already loading up when I arrived. The trailer measured four feet by five feet with an 18-inch depth and could carry only the barest essentials of food, clothing and bedding for 23 people. Everything else except for a few prized mementos would have to be left behind.

It was such a mad scramble against time. There was an unending list of items to consider—food for Finda, fuel for the vehicles, passports, official documents, cooking pots, medical supplies and tools for a breakdown. Wonderfully, one of the faithful orderlies had volunteered to stay and administer food and drugs to any lepers left at the village.

While we packed our gear our minds were racing ahead. Would we get away before the planes struck? Would the Katangese confiscate our transport on the highway? Could the vehicles even last the two-day journey to the frontier? And once at the border, could we get across? How would the Angolan government treat us? Each question raised a host of uncertainties. Actually, could we even be sure about leaving Kasaji?

Terry had strapped Grannie's wheel chair to the roof of the pickup and was finishing the last minute preparations when four Katangese appeared. "What are you doing?'' they asked.

"We're leaving,'' Terry replied. "The commandant told us to go.''

"In that truck?'' they pointed.

"Yes.''

"We need that truck right now,'' the spokesman declared.

"What for?'' Terry protested.

"We have to go somewhere but we'll bring it back later.'' It was clear that we'd never see the van again. "Give me the keys!'' the rebel ordered.

"But the commandant told us to leave right away,'' Terry objected.

"I am the commandant and I am telling you to give me the keys,'' he growled. Terry hung on for a few minutes longer but the Katangese became even more hostile. He had no choice but to capitulate to their demands. All seemed lost. Our escape had been aborted.

"What's happening here?'' a voice called out from the driveway. It was a Katangese officer, our old friend Roger. We hadn't seen him for almost a month and were wondering if he had been killed.

"Roger!'' Terry exclaimed. "Am I glad to see you!''

After the story was told, Roger turned angrily to his comrades. "Why are you harassing them? They have done you no harm and they already have lost much. Let them go in their truck. If you want to escape, use your feet! If you are men, you will stay and fight!" Sullen and resentful, the four rebels tramped off. Roger's timely appearance was God's miraculous provision.

The tractor and trailer were almost ready to roll. One last time I was drawn back to the hospital before we left. A flood of memories swept through my mind as I drove down the dispensary road. The buildings stood somber and silent, but could they speak, they would recount stories of suffering and sacrifice, tales of terror and triumph. I stopped for an instant overwhelmed by it all, then turned back up the road leaving a part of me behind in the solitude.

The caravan was set to go. Leading off on mobylettes were Walter and Anne accompanied by the sick student. Next was Peter on the tractor followed by Ruth and me on one mobylette and the McKenzies on their motorcycle. The pickup would leave shortly with 16 cramped occupants.

Hovering around the homes like vultures were the rebels, poised to pillage as soon as we left. We revved our engines. It was 9 A.M. Slowly we pulled away from the Coates's house and snaked onto the main road. We were off.

For several minutes we bounced along the highway lost in our thoughts. That all our responsibilities had been discharged was a relief. We had abandoned everything but we had deserted no one. The people had left us and we had left Kasaji to the Katangese and to the ravages of war. That hundreds of patients and students and staff and villagers had fled overnight was a tragedy and a mystery. That the few who remained would be well cared for was a blessing.

The highway was barren. There was nothing ahead of us except the vehicles and the clouds of dust they raised. Ruth held tightly to my waist as we skirted potholes and skidded through soft sand. "How wonderful that dry season has come so early this year!" she exclaimed. "I couldn't imagine traveling on muddy roads in those terrible storms." I nodded in agreement.

"Hey, look ahead!" I shouted. The first of the African civilians appeared and soon there was a steady trickle of refugees along the road. Old and young, they carried their precious possessions with them to destinations as uncertain as our own.

Walter and Anne had been driving faster than the tractor and were now out of sight. Afraid that he might accidentally hit one of the refugees, Peter directed us to take the lead in order to give the people adequate warning.

We hadn't been in front for more than a few minutes when Ruth exclaimed excitedly, "David, some soldiers have stopped Peter!"

I spun around and saw several rebels encircling the tractor. Would our vehicles be confiscated or was something much worse about to happen? I raced back, but before we arrived the Katangese vaulted on top of the trailer and Peter motioned us to carry on.

"I guess all they want is a lift," I muttered. "I hope the trailer can take it." I knew Peter wouldn't like having armed soldiers at his back but there was nothing we could do about it.

About six miles out of Kasaji and two miles after the rebels joined our bizarre parade, Terry's van passed us. It cheered us to know that they had safely evacuated the mission station and that the miracle pickup was coping with its incredible load. Just at that time, however, Peter seemed to be experiencing trouble with the trailer. He kept on looking back at his left tire, then finally ground to a halt.

"David, we should see what's wrong," Ruth suggested earnestly. "Peter is stopped again."

Harold was already working on the problem when we pulled up. The weight of the rebels had broken the spring on the left side causing the frame to rub against the wheels. "I'll wedge some timber between the axle and the body," Harold said, "but it won't hold if the camarades hop back on."

"Look at what you've done," I scolded the Katangese. "You've broken our vehicle after doing all those other bad things to us at Kasaji." I cited our long list of grievances with controlled animosity while Peter started up the motor.

"And don't you get back on our trailer or you'll break it again. We have been told by the commandant to leave and . . . " Both Peter and the McKenzies drove off while I slowed down my non-stop rhetoric and winded up with a handshake, a smile, and a *"Merci,* Camarade." Without looking back, Ruth and I roared away leaving the rebels standing in stony silence.

The journey soon became more difficult as we finally caught up with the crowds that had fled Kasaji in the night. A trickle became a stream, and a stream became a torrent. The highway overflowed with refugees and we had to proceed at a crawl through the mass of people.

It was a piteous spectacle. Mothers balanced sacks of meal on their heads and bore babies strapped to their backs. Little boys and girls carried chickens, buckets and stools. Fathers pushed unbelievable burdens on battered bikes. Old crooked women hobbled; polio victims hopped; lepers and tuberculosis patients from our wards staggered along. One woman with recent abdominal surgery was lying on a makeshift stretcher supported over the back wheel of a bicycle. Students and teachers and orderlies and technicians and elders and oh, so many friends—our hearts tugged with deep sorrow for the human tragedy that was strung out for miles.

And then we spotted our beloved Tshihinga. I couldn't force more than a few trembling words from my mouth yet with an ear-to-ear smile he said,

"The Lord will take care of you just like He will take care of us!" In a moment his face was a memory as were his words of hope and confidence. Through men and women such as him the Lord would continue to build His African church.

Our grief became more bearable after Musalika where most of the refugees veered north to Kakenge. This route enabled them to avoid the main highway and the railway line, both of which were prime aerial targets. With less traffic, we picked up speed and soon were approaching Malonga.

"Hey, look up there, Ruth!" I exclaimed. "Tanks!" I whipped out my camera for a shot of two FAZ tanks lying where they had been knocked out in a Katangese ambush before the battle at Kasaji. Farther on was a Ge'camines truck destroyed in the same encounter. We rocketed past these relics of war and swerved around a corner on the outskirts of Malonga. There was our first roadblock.

I slowed down so that Peter and the McKenzies could catch up, then together we eased our way to the barrier. A rebel emerged from the bushes and I called out lustily, *"Jambo,* Camarade!" He grinned, and we immediately recognized him as the Toothless One. He shook our hands vigorously and motioned us on.

"That was the most precious bar of soap you ever gave away, Ruth," I muttered. Our procession rolled through the center of Malonga. The people had not left the town and many of them came out to greet us. At the end of the boulevard stretched another roadblock. Some civilians manned this barrier, but two rebels jogged over from a nearby house. If it weren't Augusto and Roberto, our two military nurses!

"Camarades," I announced, "you can go to the pharmacy now and take whatever drugs you like. We left them for you."

"Thank you, thank you," they replied and they opened the gate. We motored on to the Lukoji River where we encountered a third roadblock, but this was passed as easily as the other two.

It was midday, and although we had been traveling for three hours, we were less than half way to Katoka. The suspense, however, had diminished considerably. The villages we now passed were peaceful and untouched by war. We journeyed mile after mile without encountering a soldier. Clouds screened us from the hot sun and from the view of potential aerial predators. All in all this was becoming the most pleasant part of our trip so far.

"David, Peter is stopped again," Ruth said. We swung around and sped back to the others. The problem was immediately obvious—the trailer trailed the tractor by a good 15 feet.

"It's the hitch-pin," announced Harold. "It's either broken or simply dropped out."

"Where?" Norma asked.

"Your guess is as good as mine. It could be anywhere." What a disaster! We would have to leave our luggage behind and hope that the truck could return to pick up our goods. But then how could we carry on from Katoka without the trailer? While we were talking, Harold was retracing our path along the road.

"I've found it!" he exulted from 40 feet away. The pin was repositioned and we were on our way praising the Lord.

We soon arrived at a village called Mbangu where we had quite a surprise. "Walter!" I shouted. "It's about time we found you! How are you?"

"A little saddle-sore but otherwise fine," he replied.

"Where's Anne?"

"In the pickup," he answered. "Her mobylette broke down."

"And how's the student?"

"Sherubambo? He's much better. He'll stay here with the Christians until he feels stronger. How has your trip been?"

"Rather tame—just a few breakdowns and a hijacking," I replied casually.

"What?" he exclaimed. I recounted everything in detail. He marveled that we had extricated ourselves from the rebels riding shotgun, then he asked how Norma and Ruth were doing.

"Super," I answered.

"I've never seen them dressed like that before," he commented. "Especially Norma with her fancy bonnet and ankle length dress."

"Yeah, we've already dubbed them the Pilgrim Mothers."

Walter roared his approval just as Peter mounted his tractor and started to pull out. We hurried to our bikes and the expedition curved back onto the road. Walter now took the lead while Ruth and I remained just in front of the tractor. There was a certain distance from Peter within which we had to stay, otherwise Ruth would whisper in her own inimitable style, "Peter is getting a little bit back." That was her signal to slow down and she used it countless times. Of course I always obeyed.

"Ruth, you're looking back so much that you're missing all the scenery."

"Oh, no!" she replied. "There's nice scenery behind me."

We plowed through sand traps, raced down hills and struggled up inclines. Divuma was just ahead.

"Divuma is a railway junction which connects with Kisenge," Ruth said. "Actually, we're within 20 miles of Kisenge, and I know Peter wouldn't like to stay here long."

Once more I decelerated when a roadblock loomed at the edge of town. All four vehicles came to a dead stop in front of the guardian of the gate—a lad no more than 12 years old. He was a member of the *Pionniers*, the Katangese junior militia, and these youngsters were notorious troublemakers. Walter tried to bluster our way past the barrier but the little fellow would have nothing of it. He pulled out a whistle and blew it furiously. Within seconds dozens of boys appeared from all over the town and ran towards us screaming triumphantly.

"Oh, no!" Walter groaned. The Pionniers jumped aboard the trailer and surrounded each of the vehicles. We were captured by an army of boys! Happily, a rebel soldier appeared and he beckoned the Pionniers to lead us on. We were paraded through the town; and just when we thought we were free, they forced us into the railway station and shut the door behind us. Now we were prisoners!

The situation was ludicrous. Four Katangese manned the station but none of them, not even the commandant, could give us a satisfactory answer for the arrest. When we asked about our truck they talked about transmitters and sending rebels to Katoka for our protection. Nothing made sense.

It was 2 P.M. There were still another two hours of traveling time to Katoka but we were given no idea when or if we could leave. We decided to eat and have some collective prayer before discussing our next step.

Suddenly Peter said, "Listen!" We were immediately silent. It was the unmistakable drone of a plane high overhead. The Katangese came outside gripping their rifles. Would the aircraft bomb nearby Kisenge or would they strike the railroad junction at Divuma?

"It's a transatlantic flight," Peter sighed. "Comes by once or twice a week." We breathed easily once again. The rebels, however, turned deaf ears to this danger and other arguments we raised against our detention. Forty-five minutes passed. An hour and 15 minutes passed. Would we make it to Katoka after dark? Would we make it at all?

One of the friendlier Katangese signaled to a comrade that he was going out for a beer. We had hoped that he would help us in our release. Before he left, Peter and I persuaded him to accompany us to the commandant. The officer tongue-lashed the soldier, however, and it seemed as if we had fallen into worse troubles. The commandant then turned to us. We expected another tirade but instead heard him say, "I'm sorry for keeping you here. It was all a misunderstanding of language. You can go now."

We didn't try to make sense of the nonsensical. Thanking him profusely, we climbed onto our vehicles and took off again on the last stretch of our first day's journey. We scooted through village after village and in one of them spotted the mission's new lorry, already broken down and abandoned. During the whole trip we greeted passers-by with an exuberant *"Jambo,* Camarade," in order to disarm any suspicious types we might encounter. On more than one occasion villagers recognized Peter and responded with *"Jambo sana, Munganga."*

We passed Terry's truck about eight miles from Katoka. He was driving back two Katangese to Divuma after successfully depositing his passengers at the Rews's. Rejoicing at the news of their safe arrival, we pressed onwards.

The sinking sun blinded us for the last 20 minutes of our trip but we finally entered Katoka at 5:10 P.M. feeling every bit like Pilgrim Mothers and Fathers. The discomforts were soon forgotten in our happy reunion with other equally thankful travelers.

The Katoka mission station was an oasis for the weary. We were fed a nourishing meal and had a chance to wash up after a long day on a dusty road. Then we listened to how the miracle pickup had fared. Terry, Grannie, a very big Deirdre and a very small Glenys had squeezed into the front seat while the other 13 had crammed into the back. Shortly after the truck left Kasaji, rebels carrying anti-tank missiles had given everyone a few tense moments before letting the vehicle pass. Then, at Divuma much the same drama had transpired before two Katangese climbed onto the roof of the already overloaded Chevy and rode to Katoka as "protection." Mercifully, the pickup had withstood the rigors of the trip.

That evening we prayed about the deteriorating situation and for our many displaced brothers and sisters. We also prayed for the Rews and Mary Ratter. They had decided not to evacuate with us despite Mobutu's continuing advance against the Katangese. Katoka was still well behind the front lines and they felt that such a move would be premature.

Walter and I were assigned to the Rews's living room where we set up some camp beds. After furiously scribbling away in our diaries, we recalled some of the amazing things that had happened just that day—the miracle pickup and all the other vehicles, the empty hospital and fleeing staff, the deserted villages, the scattered students, Roger's timely arrival, the early dry season, rebels on the trailer, the roadblocks guarded by the Toothless One and the military nurses, the recovered hitch-pin and the Divuma incident and countless unseen dangers. Our hearts soared with prayers of thanksgiving.

The morrow was completely unknown as were all succeeding morrows. Plans could be formulated but the reality was that we were utterly dependent upon the Lord for food, shelter, transportation and everything else. What a wonderful feeling! It would be exciting to be borne along in His hand of deliverance.

19
Angolan Midnight Express

Ring! Ring! An alarm clock wakened me from my light sleep. I peered at my watch. "Four-thirty!" I muttered. "Another one of Peter's patented early starts!"

Walter and I hurriedly packed our gear and reloaded the trailer in preparation for our predawn getaway. It was still pitch black outside and unusually chilly. Our departure was delayed by the darkness, but after a time of prayer and farewell, the mobylette-tractor caravan finally slipped away at 6:15 A.M.

The first glimmer of morning allowed a visibility of less than 30 feet on the main highway. Within minutes the mobylettes' wheels were spinning wildly in loose sand bringing us to a standstill. The tractor kept on going while we dragged the bikes off the road and started again on firmer ground. The sand traps were to menace us the whole journey.

A few miles beyond Katoka was Kahundu railway station. Here we expected to encounter our next barrier but there was none. We pressed on while daybreak continued to illuminate greater and greater stretches of road.

"There's the FNLA[2] camp," said Ruth pointing to the north of the highway. The shantytown which garrisoned the defeated FNLA soldiers now lay forlorn and in shambles. It had been abandoned in a hurry when the Katangese spilled over the border.

We pushed on mile after mile without seeing a soldier, without seeing anyone, and finally Terry's pickup overtook us at 7:30 A.M. some 10 miles outside of Katoka. By then the sun had poked over the horizon at our backs and we chased our bouncing shadows towards the frontier.

The road was a challenge. Some stretches were riven with deep rainwater gullies and threatened to throw us off our vehicles. In other places deep soft sand would swallow our tires causing the mobylettes to lurch madly and sometimes topple over onto our legs. Often we had to snake our way through elephant grass at the side of the road to avoid these pitfalls.

The rugged highway proved to be the biggest obstacle in our three-hour flight to Dilolo. No roadblocks were encountered, no Zairian planes were sighted, and not until we reached the outskirts of the city did we even see any Katangese troops.

"Where is Peter taking us?" I asked Ruth as we entered the town.

"To the Jones's old house," she answered. "They were missionaries here a few years ago."

The caravan rumbled through the streets of Dilolo attracting many a stare. The town was teeming with Katangese but the atmosphere was relaxed; most of the rebels strolled the avenues without their guns. Dilolo was a more impressive place than I had envisioned. Many larger buildings dotted the downtown area, and in its hills were nestled numerous villa-style homes. It was at one of these that we finally stopped at 9:30 A.M.

"The Jones's," Ruth announced as we tumbled off our vehicles.

"I'm so sore," Walter moaned. "I won't be able to sit down for days."

Peter unlocked the gate and we explored the mission house. There was little in it except some children's books, a few chairs and a table or two. There was no electricity or running water although the backyard did have a well, a fireplace, and a water closet. For 23 people the house was at best primitive, at worst uninhabitable.

"David," Peter called. "I'm going into town to find Terry. Perhaps he's already seen the colonel."

There were three major hurdles that faced us in our efforts to enter Angola. First of all, we needed the permission of the Katangese. Secondly, we needed the permission of the Angolans. Thirdly, we needed transportation across the border. Terry was to seek the rebel colonel to present our case.

Peter and I hadn't ridden very far into town when we spotted Terry lumbering along the sidewalk. It was great to see him and especially to hear the news.

"I haven't seen the colonel yet, but something tremendous happened," he exclaimed. "I met an elder from one of our assemblies. He's an administrator with the Angolans and has already gone across to Texeira de Sousa to organize our acceptance on the other side!" What a thrill! We had hardly arrived and the Lord was already clearing the way.

"And this afternoon around one o'clock, the colonel will see us over there," Terry continued, pointing to a nearby building. "The problem is that the Katangese have firmly refused all requests to cross the border so we'll have to pray for the Lord to overrule."

"We will," Peter answered. "I'll be back here by one o'clock." We zoomed off.

If the reports we heard were accurate, the colonel was a practicing Christian and well-known as such by his men. How or why he was involved in war we didn't know. Many believers in times past had conscientiously taken up arms for causes they believed to be just; perhaps this was what he had done. In any case we were told that he ran a clean headquarters—no liquor, no tramps, no drugs. He also conducted Bible studies and prayer times for those soldiers who would come. I certainly wanted to meet the man.

At a quarter to one we pulled up to the combat headquarters of the FNLC. On the outside walls were painted the insignia of the Tiger Commandos and slogans to the praise of Mbumba. We were ushered inside where we waited on a couple of couches. Rebels marched back and forth past us, hardly acknowledging our presence.

Finally, the colonel appeared. He was short and he wore light green battle fatigues, a weathered red beret and a pair of scuffed boots. He sank into a seat beside us looking very tired, but for 30 minutes he listened attentively to our requests, nodding and grunting and answering warmly. More than once I thought to myself that this fellow was too gentle to be a colonel.

When the interview terminated, he ordered one of his men to type up permission for us to leave the country, then told us that a train would take us across at eight o'clock that night. Bidding us adieu, he returned to his work.

We were overjoyed! It was what we had prayed for, yet it was too good to be true! Clutching the precious document we raced back to the Jones's.

"We have the colonel's permission!" Terry announced as we bounded into the mission house.

"Even without our passports?" Phyllis exclaimed.

"Even without our passports!" Terry assured. Three of the Kasaji folk had sent their papers to Lubumbashi for visas and were traveling with long-expired passports.

"And what about the pickup for the Rews?" Anne asked.

"That's also arranged. The colonel has written a letter authorizing William to keep the vehicle. The Katoka schoolteacher is driving it back tonight." This was another wonderful answer to prayer! The Rews and Mary would now have transport should they be forced to take flight.

Other amazing things happened that afternoon. We had expected to abandon our remaining vehicles at the train. After lunch, however, a local trader came by the house and offered to purchase Harold's motorcycle, the two mobylettes, the tractor and the trailer! He even took an option on the van should the Katoka folk pass through Dilolo. What we had reckoned to be a total loss was liquidated for significant cash funds, and all in much-needed Angolan currency! We rejoiced at the Lord's provision.

The Katangese also came by the house and with them they brought fresh meat, courtesy of the colonel. We received it gratefully and Harold and Hazel set to work cooking it for supper.

Meanwhile Robbie, Rachel and Ingrid were frolicking in the backyard and had stumbled upon a small metal trolley.

"Now Rachel and Ingrid," Robbie squealed delightedly, "both of you go inside." The girls dutifully obeyed and we gazed with increasing astonishment at the evolving drama.

Robbie picked up a stick, and finding it to his satisfaction, he paced back and forth in front of his penitentiary. The captives peered gleefully through the bars until Robbie pointed his gun at them and let out a thunderous "Bang! Bang!"

This turn of events had taken the girls by surprise. Rachel and Ingrid thought they were playing house, not guns and war. They crawled out of the dungeon to the great displeasure of Robbie who immediately shot them both dead. The only problem was that they didn't drop to the ground.

"You have to fall down," Robbie pleaded, but the girls would have nothing of it.

"We're not playing," Rachel announced decisively and walked from the arena. There was little that Robbie could do about the jailbirds. After a short pout, he marched to and fro in front of his empty prison firing his gun with great gusto until the hot sun finally curbed his enthusiasm.

The heat was oppressive even in the shadow of the house. Already wearied by travel and tension, several of us succumbed to the temperature—we catnapped. The waiting dragged on and on. Finally supper came and with it a ration of the toughest meat I had ever chewed.

"It's called biltong," Harold explained. "Just an old trick to preserve meat so that we can eat it for other meals."

Supper finished and still we waited. The sultry afternoon slipped into a humid evening when swarms of ravenous mosquitos forced us inside.

The trader had promised to transport us to the station in time for the 8 P.M. train. When his truck had not arrived by six-thirty, Peter and Terry set out to see what was wrong. We continued to sing and pray and wait. Someone turned on the seven o'clock news which reported that the FAZ were closing in on Mutshatsha. The minutes continued to tick by without sign of the lorry or Terry or Peter.

Finally at 7:15 P.M. we heard a rumble up the street. It was the truck. "Praise the Lord!" said Rachel, and we all rushed outside to climb aboard. We were off to our rendezvous with the train.

The railway station was a beehive of activity. During the daytime the line between Dilolo and Texeira de Sousa was closed to all transit. Trains and small motorized rail cars, called *dressines,* crossed over only in the dark when there was no danger of their being attacked from the air. As we arrived, the bustle and tear indicated to us that the Katangese were preparing for their night run. We noticed our tractor and numerous late model cars already loaded on a freight wagon for transport to Angola—the rich Dilolo merchants were trying to preserve their assets.

"Over here," the trader motioned. "Put your luggage in this railway car." The carriage had multiple holes from rocket fire but we didn't complain. Having our belongings inside was much better than on an open platform full of Katangese, Pionniers and workmen.

We found a few benches where Grannie and the families could rest, and from this vantage point we watched our boxcar. The rebels strolled back and forth along the train looking menacingly at us. No doubt our presence reminded them that the tide of the war had turned. Like so many of their comrades, several viewed us as responsible. One unpleasant fellow walked around us clutching a bottle and muttering, *"Américains! Eliminez!"* We ignored him but we realized again how little it would take for some of the Katangese to take out their vengeance against us. We yearned for the locomotive to appear and pull us out of Zaire.

But then disaster struck. A railway officer arrived with stunning news: "There will be no train tonight. The engine has been recalled to the front lines and will not be available until at least tomorrow."

"But the colonel himself told us to come on the train," Peter protested.

"I'm sorry. The engine has already gone. There's nothing I can do."

We were shocked. Everything had worked out so well. We had the permission from the Angolans. We had the permission from the Katangese. All we needed was transportation across the border and this had been promised us. Now it had been cruelly snatched away and our plans had crumbled before our very eyes.

What could we do? We couldn't go back to the mission house—it had no facilities; we had no way of getting there; and we feared that a train might pass through Dilolo unannounced. We couldn't stay indefinitely at the railway terminal—it also had no facilities; angry rebels were a continual menace; and in the daytime the station might be bombarded by the Zairian air force. We couldn't go forward to Texeira de Sousa—there was no train; there was no road bridge; and we'd never walk the 12-mile distance carrying Grannie, the children and the luggage. We were stranded, we were helpless and we knew it.

"Oh Lord," we cried, "we know that you and you alone have led us through all our troubles to this place and time. And Father, once more we've come to the end of ourselves. We can't go back, we can't go forward, and we can't stay where we are. Lord, we're in a mess; but we know that you can and that you will deliver us from our desperate situation. In Jesus' name, Amen."

And so our vigil began in Dilolo railway station amidst soldiers who moved about us murmuring, *"Eliminez! Eliminez!"* Time passed. It was getting late and we had to find somewhere to sleep, especially for Grannie and the children.

"The railway officer told us to use the waiting room," Peter said. "Let's bring the bedding there for Grannie and the families."

The waiting room was not in the best of shape. The windows were smashed, the door was knocked in, the tables were overturned and glass covered the floor. It took some clean-up before it was suitable, but finally everyone was settled.

Back on the platform Peter said, "David, I'd like you and Walter to guard the luggage in the boxcar. Just bolt the door behind you."

"Sure," I replied. "What about the rest of you?"

"We'll be in there," he said pointing to a coach on one of the sidings. "It has some rather smelly bunks but they'll have to do. If you have any problems with the soldiers give us a shout."

We all went to our respective places. What an incredible array of sleeping chambers—a battered waiting room, a moth-eaten coach and a shot-up boxcar—yet we thanked the Lord for each one. We had no idea what would happen next, nor did we even know what to expect; but we trusted God to provide for us. Walter and I lay down amidst the luggage and fell asleep.

Half an hour later I was awakened by a strange noise. "Listen," I told Walter. It was a low-pitched, rapid-fire chugging sound.

"It's a dressine!" Walter exclaimed. We leaped out of our carriage and sprinted along the platform. The noise was more distinct now and the vehicle had already entered the station. Peter, Terry and several others including a score of African women and children joined us.

The dressine stopped directly in front of us. The small motorized rail car towed an equal-sized workmen's coach and together they carried about 10 rebels and four civilians. Amongst the group was our psychotic college student and a war victim who had fled the hospital. As the last few occupants piled out of the dressine, Terry blurted out, "Isn't that Mufu?"

Indeed it was! The major crossed over the tracks and agilely mounted the platform. "Major Mufu," Terry exclaimed. "we didn't expect to find you here!"

"I am all over the place," he replied.

"How are the ribs, Major?" I asked.

"No more pain, Doctor," he answered, "but I expected to see you and Dr. Peter in Kasaji this afternoon. I was disappointed to find out you had gone."

"And everybody else too," Peter added.

"Yes, that is war, but the battles have only begun. We are entrenched at Kasaji and will soon crush the Moroccans and the FAZ." Mufu's spirit was far from broken. "I am going to Angola tonight but I will be back later," he divulged.

Terry seized the opportunity. "Do you think we can be transported across when you come back?" he asked pointedly. "The colonel gave us permission to take the train but it never arrived."

"It's possible, but it all depends on how long my business takes. Anyway," he said, glancing at his watch, "I must leave now. Good-bye." Having summoned his aides, he reboarded the dressine and pulled off into the darkness towards the Angolan frontier. It was 9:45 P.M.

Major Mufu's appearance almost three weeks since last we had seen him was another one of an endless series of miracles. We were convinced that the Lord had preserved his life, and now had brought him to us as the instrument of our escape across the border. But once more we would have to wait.

Walter and I returned to our unusual bedroom. Strollers, suitcases and boxes surrounded us, and underneath us was a blanket and a cold metal floor. The walls of the carriage were multiply punctured by bullets and mortar shells, while above us gaping bomb holes revealed the moon and the starry sky.

"Just like a planetarium," Walter commented looking at the roof.

Our conversation drifted into prayer and finally we dozed off. I slept the sleep of exhaustion until 12:15 A.M. From that time on I battled an air force of mosquitos. Most of them seemed to attack me kamikaze-style, their prime targets being my ankles and my neck. No matter how many crash-landed, waves more were circling for the kill. The struggle had dragged on for an hour when once more I picked up the chug-chug of the dressine.

"Walter, Mufu's back!" He wakened immediately and we tumbled out onto the platform.

Peter was already running across the tracks. "Quick! Let's get the luggage!" We rapidly emptied our boxcar and when the dressine finally skidded to a halt we were all ready to clamber aboard with our belongings.

Beside us, however, was a crowd of African women and children—the same ones who had appeared when the dressine first arrived. Amongst them we spotted a couple of Dilolo traders. Altogether they totaled more than 40 people, and their baggage included a large number of bulky-shaped goods. Obviously they also intended to board the dressine.

Mufu strode across the landing. "Major Mufu," Peter called out, "can we go?"

Before the major could answer, one of the African merchants mumbled something to him. Mufu then turned to us and said, "Yes, of course you can go—but there will be no discrimination. The Congolese families will leave first and then you will be taken." We were crushed.

"Could Mr. Raymond go on this trip?" Peter bargained. "He is supposed to confirm the accommodation that the colonel arranged for us."

"Sure there's plenty of room for him," Mufu replied.

While the Africans loaded their gear the major talked with us for some time. His last words were an admonition. "When you arrive home, you must give a good report. Tell everyone that you left because the Zairians were bombing your hospital. Tell the world that the FAZ are butchers and thieves. But now I must sleep. At five-thirty I leave in my dressine for the front. Good-bye," he said, shaking our hands. "Come back to the Congo. I will be here."

It was 1:45 A.M. We watched the last possible African squeeze aboard. The dressine chugged off to the frontier leaving 20 more civilians and all their baggage. Clearly a second trip would not carry everybody, and a third would be impossible before Mufu's deadline of 5:30 A.M.

"Peter, unless we think of something we won't get to Angola on the dressine," I muttered.

"I know," he acknowledged, deep in thought. Both of us stood there groping and praying for an answer to the dilemma. Once more the obstacle seemed insurmountable.

"Peter!" I called out excitedly. "What about using another workmen's carriage? We can attach it to the other two and that should give us all the space we need!"

"That sounds fine," he replied, "but where are we going to find one?"

"There's bound to be one on a siding someplace. Here, let's ask the railway officer." The lonely figure on the platform didn't know the specific location of any but promised to search the east side of the railway yard. We quickly checked the smaller western end then Terry, Peter and I ran to join the railway officer.

There was not a moment to spare. We weren't even sure that an empty, functioning carriage existed; but if there was one, our first task was to locate it. Secondly, we would have to drag it through a series of switches until it was running on the main line. Then we would have to roll it all the way to our platform before finally loading it up. All this had to be done before the dressine returned.

We fanned out across the tracks and swept eastward through the station. Far in the distance we noticed the railman. He was waving to us.

"We've got one!" Terry exclaimed.

In record time we covered the next quarter of a mile to where the empty carriage was being pushed along the rails. It was amazingly light and we were able to shoot it down the tracks and through the switches with remarkable speed. Breathless and flushed with excitement we pulled up to the platform with our miracle carriage.

All the men set to work bringing over the baggage while Peter and I packed it into every available space. It didn't seem possible but everything was finally jammed in and Harold tied it all down with rope. There were no sides on our carriage—if anything fell out, it would be lost.

It was 2:45 A.M. As yet there was no sign of the dressine. I looked around. We were such a motley band—Grannie in her wheel chair, Deirdre ready to deliver at any moment, five exhausted, confused children, women wearing long skirts and fancy bonnets, men wearing shorts and a crazy assortment of hats—how we loved and cared for one another!

At last we heard the motorized rail car struggling up the incline from the Luao River. Moments later it entered the station and stopped at the platform. We secured the dressine itself for our women and children; next we helped the Africans properly load their gear. Our five children and 12 of the adults squeezed into eight seats in the front car. The middle carriage was packed solid with the traders' families and their luggage. The overburdened caboose was occupied by the Coates, Harold, Walter and me in a space that would normally admit two. At last we were ready to go. Two quick photos of the unlikely mini-train guarded by a couple of rebels captured the historical moment.

The dressine pitched forward into the blackness—no lights were permitted. We clung to each other and to the roof overhead. Slowly we picked up speed. The land dipped towards the river and soon the railcars were hurtling along at breakneck speeds in total darkness. The carriages lurched from side to side like a roller-coaster and we clutched each other with increasing avidity lest one of us be catapulted into the night.

The land leveled off. The border was approaching. We looked back to the lights of Dilolo, now distant and dim. We would soon exit Zaire, the land of our labor and our love, but the country whose conflict had nearly cut short our lives. We would soon enter Angola, a nation also troubled by poverty and civil war. Where would we stay and how would we travel? What would we eat and when would we leave? To these and other questions we had no answers.

"There she goes!" Harold cried as we rocketed across the Luao River. I looked at my watch—it was 3:29 A.M., April 20, 1977. I reached into my pocket and pulled out the daily calendar of verses. Under April 20 was copied Psalm 62 verse 5: "My soul, wait thou only upon God; for my expectation is from him." Only God had met our every need as we struggled in Zaire. Only from Him could we expect continued deliverance as we crossed Angola.

20
Watching Africa Go By

The small open-backed pickup chased its headlights through the blackness of the Texeira night. At the wheel was a Portuguese trader named Carlos, and in his truck was a second load of weary, white refugees from Zaire. How thrilled we had been to see Mr. Raymond at the railway station and how exciting to learn that accommodation was awaiting us! Now the last of the Kasaji family was being ferried to the residence of our kind chauffeur.

Carlos was not the typical merchant. Still in his late twenties, he was a short, sunken-chested man. Tattered jeans hugged his legs and a plain shirt hung sloppily over his lean frame. His jet black hair fell in long tangles down his back and a shaggy moustache drooped over his mouth. He looked much more like a vagabond from the West than a successful businessman.

The pickup jerked to a stop and Carlos jumped from the cab. "Take the bags," he instructed in rough-spoken French. "I'll show you where the others are." We unloaded our luggage and followed him through a courtyard into the dining room of his home.

"Shhh," Phyllis whispered as we entered, "the children are sleeping!" We tiptoed over the bodies and deposited the bags in places already staked out for individual families. Off the dining room were a small kitchen, a bathroom and two sleeping chambers—one used by an Angolan soldier, and the other given up by Carlos for Grannie. Beyond the dining room was a living room where 14 African refugees were sleeping on the floor. Adjacent to them was a lounge reserved for us, and next to that a bedroom saved for Deirdre.

It was almost dawn before everyone settled. "Let's go for a walk," Walter suggested.

"Are you serious?"

"Sure," he replied. "There's hardly any floor space to sleep on. Besides I'm starting to wake up."

"I'm game if you are."

Together we set out in the first light of day. Initially we wondered if we would be stopped by sentries patrolling the neighborhood. After all, bloody fighting was going on in nearby Zaire; besides, Angola was a communist country. The streets were empty, however, and the first soldier we saw was not even carrying a gun.

Texeira de Sousa had been a beautiful town. Typically Portuguese in design, its dwellings, roadways and playgrounds had been blemished by war and neglect. Spacious pink villas had large shell holes through their walls and overgrown vegetation in their gardens. Store windows were bricked up. Building exteriors were defaced by revolutionary graffiti. A four-lane boulevard with a grassed-in median and tiled sidewalks had non-functioning street lights and crumbling curbs. In the center of town we stumbled across a spacious park with palm trees, benches, and trimmed lawns, but next to it was a playground with broken swings and slides—further reminders of the neglect in this war-torn land.

Back at the house Carlos confirmed our impressions of the town. "Texeira was a very fine place. We had everything. Our shops were many and full of anything you could possibly want—radios, watches, fine clothes, new cars, construction materials, and great varieties of food. What we lacked we ordered, and it came on the Benguella Railway. We even had cinemas in Texeira. Three thousand Portuguese lived here—it was like a paradise.

"Then the troubles came." Carlos lit up a cigarette and sat back for a moment of reflection. "The railway was cut, the civil war spread to our town and that was the end of the old Texeira. It is almost two years since the fighting stopped in our streets, but still only three shops exist and two of them are empty. The Portuguese evacuated and now there are less than 30 left. My father also went to Europe with the family but I stayed on to look after our business." Carlos stared blankly ahead as if reliving the painful memories of which he spoke.

"Carlos, what is your business?" I asked.

"We had many businesses. Shops—but they are closed. Ranches—but we have little there. There are other side interests, but we have one big business and we have done it for 10 years." He stopped to draw on his cigarette. "We supply food to the Katangese army." So that was the connection between the colonel and Carlos!

"That's how we're here!"

"Yes," he replied. "The colonel asked me to let you stay. Usually it is reserved for Katangese officers who sleep here on their way through, but," he announced to us all, "the house is yours. Use it as you like. I've brought in extra gas for the stove and there is plenty of water and electricity. You can stay here as long as you like. But now I must attend to some affairs." We thanked him for his generosity and he left.

Despite Carlos's hospitality we weren't hoping to stay for a long time. Our food supplies would last only a few days, Deirdre's delivery was imminent, and we simply wanted to keep moving. We decided to wait until late afternoon for the authorities to approach us, but if they didn't, Peter would try to arrange onward transport through the Katangese army or whatever city officials he could find.

Meanwhile, Mr. Raymond would inquire at the railway station about train schedules. "It will give me a chance to practice my rusty Portuguese," he chuckled.

Most of the Kasaji family wanted to rest that morning. However, having been rallied by a little breakfast, Walter and I were anxious to pursue our earlier investigations. "Let's go back and see if that really was the hospital," I suggested.

"May I come?" Glenys interjected. "I'd like to visit the hospital too!" We were delighted to have the female company.

All the way to our destination I recalled the boastings of Alexis the Great, Edouard, and the other military nurses: *In Angola we have so many drugs, so much penicillin! Fill out a requisition and we will send for them.*

You don't look after our soldiers well! We are taking them to Angola for better treatment!

Later on we will bring you more doctors from Angola because here you do not have enough.

Many of the Katangese claims were undoubtedly exaggerated but I expected the Texeira hospital to have reasonably good standards because of its proximity to the fighting.

The building itself was impressive. It was bigger than any of our wards and from the outside it looked much like some rural Canadian hospitals that I had visited. When the director invited us inside for a tour, however, I experienced some of the most heartrending moments of my life.

In the first room there were 12 wounded Katangese. One teenage rebel was lying on a bed which had no mattress, just a spring. Shot in the stomach the day before, he appeared to be almost lifeless, his abdomen rigid with peritonitis.

"Where's the doctor?" I asked the hospital director.

"We have no doctor," he replied. I was stricken.

"No doctor?" I cried.

"No. The nearest doctors are 200 miles away at Luena Hospital. We send the sick ones there as soon as there is transport. It may take a day or two.'' I couldn't believe what I was hearing. No doctors, no transport—this fellow was going to die!

I quickly rounded on the others. Some of the Katangese were critically ill and others had been carrying bullets and shrapnel in their bodies for days. A couple lay on the floor for lack of beds. All had received negligible treatment.

''Where's your operating theater?'' I asked, thinking we could do something. The director led us down the corridor.

''A sterilizer room, a scrub room, a separate anesthetic room, a theater—this has potential,'' Glenys said.

''What about scalpels and forceps and sutures?'' I asked.

''We have almost no instruments. Everything was taken during the war. There has been no surgery since the Portuguese left.''

''X-rays?''

''No.''

''And what about drugs? Penicillin?''

''Our supplies are very small,'' he answered defensively. ''After all we have had a crisis in Angola since the civil war. Our country is only now rebuilding.''

The rest of the tour revealed much the same conditions and I counted less than 20 other ward patients in the whole building. Alexis, Kabeya and others had lied to us. I left the hospital deeply grieved. The spectacle I had just witnessed shattered any lingering confidence I had in anything else the Katangese had said. I pitied the suffering soldiers inside who were receiving ''better treatment.'' I pitied the rebels whose minds were so distorted by ideology that they could fanatically spread deliberate lies. I pitied the poor Kasaji population whose well-equipped hospital had been ruined by men who had little to offer in return. Our walk home was slow and somber.

Back at Carlos's, however, there was something to lift the gloom. The Katangese had brought us two legs of beef and granted us a permit to buy bread. These little acts of kindness helped to restore a truer picture of the rebels. They were a mosaic of good and of evil, just like the rest of humanity.

''Here, David,'' Phyllis said, ''try some warm bread.''

''Did you know that Texeira has been without bread for months?'' Ruth marveled. ''Just a few days ago the bakers received some flour so that now, when we arrive, there is plenty to eat.''

''It makes me think of the Lord's Prayer,'' Phyllis said. '' 'Give us this day our daily bread.' '' And so in Texeira the Lord's daily provision continued.

Since the authorities had not appeared by late afternoon, Peter and I sought out the Katangese headquarters. We walked through the streets of Texeira passing groups of intermingling MPLA and FNLC troops. There was less an Angolan military presence in the town than we had expected and the Katangese seemed to be in control. However, neither army looked concerned about the ongoing war—very few soldiers carried weapons.

We finally found the FNLC command post but our visit produced no concrete results. The commandant was out and the information we received confirmed Mr. Raymond's report of trains every Tuesday and Saturday to Luena. Our sole consolation was that the Katangese gave us some macaroni which we enjoyed for supper along with beef, bread and, of course, tea.

A city official unexpectedly visited that night gathering information from each of us—name, date of birth, occupation, citizenship, passport number and other pertinent data. Then he disclosed the possibility of our leaving in the morning on the provincial commissar's special train. We were all excited.

"I'll telegram Luena first thing tomorrow for hotel accommodation," Mr . Raymond said. "We must be ready to go at any time."

This was our first night outside of Zaire and we reviewed the many goodnesses of the Lord since we left Kasaji. Overwhelmed by a sense of God's greatness and our unworthiness, we poured out our hearts in thanksgiving to Him. Our prayers continued for our scattered African brethren and for the missionaries who were still in the occupied zones of Shaba province.

An early bedtime came for all. The 38 of us used the single bathroom in shifts and then retired to our respective corners. Since the lounge had no available floor space, Walter and I moved to the dining room where we made beds out of rows of chairs.

"Well," I said, as we drifted off to sleep, "last night a carriage wagon and now Carlos's chairs!"

"I wonder what's next," Walter whispered.

Thursday, April 21, started off with the prospect of departure, but this hope was soon dashed. The provincial commissar's train didn't come and we would not leave before Saturday. At first disappointed, we once more acknowledged God's timing was best. Even from our own perspective there were advantages. Grannie and the children were not quite recuperated from our travel. Terry's month-old phlebitis had become worse and he too needed rest. Finally, Mr. Raymond hadn't been able to book hotel space as yet. We settled back to wait until Saturday.

That morning, Mr. Raymond, Walter and I went to the Mercado Municipal to buy some fresh fruit and vegetables. Although there was room for 32 farmers at the food stalls only two were there, and all they sold were a few tiny tangerines and a lettuce-like vegetable. Apparently, Texeira's market had been barren since the civil war.

"There are quite a few Christians in this area," Mr. Raymond remarked as we walked home. "Missionaries have been gone for years but there are many indigenous assemblies. I think I'll try to find some." And he did. He was able to visit with them at least a couple of times in the surrounding villages and brought back heartening news of the strength of the Christian church.

"Look at what a couple of elders gave me," Mr. Raymond said showing us a letter. "They've listed the names of 193 believers who are in the assembly. They say that there are 11 other similar-sized fellowships in the area and several smaller ones as well." We were thrilled to learn of the continued growth of the Angolan church despite the hardships of the civil war. Frederick Stanley Arnot would have been pleased to hear it too since this was the area he had pioneered almost 100 years before.

The local Christians were not content just to know that we were in Texeira de Sousa. They had to do something. Fresh produce was brought in from their farms—large tangerines, bananas and a whole sack of maize flour for porridge. They also insisted that we accept money to help us on our journey and they vowed to pray for our safe passage home. Out of their poverty and want flowed an abounding generosity.

Early Thursday evening after the oppressive daytime heat had relented, Walter and I went out for a stroll. "Let's visit the old UNITA head-quarters," I suggested.

Led by Dr. Savimbi, UNITA was one of three rival nationalist move-ments that struggled for control of Angola when the Portuguese relin-quished the reins of government. Allegedly supported by the U.S. and South Africa, UNITA had been beaten back by the MPLA and Cuban military might, although vast areas of the country remained under its influence. In Texeira de Sousa, however, its presence had not been felt for several years.

The devastated headquarters lay on the edge of town beside the military airport. At its entrance stood a rusty sign which announced that a certain company of UNITA's troops were stationed there. We slipped past an observation booth into the camp. The dozen or more buildings were all badly pockmarked. Three long slender barracks were without roofs and appeared choked by the tall weeds that clutched up their walls.

I was especially attracted to a slogan painted on the inside of one building. "Look, Walter: *'Dr. Savimbi, Symbolo Da Paz, Patria Ou Morte, Unidos Venceremos.'* "

"I don't know any Portuguese," he replied, "but I think it translates, 'Dr. Savimbi, symbol of peace, country or death, united we shall con-quer.' "

"Sounds familiar, doesn't it? Except for the leader's name, the slogans could belong to any liberation movement."

We waded in single file through the chest-high grass to inspect one of the four abandoned army trucks in the camp.

Suddenly Walter called ahead to me, "Tell me if you step on any mines.'' The possibility hadn't occurred to us until this point, but we deemed it prudent to retreat to safer soil leaving the desolate UNITA headquarters to the continued ravagings of time and the elements.

Our numbers swelled to 48 that night with the arrival of eight Roman Catholic nuns and two priests. They were from Mutshatsha and Dilolo and had actually stayed at their Dilolo mission for several days until a train finally carried them across the border. How thankful we were for Mutu's dressine! It had saved us from a 48-hour vigil in the railway station or at the abandoned Jones's house. Instead we had lived in Texeira in relative comfort and ease.

Since the house was already bulging, Carlos opened up the family store that was connected to Deirdre's bedroom. We helped our fellow refugees lug their crates and trunks into their new quarters and invited them back for tea.

The nursing sisters from Mutshatsha described fierce aerial attacks: ''Sometimes the planes came two or three times a day,'' one Italian nun said. ''They flew low and strafed the town. Finally we had to go into the bush with the patients during the daytime and then return in the evening.''

''Look over here!'' said another nun, ''This is where a bullet came in and this is where it went out.'' She pointed to holes in the front and back of her blouse. We all looked aghast. ''But I wasn't inside,'' she chuckled.

''What happened to the mines' doctor and the FAZ doctor who worked at the hospital?'' I asked.

''On the night before the train brought us to Dilolo, they fled towards Zambia with a couple of guides.''

''Did they make it?''

''No. We heard that the rebels caught them near the border.''

''And?''

They hesitated for a moment. ''Some say they shot them.'' Although it was only a rumor, it was solemnizing anyway. Some of the Katangese were fully capable of doing it.

The priest from Dilolo changed the subject. ''Do you have any information about transportation to Luena?'' he asked.

''We've contacted the authorities here,'' Mr. Raymond explained. ''There's a train to Luena on Saturday at fairly reasonable rates. We don't have any confirmation yet, but we hope to go on that. If you like, I'll try to make arrangements for you when I meet the officials tomorrow.''

The next morning we noticed that our Roman Catholic friends were not the only arrivals from Dilolo. Parked in Carlos's driveway were a couple of trucks, a tractor and several private cars, all bearing Zairian license plates. At least three of the cars were virtually brand new. One was a shiny Renault 17 fastback with numerous accessories, including a four-speaker, Pioneer stereo cassette system. The Dilolo merchants were preserving their assets.

Once more we saw that Katangese socialism patronized the privileged few.

A terrific downpour hit Texeira on Friday, our first rain in more than a week. This was no small storm. Visibility was cut to 20 yards, and brimming rivulets raced across the streets.

"Ruth," I said, "there's one thing that I've missed since leaving Kasaji and I think that it's about time I had one."

"What's that?" she asked with a quizzical look.

"A shower."

"Out in the rain?"

"No. At the end of the eavestrough."

It was a little too unconventional for the Kasaji folk, but most of them watched Walter and me with envy. No one had been able to have a proper bath since we left Katoka, and that for an Englishman was a tragedy. Finally, a couple of the men broke down and went to change, but alas, the rain was turned off and so was the shower.

That day we received more news about the war. Radio reports indicated that Mobutu had surrounded Mutshatsha and a rebel officer told us of repeated aerial bombardment at Kasaji.

Carlos had news of his own. "Three nights ago anti-aircraft guns were taken across. It's a good thing you got out. This war will go on for a long time." He paused momentarily then said, "It is not even safe in Texeira. Last year Mobutu's planes dropped bombs on our town—just like that!" he exclaimed snapping his fingers. "Maybe he will come again."

We were happy when night had fallen. We were even happier when a Katangese commandant arrived and confirmed our places on the morning train. When he told us that the FNLC would pay our fares, we were staggered. We thanked him and busily packed our luggage. Our food for the trip would include tinned meat, extra bread from the bakery, fruit and maize flour from the African Christians, and more beef from the Katangese army. We cleaned up Carlos's house as much as possible then assembled for prayer.

What a joyful time! The Lord had very specifically answered our requests for food and onward transportation. We praised Him for the incredible list of blessings that were ours and remembered the words of Scripture: "His compassion never ends. It is only the Lord's mercies that have kept us from complete destruction. Great is his faithfulness; his lovingkindness begins afresh each day" (Lam. 3:22,23, *TLB*).

We still had one small problem—no accommodation in Luena. The Catholics had wired ahead to their mission and expected to stay there but the answer to Mr. Raymond's telegram was that there was nothing available for us. We committed this very obvious need to the Lord and then retired for the night.

At 4:30 A.M. we awoke. Confusion reigned until six o'clock when

Carlos started to ferry us to the railway station. We weren't the only ones going to Luena; hundreds of Africans jammed the platform in eager anticipation of the journey.

"Carlos," Mr. Raymond said, "we cannot express how thankful we are for all you've done. To give up your home, your time and your vehicle—it was something we'll never forget. We are very, very grateful, We will pray for you, Carlos."

"It was good for me also to live with you missionaries. Maybe I will visit you one day in your country." We watched him drive off. Carlos was such a likable man in such an unlikely place, but he was a white child of Africa and there he would stay.

We brought our luggage into a steel cage in a special compartment which was under the surveillance of two armed guards.

"Why all the precautions?" I whispered.

"Theft," Walter replied. "You'll lose the shirt off your back if you're not careful."

We returned to our coach to find that many of the local Christians had come to say good-bye. Some had walked several miles to be there before our 7 A.M. departure and we thanked them for all their kindnesses.

"Let's get Mother up," Terry said.

"Careful now," Grannie directed as we hoisted her into the train. "That's better. Now put the chair over there on this back platform. I want to watch Africa go by."

The whistle blew and the train lurched forward down the tracks. Zambian, Zairian and Rhodesian freight cars were lined up on the sidings, stranded there for years due to Angolan-Zairian tensions. Finally we pulled away from the station and rolled onwards into the open countryside.

Our seating was in a third class carriage. Four rows of wooden seats ran longitudinally providing ample space for the nuns, priests and us. Compared to the rest of the travelers, we were very comfortable. Everywhere else it was standing room only and many were crammed into open goods wagons. The Katangese had taken good care of us.

Our children were having the time of their lives. When they became tired gazing at the passing scenery, they played on their own. When they became tired playing on their own, they had many uncles and aunts to entertain them. When they finished with us, they visited the nuns and then went back to the scenery. And so the miles and minutes raced by.

Grannie sat in her wheel chair outside on the platform. She shared the gospel with the many Africans who gawked at her from the next coach. She played Scrabble with any challengers and wistfully watched Africa go by.

"This is the land through which Arnot traveled," she said. We were now journeying through a stretch of country with few trees, fewer people and even fewer sources of food. "Arnot and his carriers nearly died of starvation here on his first expedition into Central Africa. But he made it, and over the years all those mission stations were founded.''

''I've been thinking about Arnot too,'' I replied. ''We're retracing his steps. He came in this way in order to establish a belt of Christian testimony across Central Africa and we're leaving the same way with that testimony already established. Look at Texeira. The assemblies are thriving without the missionaries. Perhaps the Lord is taking us away for a time to show us that He upholds His church and not us. After a building is erected, the scaffolding disappears.''

''That's possible, but I do hope that some of you return,'' she replied from a heart that ached.

The Zaire frontier became more and more distant. We exchanged food with the nuns and priests, and we traded war stories. We watched the fishing villages in the marshland come and go. We chatted with the MPLA soldier who guarded our coach. We sang hymns and read Scriptures. Some held the children, others slept, a few played Scrabble. A couple expressed their deep sorrow at leaving their adopted country behind.

''It's true I can't wait to get to New Zealand, but I'll tell you one thing,'' Harold sighed, ''I'll really miss Africa!''

When I asked Brian how his diary was faring he replied, ''I had to give mine up. I've been too sad to write anything.''

We traveled on—six, eight, ten hours and finally our destination was close at hand. There were many unknowns lurking ahead. How would the government react to 33 white refugees from war-torn Zaire arriving unannounced in the heart of Angola? Would their political embarrassment influence how they treated us? Would we be interrogated and what would they do to my extensive diary and 30 precious rolls of film?

There was one other small problem. Where would we sleep in a few hours time?

It was 6 P.M. when we touched the outskirts of Luena. Soon we could see the railway yards.

The locomotive slowed down.

We entered the station.

The train stopped.

21
Confined to a Palace

"Let's get the luggage!" Peter exclaimed. Walter and I dashed after him leaving the others behind.

Mobs of travelers scrambled noisily off the coaches and fought their way towards the single exit. Suddenly, two gunshots rang out. The pandemonium settled quickly and the people conducted their exodus in more orderly fashion. The Angolans had an effective and certainly unique method of crowd control.

We unloaded the carriage and stood guard over our belongings while soldiers and civilians gathered round quizzing us in Portuguese and Chokwe. Meanwhile, an Angolan railway agent spotted our party and rushed over to investigate. At the same time a Catholic priest appeared with a few white men and then some government officials arrived demanding further explanations of our presence. The situation was chaotic.

The authorities hadn't been warned of our coming and didn't really know what to do. Finally they told us to wait until the station had emptied. Only then would they deal with our case.

It took more than two hours for the station to clear. We entertained the tired children, walked the platform and rested on our baggage, all the while wondering what would happen next.

"There are no hotels, hostels or lodging of any sort available," Mr. Raymond quietly disclosed. "They'll have to find a place for us or I guess we camp out at the station." That wouldn't be the first time, yet it was a dismal prospect, especially for Grannie and the families. We prayed on.

After the civilians had been processed through the departure area, about 300 MPLA militia men filed past the gate. Their clothes were ragged and they bore guns of all shapes and sizes. When one poor chap spilled his sack of tangerines, several officers pushed him on while they picked up and ate the fruit.

Now it was our turn. "Get your bags and stand in front of me," a young Angolan official hollered. We piled everything near the exit while he and an associate scrutinized and retained our passports. We didn't like surrendering our documents but we had no choice.

The children had become increasingly irritable and Grannie was noticeably fatigued. As yet we had no idea where the authorities would take us, but soon they would have to say something. We slowly moved up the line.

The two security agents poured over Anne's papers, then the McKenzie's. Each page, each entry was studied by the zealous young men. Harold's passport was in Lubumbashi and he fully expected problems with the cancelled one he presented them.

"Very good," they said. "Next."

I handed them my Canadian passport. They read the bilingual preamble although neither of them spoke English nor more than a few words of French. They grunted at Kenya's stamp and glanced at each other when they saw Zambia. Just as I was ready to go, one of them snatched Mr. Raymond's army-like hat off my head. He looked at it, eyed me, and then handed it back.

In the foyer, our luggage was examined. The security agent assigned to me barely ruffled my belongings and didn't even open my bag of films. Others' cases were meticulously searched and one soldier curiously fingered through our emergency medical kit, but eventually we all cleared inspection.

The Catholic priest approached Mr. Raymond. "Do you have any accommodation?" he asked.

"No. Not yet."

"Would you like to stay at our mission? You'll have to sleep on the floor, but there is plenty of room," he explained.

"You are very kind and yes, we will come," Mr. Raymond replied gratefully.

"Good. The vehicles are outside waiting for us." What a wonderful way everything had worked out! If we had caught the provincial commissar's train on Thursday, we would have arrived without lodging. The Lord had delayed us in Texeira de Sousa so that our Catholic friends could catch up with us and bring us to their residence.

While we were gathering our baggage, the Angolan soldier who had rummaged through our medical supplies slipped over to me and whispered, "Give me two or three of your vials of morphine."

I was startled. "No," I replied.

"Please, just two or three."

"Of course not," I answered in a louder voice.

"Just one."

"Never. If you are sick, go to the hospital."

He turned from me to Peter who likewise refused his request. However, the soldier continued to hound us. He followed at our heels while we ferried the luggage to the vehicles, and even while the engines were revving up to leave, he badgered us. Finally, our jeep roared off leaving him there arguing to the wind. The whole incident had surprised me. Narcotic abuse was prevalent even in this corner of society.

It was 9:30 P.M. The motorcade whisked through street after empty street in the dimly-lit city. Even in the darkness we could tell that many neighborhoods were empty and many large buildings little more than rubble. After a 10-minute drive we turned onto a broad boulevard which was well-illuminated by bright street lamps. Alongside the avenue ran a promenade with flowers and trees, and there at the end of the block stood an imposing two-storied structure bathed in floodlights. This was no ordinary mission house. This was the Catholic bishop's palace!

The vehicles filed through swinging iron gates into the semicircular driveway and slowed to a stop. Awed by the building's grandeur and feeling somewhat guilty at our good fortune, we trailed the priest through double doors into a large beautiful foyer. Minutes later we had carried Grannie and all the luggage up two flights of stairs to our new quarters, the *Sala de Reunioes*, or conference room.

This great hall had a wood-tiled floor, long tables, padded chairs and large curtained windows which looked out over a balcony to the promenade. The conference room, a library, a wing of bedrooms and the top of a chapel towered above a square courtyard with its pool, shrubs and papaya trees. Surrounding the whole residence were gardens, lawns and walkways. What a majestic setting for our new home!

This magnificent structure, however, had not escaped the fury of the Angolan civil war as hundreds of bullet holes grimly testified. Damage had been even more extensive, and after lengthy repairs, the restored palace had been blessed the previous week for the use of a new black bishop. The only occupants were a Catholic priest and the bishop who was away on business. Just two days before we arrived, all the nuns had evacuated because conditions in Luena had prevented them from doing their work to their satisfaction. Their departure, however, had made it possible for us to move in!

The priest came by after we had unpacked. "We can give you a bedroom for two," he offered.

"That's very kind of you," Mr. Raymond replied. "Thank you so much."

"I have some other information," the priest continued. "The lights will go off any minute as we use them only from dusk to 10 P.M. As for bathrooms, there is one downstairs beside the offices and another in the bedroom. We have running water every day at 6 A.M. for 30 minutes. That's when we fill up our bathtubs so that we have enough water for the rest of the day. If you have any problems let me know. Good night.''

"Thank you again," Mr. Raymond said. "Good night."

After prayer, a wash and a bread roll we retired to our quarters. Wonderfully, for Grannie and Deirdre it was again a bedroom. For most of the others it was the *Sala de Reunioes,* and for the Fishers, Walter and me it was the second-floor landing. There we arranged the padded chairs Texeira-style while Walter commented solemnly, "First a carriage, then Carlos's house, now a Catholic palace—each refuge more luxurious than the last. I can't imagine what the Lord is preparing next."

He was so right. The God who had preserved us through death threats and bombardment was now putting food in our mouths and a roof over our heads. His sufficiency was operative in matters big and small, in the spectacular and in the ordinary. Moreover, not content to let us merely wander out, the Lord was leading us forth with a high hand to show us His power. For this reason there was no basis for guilt at our present situation, rather thanksgiving and praise. It was He who had provided for us and it was He who would provide for our African brethren—not in dressines and palaces, but in ways most appropriate to their needs.

At dawn the next day, I read the following confirming promise: "The Lord also will be a refuge for the oppressed, a refuge in times of trouble" (Ps. 9:9).

Texeira bread, Texeira corn flour porridge and tea comprised Sunday breakfast, and over it we discussed our plans. "Our passports are in the government's hands," Mr. Raymond reminded us, "so we cannot move until they're returned."

"However, we can still make inquiries about onward transport," Peter said.

"It will have to be by plane," Terry interjected. "The trains stop here because UNITA has paralyzed the railway beyond Luena."

"Well, let's check into air schedules and fares," Mr. Raymond concluded. "I'm sure the authorities will show up sometime with our papers."

That morning our whole situation threatened to change. There had been a difference of opinion amongst the nuns and priests over the wisdom of our remaining in the palace. Since some felt that our presence would be an embarrassment to the black bishop on his return, they escorted Mr. Raymond and the Coates to an abandoned school dormitory about one mile away where they suggested we stay.

While they were gone, the authorities arrived—a different group of men than had interrogated us at the railway station. They were quite angry with the Catholic friar for not notifying them that 33 white refugees had come during the night. The poor priest was the innocent victim of the lack of communication between Angolan officials.

To make matters worse, the two nuns, Mr. Raymond and the Coates trooped in at this juncture. Immediately we were all placed under house arrest and two armed guards were posted at the front of the bishop's palace. We could neither leave nor communicate with the outside world until further notice.

This certainly solved our problem of moving to what the others considered very undesirable quarters. It also unburdened our Catholic friends from the responsibility of our presence at their residence. All in all, it was an answer to our immediate needs, and the obstacle it did present—that of being under house arrest—was simply another opportunity to trust.

The authorities had told us that they would return for a full interrogation at 2:30 P.M., but when no one had appeared by 4:30 P.M., we began our regular Sunday afternoon Bible study. Fifteen minutes later, they arrived.

"Everyone must come to the lounge," they ordered.

"Even the children and their mothers?" Mr. Raymond asked.

"Everyone!"

"We have one elderly lady who cannot walk the stairs," Mr. Raymond interceded. "Could she please stay in her room?"

"No," was the stern reply. "Everyone must come."

Four of us carefully carried Grannie in her chair down the staircase. She didn't fancy the little journey with its hazards but she certainly did look forward to the action. When we wheeled her into the lounge she smiled and waved at the two army-uniformed officials. They were completely disarmed. Grannie's presence was always a formidable advantage.

Using very broken French, the spokesman told us not to worry, then proceeded to ask how many of us were from the respective missions at Dilolo, Kasaji and Mutshatsha. After ascertaining the approximate geographical relations between the three towns, he dismissed us except for representatives from each station.

"Is that all?" Grannie muttered as we hauled her back up to the second floor. To her and to us the five minutes hadn't seemed worth the effort. We would have to bide our time until Mr. Raymond returned from the interview with some news.

Half an hour later he came back upstairs. We could tell by the look on his face that our questions had not been answered.

"Did they give you back the passports?" Colin asked.

"No, Colin, they didn't even have them. They're not the authorities—they're news reporters." We all groaned.

"So what did they ask you?" Brian inquired.

"My name, my job and my country," he stated. "Then they quizzed me about the war: when did the Katangese come, how many, how were they received, did they recruit, what was the name of the Zairian commandant, and on and on it went." The story didn't seem to fit. How could they have been so ignorant about the whole war? As for Katangese recruits, we had already seen them jogging and chanting along the road past the palace. Surely the Angolans were aware of the Katangese presence! Thus, instead of offering hope of an early release, this visit had brought even more confusion.

Monday marked one week since we had evacuated Kasaji. Although we were in good spirits, we were concerned about some of the medical problems. Terry's phlebitis hadn't improved and Robbie was gripped with abdominal pain. Deirdre's delivery was uncomfortably imminent and Grannie was "out of sorts." Norma had a violent gastroenteritis and Colin was suffering from a severely infected finger reminiscent of my own Napoleonic thumb. However, under the circumstances we could be thankful that our ailments were so few.

Our food had lasted but would have been gone without the gifts we had received. Even then we had enough for only two more days and that was stretching it. It became a real matter for prayer, especially since there was no food to be bought in Luena. There had been no meat in the city for two years and no bread for two months. Where hundreds of shops had catered to every need, only two or three were left in the wake of the civil war and the Portuguese exodus. Nine thousand of Luena's 10 thousand Europeans had fled the country and the much larger urban African population had been reduced in similar proportion. Thirty-three battles had waged back and forth through the provincial capital, the last one raging for seven days just over a year previously. This was not the land of milk and honey that the Katangese had deceivingly portrayed for us. It was a country struggling to rebuild from the ruins of a brutal war.

The armed guards had been removed, but on Monday morning more Angolan officials appeared. Once more we were called to the lounge and once more there was no news of departure. Instead, when it was time to go I received a terrible shock.

"Now you can all leave," the official said, "except Camarades Raymond and John David." I cringed. They were obviously referring to me. "Camarade John David first." The others filed out of the room.

"Take this chair closer to us," they motioned. Three sat on the couch and a fourth paced around the room chain-smoking.

"What is your name?" the spokesman muttered. I strained to understand his fractured French.

"David John Dawson."

"Where were you born?"

"Montreal, Canada."

After several more basic questions he said, "I notice that you are a student."

"I was a medical student four years ago when my passport was issued, but six months later I graduated as a physician." He repeated the story to the other three who obviously spoke less French than he.

"I have a few other things to ask," he said, "How many Zairian soldiers fought in the battle at Kasaji?"

"I really don't know. I never saw them all because we stayed at the station."

"How many do you think there were?"

"Any answer would be a guess. I really don't know."

"Make a guess."

"One thousand, two thousand, three, four thousand. I don't know." He didn't like my answer, but all I could say was the truth.

"What did Radio Kinshasa report during the war?" he asked.

"I don't know."

"Didn't you listen to Radio Kinshasa?"

"No."

"Why not?" he contested angrily.

"I never wanted to. I listened to Radio Canada, BBC and others." I dared not mention Voice of America.

"Don't you think you should have listened to Radio Kinshasa?"

"Frankly, I was satisfied with the other stations." He didn't like my answer, but all I could say was the truth.

"What other soldiers did you see fighting for the FAZ?" he began again.

"I only saw Zairian soldiers with the Zairians."

"Were there no others?"

"I didn't see any others."

He grew angrier. "I thought you listened to the radio. You know that Moroccans were fighting with the FAZ," he challenged.

"That's what the radio says. You asked me what I saw. I only saw Zairians."

"And no Moroccans?" he growled.

"No Moroccans."

"If the radio says they were there, why didn't you see them?" he lashed back.

"Because they were at the front lines and we were 120 miles behind the lines at that stage."

"So you admit that they were at the front lines."

"That's what the radio says. I myself didn't see any." He continued his interrogation trying to extract from me firsthand testimony of foreign involvement in Zaire's armed forces. Since I had none to give, I was not going to compromise. The minutes ticked by and still the questions tumbled out. Ten minutes, 20 minutes, half an hour. The smoker continued to pace. The others looked on. The challenges, the insinuations, the jabs continued relentlessly and I realized how easy it would be to satisfy him with a few vague admissions. However, I thought back to that morning and the psalm I had read:

"Lord, who shall abide in thy tabernacle? . . . He that walketh uprightly, and worketh righteousness, and speaketh the truth in his heart" (Ps. 15:1,2). There was no way I could do anything but speak the truth that was in my heart.

Forty minutes, 50 minutes passed. "How long did the planes bomb you?"

"Four to five minutes and they were gone."

"What was the damage?"

"Not much. A few big holes were made but no strategic targets were hit." He seemed to like that answer.

"Who flew the planes?"

I couldn't believe my ears, "I'm sorry. What did you say?"

"Who flew the planes?"

"How could anyone possibly see the pilots?" I asked. "Besides I never stopped to look—I ran for the nearest cover."

"Are you sure that you don't know?" he pressed.

"Of course I'm sure."

"Then who do you think were flying the planes?"

"I'm sorry. I can only tell you what I saw."

"Do you think the Zairians are capable of flying those planes?" he asked scornfully.

"I'm sorry. I can't help you."

They turned to consult each other in Portuguese. The whole interrogation had lasted an hour and I hadn't enjoyed it at all. Nor was I prepared for what they told me next.

"Camarade David, we want you to get Camarade Walter, the young Raymond. But first we have some suggestions. Your answers have not been satisfactory. We want you to think a little harder for a few hours. Try to come up with some good answers. We will come back for you at three o'clock this afternoon."

22
"Then the Earth Shook!"

I staggered out of the lounge. Finding Walter, I quickly briefed him then sent him along with a prayer. Forty-five minutes later he emerged after undergoing similar grueling treatment. His answers had also been inadequate and they were coming back for him, too. When Mr. Raymond heard this, he strode to the front door and called to the security men.

"None of us can tell you what we haven't seen," he said.

"We'll be back at three o'clock," they replied coldly.

Why had they chosen us out for such harassment? Perhaps it was because both our passports listed us as students. Perhaps it was because we were both single and they wondered whether or not we were real missionaries. In any case, this was a time for prayer. How often we had come to the Lord for situations just as ominous! How often He had led us out of each dilemma! We desperately needed a display of His power that afternoon.

At 2 P.M. there was a racket at the front door. Several soldiers had stormed in demanding to see all the men. The priests joined us in the lounge while yet another group of Angolan army men interrogated us. After a barrage of questions, they were satisfied that we were missionaries and they left as speedily as they had come.

Three o'clock came but the security agents hadn't. Time dragged on. I read a bit. Fifteen past three. I played with Timmy and David. Three-thirty. Still no sign of them. I sat on the back balcony. Quarter to four. Rosary in hand, the Spanish nun came by. "I'm praying for you," she said.

"Thank you," I replied. "Thank you very much."

Four o'clock. They hadn't come—and they wouldn't. Whether Mr. Raymond's parting words had touched them, whether they had already rattled their sabers sufficiently or whether some other business had intervened, the Lord had kept them away and we thanked Him from grateful hearts.

After supper we again chatted with the nuns and priests. We talked about our mission stations and our work. We discussed the events of the day. We shared morsels of information that we had gleaned. The Italian nun related that they had heard about a plane leaving on the morrow. This would be an unscheduled run because generally there were only two nonmilitary flights a week, and those were on Wednesday and Saturday. Perhaps tomorrow's would be ours!

That evening the radio news brought us back to Kasaji: "President Mobutu is on the front lines tonight. He claims that his troops, including a company of Pygmy fighters armed with poisoned arrows, have found Mutshatsha abandoned and neighboring villages razed by the retreating Katangese. The Zaire army, led by crack Moroccan commandos, are now headed for Kasaji, the next largest town on the way to the Angolan frontier. Meanwhile, British government sources state that Brethren missionaries at Kasaji have not been heard of since early March when the conflict began."

Several moments of silence were broken by Peter. "Well, that just proves that none of the messages we sent through the Katangese ever made it."

"I just hope we can send word home before the FAZ find Kasaji abandoned." Brian sighed. "Poor Deirdre's family!"

"And mine!" exclaimed Sue. And all of ours. If only they could know! But they couldn't. We were under house arrest and even if we could leave the palace, there weren't any ways open for us to dispatch messages. We and they would have to wait.

Tuesday came and our house arrest was still in effect. The families had slept better due to the kind gift of four mattresses by the nuns. Everybody was expectant—perhaps a plane would take us today.

But it didn't. Neither did two others we watched climb away from Luena that morning. Nor did we hear any news whatsoever from the authorities. One uplifting consolation, however, was that I received permission to use the small chapel organ. At first I played the hymns that I had heard the nuns sing, and then I was carried into a myriad of other psalms and melodies that expressed the feelings of my heart. Music was ever a wonderful gift from God.

Wednesday, April 27. The situation was deteriorating. We had not spoken to Angolan officials for two days. The children were becoming increasingly hard to manage. The palace had run out of gas for its stove, forcing us to cook everything over a wood fire. Food was precariously low. Our Texeira bread was gone and almost all of our tinned meat and fruit had been eaten. The last of the corn flour porridge would be used up in one more sitting. The nuns had kindly given us macaroni when our rice was finished, and on his own the palace cook had compassionately handed us some meat. Since there was nothing to be bought in Luena, we ate macaroni twice a day with soup mix or beans or a piece of meat. We certainly weren't starving but things couldn't go on like that, especially for the children. Actually, the ladies were keeping it quiet—all our food would be gone the next morning.

At dawn I was reading in the Psalms. David was a fugitive and round about him were treacherous men. In his overwhelming distress, he called upon the Lord who heard him "out of his temple . . . Then the earth shook and trembled; the foundations also of the hills moved and were shaken, because he was wroth. . . . He sent from above, he took me, he drew me out of many waters. . . . He brought me forth also into a large place" (Ps. 18:6,7,16,19). I wondered if this would be the day for the Lord to shake the earth.

That morning Mr. Raymond and Peter decided to break house arrest. They would try to make it directly to the provincial commissar and explain the situation for all 33 of us. When they left, the rest of us met for prayer and I shared the passage I had read earlier. Grannie glowed the whole way through.

"Why did you choose Psalm 18?" she asked after I had finished.

"I came across it today in my regular reading," I explained.

"How marvelous!" she declared. "I read the same psalm about the earth being shaken just an hour ago, and I even discussed it with Walter."

We went to prayer with real expectation that the Lord would speak, and there we lingered until Mr. Raymond and Peter returned. They slipped quietly in amongst us and when we had finished, Mr. Raymond said, "We have no news about a flight yet, but our passports are ready and this afternoon we will hear about tickets."

"Also, house arrest is officially over," Peter added. No earthquake had struck but we could feel a few premonitory tremors.

Walter and I decided to walk around Luena. Leaving the palace, we turned south and soon arrived at the Cuban military headquarters. Despite all the news reports, none of us had seen any Cubans at Kasaji or Dilolo or any other place in Shaba province. However, their presence here in the heart of Angola was not a secret. We passed by a manned sentry booth in front of the headquarters.

"*Bon dia,*" we called out to the Cuban guard.

A sullen soldier with a battle helmet squashed over his ears and a machine gun in his hands glared at us and gruffly muttered something incomprehensible. We made an abrupt right-angled turn and strode off.

"He didn't look too happy, did he?" Walter commented.

"Not in the least." We proceeded west along a pretty side street. Along the whole length of it we were surprised to find no severe war damage. Yes, slogans and propaganda posters adorned the vacant walls and there had been a moderate peppering of all the villas, but so far it was not as bad as we had anticipated.

Every fourth person we passed was a soldier and when we arrived at a crossroads in the commercial section of Luena, several hundred militia marched by. ''They look like the troops we saw at the station,'' I said.

We crossed the boulevard and Walter pointed to a shop that seemed to be open. ''Let's go in.''

About 20 women in each of two queues were showing pink tickets to the Portuguese men behind the counter. The commodities they purchased were cooking oil and soap—there was nothing else for sale. Five or six sacks of meal lay on the floor but apparently none were being distributed. A couple of hundred shopping carts on the second floor represented a sad, yet constant reminder of better days.

As we left the store, we heard a loud, *''Docteur, Docteur,''* and saw four Katangese soldiers running towards us across the street: one was Roberto, the military nurse; the second was the infamous Hernia Man clutching a bag of tangerines; and the other two were vaguely familiar. All of them greeted us like long lost comrades and then proceeded to give us their version of the war.

''At Kapanga we have captured 30 Moroccans alive and 14 armored cars,'' Roberto announced.

''And since you left, there has been no more bombing of Kasaji,'' the Hernia Man declared. Eyewitnesses had told us quite the opposite.

A third said, ''Now our forces are in Mutshatsha.'' That was also a lie.

''How long have you been in Luena?'' I asked them.

''Just since the train came yesterday,'' Roberto replied.

''But we're going back as soon as we can,'' the Hernia Man interrupted. He pointed to his bag of tangerines. ''That's all we could buy. There's no food here,'' he mourned. We said good-bye and they wished us luck on our journey.

''Imagine that,'' Walter said as we walked off. ''They themselves say there's no food here.''

''And after all their boasting about the conditions on the other side,'' I replied.

We continued westward, soon discovering a sprawling hospital. Outside we met five more Katangese guerillas who told us that many comrades had been treated there recently but most had been discharged.

''Do you think the Angolans would let us in, Walter?'' I wondered.

''We can always try.''

We climbed the stairs and walked through the main entrance. A clerk greeted us, and as we introduced ourselves, a familiar face appeared in the corridor—Safi was here! I was overjoyed to see her. She had come to Angola at a commandant's insistence arriving in Luena just the previous night. She showed me her beautiful baby and I was delighted to find out that the thigh wound was almost healed.

We met others at the hospital: the psychotic college student, a wounded Katangese officer who claimed that he had been living at the Coates's house while Mufu was living in the girls' house, and a pleasant Cuban doctor who briefly showed us around. We saw a large ward for Angolan soldiers, many of whom were amputees. Several other Katangese stopped us, including one injured captain who insisted that I remain in Angola as the doctor for the rebel army. I shuddered.

"I already have a job back in Canada," I replied. "I'm leaving as soon as I can."

"No, you're not," he retorted. "You'll be staying here." I hoped he was bluffing but I didn't linger to discuss the issue. I left the hospital with that fearful prospect hanging over my head and I prayed that our air tickets would be secured as soon as possible.

We retraced our steps to the business section of the city. Here the havoc of war was more evident. Row upon row of emptied bullet-riddled shops lined the boulevard and glass still littered the sidewalks where it had fallen. A couple of buildings had received more than their share of punishment and were reduced to mounds of rubble.

"Look over there!" Walter exclaimed, pointing across the street. It was the Luena Hotel. The four-storied structure lay stark and abandoned, not a window unsmashed. Everything had been stripped from the premises and the purple-tiled outdoor swimming pool was full of rain water, glass and drifted garbage.

"No wonder there was no accommodation," Walter muttered gravely.

We were soon approaching the bishop's palace. Since my unfortunate encounter with the Katangese captain, I had been wondering more than ever how Mr. Raymond and Peter had fared with the provincial commissar. How much longer would it be before we could leave Luena behind?

"It's only tentative," Peter cautioned, "but we'll probably receive tickets late in the afternoon for tomorrow's flight. If we go, we must be at the airport by nine o'clock." The earth tremors were becoming more marked.

Mr. Raymond and Peter returned downtown to the travel office where the officials were slowly getting around to our business. Peter parked himself on a chair by the ticket agent's desk and waited.

"You don't have to stay here," the official said to Peter. "Come back at 5 P.M. and we'll give you the tickets."

"Thank you very much, but I have nothing else to do," he replied. "I'll just sit here and help you if you have any questions." Peter was not budging; he wanted to keep vigil until everything was delivered.

At four o'clock Mr. Raymond reappeared at the palace. We had been cleaning the premises and washing and packing in anticipation of the morrow. His return without the tickets bothered us but he said, "Don't worry. Peter is hovering over the official's desk. If it's possible to be done by 5 P.M., it'll be done.''

A few of us accompanied Mr. Raymond back to the airline office.

''It's good I stayed,'' Peter breathed quietly. ''It was a lot more work than they thought and they've had questions on almost every ticket. I still don't know if they'll finish on time.''

We left him there, and with Mr. Raymond's instructions found one of our assemblies just around the corner. It was a beautiful little building and a couple of Christians happened by while we stood outside. To meet them was a thrill. They spoke about many missionaries who used to be in these areas, especially the Clifford Beggs who had worked at this chapel for years. Then they ushered us into the attractive balconied hall which had been restored since the war. Here the 130 in fellowship worshiped, and we very much wished we could have joined them the previous Sunday.

Saying good-bye, we returned to the travel office just as the business was being concluded. Peter was exultant.''We have all 33 tickets,'' he beamed clasping the precious bundle in his hand, ''and what's more, they've cost us nothing! The Angolan government has paid for our trip!''

Then the earth shook and trembled!

At 4 A.M., April 28, Harold was building a fire. By 5:30 A.M. the last of our corn flour porridge was being prepared and an hour later we were waiting outside with our baggage. A lorry and a Volvo appeared shortly, and after deep expression of thanks, we left the bishop's palace.

Our arrival at the terminal, however, preceded that of any of the officials, and thus we had time to stroll around. We soon found out by the number of Cubans present that the air base was a heavily restricted military zone. To our surprise a large field gun was swiftly towed across the tarmac before our eyes. A military helicopter landed but what intrigued us most was a 15-foot high mound that ran alongside the runway.

At eight o'clock the officials showed up. Our passports were returned, our tickets were checked and our seats were allocated. Now all we needed was an airplane. Eventually it came but once again all of our luggage was searched. At last we crossed the landing area and clambered aboard, leaving Luena and the Katangese captain behind.

The anti-aircraft guns on the other side of the mound reminded us of the conflict in Zaire and the guerilla warfare still waging in Angola. We lifted past the weapons into the air heading for the capital city. Once more we had no accommodation booked, and now we had no more food. We didn't know if the interrogations would intensify or if we would finally be whisked home. What we did remember, however, were the other words in that Psalm 18: ''He sent from above, he took me; he drew me out of many waters . . . . He brought me also into a large place.''

Luanda was two hours off. The grand climax drew near.

23
"Great Is Thy Faithfulness"

The jet whistled down the Luanda runway and taxied to a stop in the debarkation zone. When all the other passengers had vacated the aircraft, we carried Grannie down the gangway to the waiting bus. She had fared poorly on the flight, requiring oxygen for chest discomfort and palpitations, but now she was feeling better. The midday swelter of this coastal city, however, would not improve the situation. Waves of furnace-like heat swept over us as we pulled up at the terminal. We hoped for speedy dealings with the authorities.

After picking up our luggage we stationed ourselves in the corner of the main airport foyer. From here some went off in search of food while a few looked for the ticket office to book the earliest onward transport. I set off to find a Luanda telephone directory and call anything Canadian. Perhaps I'd be able to send a message home.

My hopes were soon dashed. Neither Canada, nor any of our countries maintained embassies or commercial representatives in Angola. Most had evacuated the country during the civil war.

News from the ticket office was far from encouraging. "The earliest flight is to Lisbon 12 hours from now," Mr. Raymond said, "but there are only a few seats left."

"The next plane for Europe leaves in three days and there's no room on that one either," Peter added.

"Whatever happens, we'll have to wire 'Echoes' for more money. We don't have enough to pay all our fares."

The women soon arrived. They had discovered an airport restaurant just before it closed and had purchased a bread roll for each one of us. "That's all they had," explained Ruth, "but perhaps we could take a cab into Luanda to buy more food."

"There are no cabs," Mr. Raymond replied, "and from what we've been told, food is hard to come by."

"The ticket agents also doubted that we would find lodging for everybody," Peter stated.

The total picture looked bleak. We had run aground in all three crucial areas—food, accommodation and transportation.

Moreover, by this time the airport officials had suspected that we were not ordinary travelers. Apparently they had received no communication from Luena about us, but when they finally discovered that 33 white refugees from embattled Zaire were wandering around the terminal, they were jolted into action.

First of all our passports were seized. Then we were placed in custody in a suffocating airport lounge and were denied access to both telephones and washrooms. They held us there incommunicado, telling us simply that our case was being considered. We realized that our presence raised politically explosive issues and that some high-level decisions would have to be made. Therefore, drawing upon our vast experience in waiting, we began yet another prayerful vigil.

It was hot, very hot. The children were tired and burning up with the heat. Parents, aunts and uncles employed all their collective talents to keep them from howling. Grannie was holding on too. She sagged in her wheel chair but when we came by she would smile weakly. The rest of us were also wilting, but even worse off were the nuns dressed in their long robes.

By 4 P.M. we had been waiting for three hours in these stifling conditions without any news at all from the authorities. Since our early breakfast the children had eaten only a few raisins and two bread rolls. They were hungry and even more restless. By now the temperature was nigh unbearable.

Around five-thirty Terry was becoming very agitated over Grannie's condition. "Look at her!" he urged the airport staff. "Do you know how old she is? Do you know she has heart trouble? How much longer will it be before you help her?" The attendants looked on sympathetically but nothing was done.

By 6:15 P.M. a slight breeze had arisen and we were permitted to wheel Grannie outside for some relief. About the same time, they finally allowed us to visit the washrooms, but only in twos and escorted by airport personnel. When Peter and Ruth returned, I witnessed an incredible sight. They placed a small gas cooker on the cement and started a fire. I was about to ask if the heat had driven them mad when suddenly they produced a little pot of water.

"You're not doing what I think you're doing!" I exclaimed as they lowered it onto the single burner.

Peter glanced up with a broad grin. "I think it's about time we had a cup of tea, don't you?" I shook my head in disbelief but inwardly I had to congratulate them for such remarkable resourcefulness under the circumstances.

The time crawled along. It would soon be six hours and still no word from the officials. Grannie looked as if she would collapse at any moment. Finally she muttered, "Please, let me lie down somewhere."

We rushed her inside, blew up a rubber mattress and eased her onto it in full view of the airport personnel. She was soon comfortable and I didn't fear for her, but this was an opportunity not to be missed, Walter and I proceeded to fan her vigorously while the attendants grew increasingly alarmed. Perhaps now they would do something to hasten our release.

At 7:15 P.M., while we still hovered over Grannie, several officials strode into the lounge waving papers in their hands. "You are going home," they announced. "The government of Angola is repatriating you at its expense!"

Immediately a mighty tide of joy and thankfulness inundated our little lounge. There was no frenzied crying or exuberant shouting, just a quiet spirit of rejoicing in our midst. Once again the Lord had shaken the earth.

More was to come. Government photographers soon descended upon us and started to shoot movies of the whole pageant: local officials talking to us and taking our names for tickets; weary children clinging to their relieved and happy parents; and Grannie. Grannie had been sleeping peacefully throughout the proceedings but when the bright lights shone her way and the film was spinning, she woke up. From her death-like stillness on the mattress, she sat up swiftly with a look of amazement, noticed that everything was trained on her, then waved wildly and flashed a captivating smile for the camera. Once more she was the star of the show.

Moments later other reporters appeared including a BBC correspondent and a French radio and television crew. They told us that our arrival from Zaire meant a real "scoop" for them. Except for FNLC communiqués, there had been no news from our end of Shaba province since the war began. While this was going on, our luggage was once again meticulously searched, but apart from what they called a "dangerous" knife, nothing was seized. We still had no idea when we were leaving Angola or where we were staying in the meantime.

"There may be a plane late tomorrow night but perhaps not for a few days," the senior official informed us.

"In a few minutes," his associate continued. "we will be sending you to the refugee center."

The few minutes were up and we were soon racing towards Luanda in vehicles provided by a Roman Catholic mission and by the United Nations. Veering south of the city onto a dark and bumpy highway, we drove on in the twilight to our unknown destination.

"What are you thinking about?" I asked the silent Walter.

"Oh, just about the refugee center," he replied. "I'm not sure what that means."

"Nor am I."

Five minutes later we pulled into a crescent-shaped driveway and came to a stop at the front entrance of a magnificent hotel—the Costa da Sol. We filed into a plush lounge, registered at the desk then walked up carpeted staircases and along brightly lit hallways to our air-conditioned rooms. Double boxspring beds, lamps, dressers, showers, hot and cold running water—could we be dreaming? Floor-to-ceiling sliding windows opened onto balconies which looked over a cliff and across a sandy beach to the shimmering Atlantic Ocean.

Those words came back to us: "He sent from above, he took me, he drew me out of many waters . . . He brought me forth also into a large place."

At 9:30 P.M. we gathered in a finely-set dining room. Waiters served us bowls of soup, platefuls of chicken and rice, and tall glasses of refreshingly cold water.

"The government is certainly trying to make amends for that dismal reception at the airport," Walter commented. "This was supposed to be a refugee center!"

"A refugee center for visiting dignitaries," Peter interjected. "Fidel Castro stayed here two weeks ago!"

"Who told you that?" I asked incredulously.

"One of the priests who drove us," Ruth replied.

"Amazing!" Walter exclaimed.

"Well, I'll tell you one thing," I said. "With the clothes we're wearing, none of us look like visiting dignitaries. If President Neto could see us in here like this maybe he'd toss us on the next plane to England."

"That would suit me fine," Peter replied. "I won't be happy until we're on that plane. In Africa, anything can happen!" He was right. We could rejoice in our present circumstances but we still weren't home and we didn't know what the Marxist regime had planned for us between now and that indefinite departure. We hoped there would be no more interrogation.

We finished our meal and retired to our comfortable rooms.

"Well," I sighed, "from a carriage, to Carlos's house, to a Catholic palace, to the Costa Da Sol—who'd believe anything so fantastic?"

"Lots of people," Walter laughed. "They'll have to. We've been there." Then he became more thoughtful. He rolled onto his bed and stared up at the ceiling.

"You know," he continued, "you're right in a way. Sometimes when I think of our confinement at Kasaji and our incredible escape it does seem like a dream; but that reminds me of what the Jews stated when the Lord miraculously led them out of captivity. Listen," he said as he looked up Psalm 126: " 'When the Lord turned again the captivity of Zion, we were like them that dream. Then was our mouth filled with laughter, and our tongue with singing. . . . The Lord hath done great things for us; whereof we are glad' '' (vv. 1-3).

We pondered those prophetic words in silent wonder. The Lord had done great things for us too. Then, in my mind's eye I saw Tshihinga standing on a dusty, refugee-filled Zairian road, and I could still hear him confidently say, "The Lord will take care of you just like He will take care of us!" Would we ever hear about those great things that the Lord had done for them?

The *Jornal de Angola* splashed our story across next morning's front page under sensational headlines: "European Missionaries Flee Mobutist Terror to Find Humanitarian Asylum in Angola." The regime was striving for maximum mileage from our presence.

We expected the authorities to show up that morning with information about our departure but no one came. We caught up on our rest and then at 1:00 P.M. sat down for another banquet-style meal of chicken and rice.

"Do you have any news, Mr. Raymond?" Colin asked.

"No, nothing at all. I should think the officials would appear sometime before supper."

"Daddy, will you take me to the sea?" Robbie implored.

"Yes, son," Brian replied. "But it's not the sea, it's the ocean. Angola has an ocean, but England has a sea."

"I was born in England," Robbie proudly informed his contemporaries.

"So was I!" Rachel retorted with equal flourish.

"Ingrid wasn't born in England. She was born in Kasaji," Robbie countered. "And so was Timmy."

"My David was born in Kasaji, too," Rachel said squeezing her brother. The chubby little fellow continued to eat, untouched by the claims to citizenship and fatherland that swirled about him.

"Anyway," Robbie announced, "I'm going to swim in Angola's ocean!"

Our afternoon was spent in patient waiting, but again there was no word from the government officials. At 4 P.M. we gathered for a Communion service, realizing that if we left that night, this might be the last time we would break bread together.

It was a moving experience. Each person in the room meant so much to the other. Our fellowship in joy and in sorrow, in prosperity and in adversity had long preceded the war, but through the troubles we had grown to love and cherish one another even more. Together we read the Messianic Psalm 22 and realized that, whereas deliverance had been granted to us, none had been accorded to Christ. Together we shared the bread and the wine, and together we marveled at God's love, and in response to it, our minds and our hearts sang:

Were the whole realm of nature mine,
That were an offering far too small;
Love so amazing, so divine,
Demands my soul, my life, my all![3]

Late that afternoon our story finally spilled out over BBC—the battle at Kasaji, the occupation, the bombardment, the flight to the border and the journey across Angola. Our families would now know that we had arrived safely in Luanda. Other news turned our minds back to Zaire where Mobutu's paratroopers had reportedly dropped deep into enemy zones. No doubt this was the push towards our little Kasaji.

That evening we once more dined in comfort, though the menu of chicken and rice was becoming strikingly familiar. As we ate, Mr. Raymond said, "Although there has not been a whisper from the government all day, I still think we should be ready to leave this evening. I'll let you know the moment we receive any information."

Seven, eight, and nine o'clock passed. We were beginning to wonder if we would be kept here for another day or longer. Suddenly, at 9:15 P.M., there was a sharp rap on the door.

"Quickly," Peter urged. "go downstairs for your passports and tickets. We're leaving in five minutes!"

There was a mad scurry to the reception desk. Most of the others had been informed before us and had already picked up their papers. Some were even carrying their luggage to the lobby. I verified my ticket, charged upstairs, packed the last few articles, and ran back down to the entrance.

Our driver was in a hurry. We raced down the same bumpy, unilluminated highway that we had traveled 24 hours previously. Besides the dangerous potholes, there were several tree branches that inexplicably lay over the edge of the road. I held on grimly as we navigated the obstacle course at 75 miles per hour. I finally leaned over to Walter and said, "Can't you just see the headline: 'Fugitives Escape War, Bombardment and a Thousand Miles of Danger But on Way to Last Flight Home, Die in Car Accident'?"

"No," he replied. "It's too long for a headline!"

We reached the Luanda terminal without incident, however, and prepared our baggage for the flight. Then we were ushered into the departure lounge—the one we knew so intimately from the previous day's marathon wait. Tonight, however, the room had already cooled and we even wore sweaters and jackets in order to stay warm.

The plane's takeoff was delayed and we prepared ourselves to spend at least part of the night in the building. I watched Grannie arrange and rearrange a blanket and a pillow on the narrow seats of the lounge until at last she was satisfied. What a remarkable woman! Not many her age would have withstood the rigors of our travel. Not many had accomplished so much in their time.

Not until 6 A.M. did we board the aircraft. Most of us had not slept a wink all night but everyone was alert as the engines revved and we lurched forward. The airplane taxied to the end of the runway and turned around, poised to sprint past the terminal. Then, with everyone belted down and engines opened full, the jet screamed down the track and lifted into the early light of daybreak. Higher and higher it climbed and twisted, and finally rolled out over the ocean while our misty eyes peered down at Angola and beyond that to a faraway mission station.

The plane chased up the coast as many minds played and replayed memories that bordered on being nightmares. Countless dramas were reenacted, and a host of sights and sounds and feelings were keenly experienced. Who could forget the tingling freshness after a Kasaji rain, the clangy strumming of a homemade guitar, or the austere visage of a lonely anthill? What about the eager students, the grateful patients and the joyful believers? Yes, some pupils had been disappointing, some medical cases discouraging, and some Christians disheartening, but in each situation we had struggled with human life and learned something in the process.

Then came the invasion with the panic, the flight and the battle. There was the teenage soldier, pleading for deliverance while being dragged off the table to his execution. There were the putrifying smells of a corpse-laden Kasaji and the same rotting stench amongst the hospital's war wounded. There was the hateful invective of the Easter death threat and the screeching Mirage that mercilessly rocketed the heart of the mission.

Our escape flashed by in word pictures—the miracle pickup, the dressine, Carlos, the palace, the Costa da Sol—each representing clusters of uncertainties, prayers and miracles. Attached to these and many more recollections were an incredible cast of characters: Mufu and the Toothless One; Alexis the Great and Vaincre ou Mourir; and Blackbeard and the Colonel.

Then I looked around me at the Kasaji family. Where were they headed? Several were already discussing a return to non-troubled areas of Shaba as a stepping stone back to Kasaji. Some were withholding decisions pending the outcome of the conflict while others, such as Grannie, would never go back.

Just hours before, I had listened as she spoke. "Africa has been my beloved home for 63 years," Grannie said, "and I wanted to die here and be buried next to my husband. But now that I'm leaving, I'm leaving for good." Her voice trembled ever so slightly as she concluded, "David, my work in Africa is finished. I know the Lord wants me in England or else He would have taken me in Kasaji or somewhere along the way. He's never let me down, though I've failed Him often. Go on trusting the Lord. He's faithful.''

The jet leaned far across the Mediterranean Sea, reaching for the coast.

''Look, Ruth!'' Peter shouted excitedly as he stretched for the window. ''There's Europe!''

Yes, there was Europe. Kasaji, Zaire and our journey to the coast lay far behind, but what legacy had they left us besides abandoned buildings and a fleeting trail? What would we carry with us into the rest of our lives?

Kasaj was not just a mission station or a battleground. It had been one of life's classrooms where unforgettable lessons had been learned and applied. Before the war the Lord had proved Himself to be utterly faithful and loving in all our joys and struggles. During the war we had been forced to the limits of life itself, and as we faced death and its grisly entourage, we discovered that the Lord was again sufficient for all our needs. It mattered not how desperate or delightful our circumstances had been; it mattered solely that we knew the reality of His nearness.

Life in the homelands or wherever we went would also have its troublous moments. Each of us would again be subject to the uncertainties that plague all mankind. Yet we could confront the unknown with incredible boldness because we carried with us the unshakable conviction that Jesus was Lord over every situation. The eternal God was indeed our refuge and our strength. There would be no fear in His presence.

NOTES

1. Garenganze: Old word for Central Africa and name given to Brethren missionary work in southern Zaire since 1902. See *Turning the World Upside Down,* by William Willimon and Patricia Willimon (Lexington, SC: Sandlapper Store, Inc., 1972), Bath, Somerset: Echoes of Service, 1972, p. 394.

2. FNLA: One of the three rival liberation armies that had struggled for control of Angola during the civil war. The victorious MPLA had paid the Katangese to fight off the FNLA.

3. ''When I Survey the Wondrous Cross'' by Isaac Watts.

CHRISTIAN HERALD ASSOCIATION AND ITS MINISTRIES

CHRISTIAN HERALD ASSOCIATION, founded in 1878, publishes The Christian Herald Magazine, one of the leading interdenominational religious monthlies in America. Through its wide circulation, it brings inspiring articles and the latest news of religious developments to many families. From the magazine's pages came the initiative for CHRISTIAN HERALD CHILDREN'S HOME and THE BOWERY MISSION, two individually supported not-for-profit corporations.

CHRISTIAN HERALD CHILDREN'S HOME, established in 1894, is the name for a unique and dynamic ministry to disadvantaged children, offering hope and opportunities which would not otherwise be available for reasons of poverty and neglect. The goal is to develop each child's potential and to demonstrate Christian compassion and understanding to children in need.

Mont Lawn is a permanent camp located in Bushkill, Pennsylvania. It is the focal point of a ministry which provides a healthful "vacation with a purpose" to children who without it would be confined to the streets of the city. Up to 1000 children between the ages of 7 and 11 come to Mont Lawn each year.

Christian Herald Children's Home maintains year-round contact with children by means of an *In-City Youth Ministry*. Central to its philosophy is the belief that only through sustained relationships and demonstrated concern can individual lives be truly enriched. Special emphasis is on individual guidance, spiritual and family counseling and tutoring. This follow-up ministry to inner-city children culminates for many in financial assistance toward higher education and career counseling.

THE BOWERY MISSION, located at 227 Bowery, New York City, has since 1879 been reaching out to the lost men on the Bowery, offering them what could be their last chance to rebuild their lives. Every man is fed, clothed and ministered to. Countless numbers have entered the 90-day residential rehabilitation program at the Bowery Mission. A concentrated ministry of counseling, medical care, nutrition therapy, Bible study and Gospel services awakens a man to spiritual renewal within himself.

These ministries are supported solely by the voluntary contributions of individuals and by legacies and bequests. Contributions are tax deductible. Checks should be made out either to CHRISTIAN HERALD CHILDREN'S HOME or to THE BOWERY MISSION.

Administrative Office: 40 Overlook Drive, Chappaqua, New York 10514
Telephone: (914) 769-9000